More Praise for *The Progress Illusion*

"Given that the Arctic has mostly melted, it seems axiomatic that our planet's economic system is not working very well. But Jon Erickson explains—in simple and powerful terms—just why that is, and just what would need to change if we were to actually build a world that worked much better. It's a real gift to all of us!"

—**BILL MCKIBBEN**
author of *The Flag, the Cross, and the Station Wagon*

"In accessible language filled with stories, ecological economist Jon Erickson shows how growth-driven economies, worsening inequities, and greenhouse gas emissions are interconnected, and thus it is possible to envision alternate paths forward which address all three."

—**PATRICIA (ELLIE) PERKINS**
Professor, Faculty of Environmental and Urban Change, York University; editor of *The Routledge Handbook of Feminist Economics*

"This book is a must-read for those who wish to understand how a promising discipline strayed inexorably from a more humane path to one that extols unbridled materialism, inequity, and environmental destruction. Economics can be rescued from its self-destructive path by having more courageous, assertive, and iconoclastic scholars like Erickson."

—**STEVE ONYEIWU**
Andrew Wells Robertson Professor of Economics, Allegheny College; author of *Emerging Issues in Contemporary African Economies*

About Island Press

Since 1984, the nonprofit organization Island Press has been stimulating, shaping, and communicating ideas that are essential for solving environmental problems worldwide. With more than 1,000 titles in print and some 30 new releases each year, we are the nation's leading publisher on environmental issues. We identify innovative thinkers and emerging trends in the environmental field. We work with world-renowned experts and authors to develop cross-disciplinary solutions to environmental challenges.

Island Press designs and executes educational campaigns, in conjunction with our authors, to communicate their critical messages in print, in person, and online using the latest technologies, innovative programs, and the media. Our goal is to reach targeted audiences—scientists, policy makers, environmental advocates, urban planners, the media, and concerned citizens—with information that can be used to create the framework for long-term ecological health and human well-being.

Island Press gratefully acknowledges major support from The Bobolink Foundation, Caldera Foundation, The Curtis and Edith Munson Foundation, The Forrest C. and Frances H. Lattner Foundation, The JPB Foundation, The Kresge Foundation, The Summit Charitable Foundation, Inc., and many other generous organizations and individuals.

The opinions expressed in this book are those of the author(s) and do not necessarily reflect the views of our supporters.

THE PROGRESS ILLUSION

THE PROGRESS ILLUSION

Reclaiming Our
Future from the
Fairytale of Economics

Jon D. Erickson

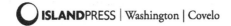
ISLANDPRESS | Washington | Covelo

Library of Congress Control Number: 2022931806

All Island Press books are printed on environmentally responsible materials.

Manufactured in the United States of America
10 9 8 7 6 5 4 3 2 1

Keywords: Adam Smith, capitalism, carbon tax, classical economics, climate change, ecological economics, economic inequality, environmental economics, feminist economics, *Freakonomics*, free market, GDP, Herman Daly, Keynesian economics, laissez-faire economics, macroeconomics, microeconomics, natural resource economics, neoclassical economics, Occupy Wall Street, supply-side economics, *The Limits to Growth*

to Louis and Jon

my inspiration
to be a good ancestor

Contents

Foreword

So what kind of economist are you?

Jon Erickson's answer to that common question is that he is an ecological economist. He explains what led him from standard training in neoclassical economics at an elite university to this rebel faction that seeks to reconstruct economics from a new foundational paradigm. Ecological economics is based on a new preanalytic vision of the economy as a dependent subsystem of an ecosystem that is finite, nongrowing, and subject to the biophysical laws of thermodynamics and ecology. Such a revisioning is quite unfriendly to the ideology of growthism that rules the politics and economics of our time. It is not the glide path to professional advancement, much less to the profitable Wall Street career in finance that many of his Ivy League contemporaries chose.

That makes this book sound rather theoretical and abstract, but the story is told as a personal narrative by someone born in 1969 and experiencing the social, economic, and political history of his generation, all the way from his student days to his current position as a distinguished professor and leader in ecological economics. The narrative includes instructive retellings of the political and economic struggles of his generation, which overlaps the generations of us readers so we can personally identify with his story. It helps that Jon is a good storyteller, a talent that carries over from his work as a documentary filmmaker. He describes and explains his increasing dissatisfaction with the unwillingness and inability of today's leading economists to seriously confront the related catastrophes of ecological destruction and economic breakdown that we are experiencing.

What were the specific conflicts and anomalies that brought him to ecological economics? I will leave that for him to tell, but one big one I will mention is the belief that ecological economics should be the cornerstone for economics as a whole rather than a minor subcategory. In the *Journal of Economic Literature* classification of over seven hundred subject areas, ecological economics is indexed way down the list as Q57. The idea that the 720th brick should be removed and refashioned to replace the cornerstone of the whole edifice is not an easy idea to sell, especially to the original builders who still live in that structure and control entry into it.

As should be expected, the same independent mind that was not satisfied with neoclassical economics will not uncritically accept everything written in the name of ecological economics. In particular, Erickson rightly urges stronger emphasis on distributive justice, as well as on sustainable scale, and cautions against empty empiricism, such as pricing nature by econometric estimates of individual willingness to pay for environmental benefit or to accept payment for environmental loss. On the latter he quotes Keynes's caution that such economistic numerology is "like those puzzles for children where you write down your age, multiply, add this and that, subtract something else, and eventually end up with the number of the Beast in Revelation."

In addition to Keynes, Erickson's critique of the mainstream neoclassical growthists draws on the forgotten classical economists, as well as more recent economists unjustly ignored, such as Henry George, Karl

Polanyi, and Nicholas Georgescu-Roegen. Careful attention is given to the history of economic thought, with appreciation for good ideas regardless of their ideological origins.

I strongly recommend this insightful book to all citizens because the errors of economists are disastrous, and we are currently suffering from them. In addition, I especially recommend it to university students who are struggling, as Jon Erickson did, to choose a worthy and sustainable path for their studies and future work. They will be instructed and inspired by his example.

Finally, in an age of online university courses, I cannot resist pointing to some ecological economic virtues secondary to high intellectual content: This book requires no access to computers, smartphones, or internet connections, uses no electricity, is easily portable, and can be reused often by different people at different times. You will be glad you bought it!

Herman Daly
Emeritus Professor
School of Public Policy
University of Maryland

Preface

Promises of an Ecological Economics

"I'm not that kind of economist."

This is a defense I've retreated to on many occasions, often when trying to explain that my profession has no magic answers to intractable questions. What's the value of the climate to the economy? What's the tradeoff between jobs and the environment? What's the worth of a songbird?[1] Economics is often used to sidestep moral judgments about what we value. It's not us who's choosing winners and losers; it's simply the market. But putting a price on everything presumes people and planet are disposable, tradable, and otherwise here to serve the invention we call the economy.

In other settings, my qualification has been a rejoinder to the old joke about economists, lawyers, and politicians alike: "What do you call a thousand economists at the bottom of the ocean? A good start." When attacked by those who vilify economics as arrogant, ahistorical, and narrow, I wholeheartedly agree, but then I argue for a more modest, reflective, interdisciplinary economics. An economics that can contribute to, not replace, democratic decision making. An economics that learns from, not ignores, its own history. An economics that partners with, not dominates, other disciplines.

In essence, this book is an answer to the question, "So what kind of economist are you?" My long-winded response begins with unpacking the term itself. *Economics* is derived from the Greek word *oikonomia*, "the management of the household." In ancient Greece, *oikos* referred to the family, the basic unit of Greek society. But oiko-nomists today study households of all shapes and sizes. Microeconomists study the resources that make things, the people who consume things, and the things themselves. Macroeconomists study the whole, the sum of the parts that make up local, regional, and national economies, as well as the systems of money, law, governance, and trade that stitch the parts together.

Beyond these two broad distinctions, economics splinters into many specialties. There are labor, business, agricultural, consumer, behavioral, and even neuro economists. There are microeconomists who study the sports economy, tourism economy, forest economy, transportation economy, and on and on. There are macroeconomists who specialize in specific countries, time periods, or even other economists. If there is an activity, resource, place, or person connected to the economy, there's probably an economist who has claimed it as the household of their specialization. In all, the *Journal of Economic Literature* (JEL) classification is broken into twenty categories with over seven hundred subject areas. From A10 to Z39, the domain of today's oikonomia is the entirety of humanity.

My own affinity has been with Q57, ecological economics. Early in my education I discovered ecological economics as a scientific understanding of the economy that is guided by sustainability, inclusiveness, and fairness. Tellingly, *economics* and *ecology* share the Greek root, *oikos*, together the management and study of the household. Ecology's household has historically been focused on nature separate from humans, and economics has focused on humans separate from nature. Ecological economics was intended to embed the human system within the ecosystem, blurring the lines between the natural and social sciences. The formalization of this transdiscipline in the late 1980s challenged a growing economic imperialism that defined humans as consumers, society's purpose as growth, and our relationship with the Earth as overlord.

Among the JEL codes, Q57 is a more recent addition, lumped in with agricultural, natural resource, and environmental economics. In some respects, an official code represents a maturing of the field, a legitimization of ecological economics as a worthy subject area. However, the JEL designation also implies a specialization *within* economics, not a reframing *of* economics. Q57 has come to represent the mainstreaming of ecological economics, most prominently the idea that nature's services should be assigned an economic value and lumped in with all other economic consumption. When I joined the ecological economics tribe nearly three decades ago, I thought I was signing on to a revolution to upend the economization of everything. More recently, I fear we have succumbed to a worldview we were meant to challenge and replace.

In articulating the kind of economics (and economists!) I think the world needs, I have revisited some of the original aspirations of ecological economics. Books such as *For the Common Good* (1989) by Herman Daly and John Cobb inspired a generation to question the dominant economic worldview and work toward a vision expressed in their own subtitle, "Redirecting the Economy toward Community, the Environment, and a Sustainable Future." They provided another link in a long chain of thought that asks for humility in the face of uncertainty, reverence for the majesty of life, and courage to fight for justice.

But today we are long past the need for merely "redirecting." Interdependent economic and environmental systems are unraveling worldwide. Neocolonial empires built on the exploitation of people and planet have run their course. Climate instability, mass extinction, and unprecedented inequality are the results. In response, the mainstream of economics has doubled down on an illusion of progress with the fate of humanity and life on Earth in the balance.

But preparations to reclaim our future are under way. A new story is emerging that unpacks the human-centered narrative of modernity, reveals the ecocidal pact of the status quo, and advocates for a less trodden path of compassion and care. A new economics is being forged from a critical look at history, renewed alliances with the natural sciences, and a new social contract for education. A new economy is evolving from the diversity of voices and life experiences beyond the failures of a winner-takes-all society and the ashes of mainstream ideology.

We have the will. I hope sharing my own journey can help illuminate the way. Thanks for sharing the ride.

CHAPTER 1

The Education of an Economist

The point is, ladies and gentlemen, that greed, for a lack of a better word, is good.

—Gordon Gekko, *Wall Street*

I graduated from high school in 1987, the Year of the Gekko. My classmates and I set aside our boyhood dreams of becoming the adventurous Michael Douglas who won the heart of Kathleen Turner in *Romancing the Stone* and turned our teenage idolatry toward his portrayal of Gordon Gekko in *Wall Street*, a role that defined the go-go '80s. The "greed is good" speech impaled our teenage brains, and every young man in my graduating class was encouraged to do the same thing: Study economics, major in business, and make lots of money.

Reporting from the New York Stock Exchange in a 1987 special for NBC News on "Money, Greed, Power," Tom Brokaw reflected on the turning point in America when greed became an asset and morality a liability. When Michael Lewis published *Liar's Poker* two years later, a best-selling *exposé* of the excesses and culture of Wall Street, a generation of twenty-somethings had already drunk the Kool-Aid. More money was the goal, and the gateway to enlightenment was Econ 101.

Business programs and degrees exploded in the '80s, with freshman economics at the base of the boom. Nearly 60 percent of the high school class of 1982 who went on to college registered for principles of micro and macroeconomics, surpassed only by enrollment in freshman composition and general psychology, the only courses over the 50 percent mark.[1] My guess is the class of '87 was north of 70 percent. Economics had become essential to degrees in business and engineering but also core to a liberal arts and science education. By the end of the decade, millions of young minds were armed and ready to conquer the world.

My own decision about what to study in college went something like this: "Pop, what should I study in college?" "Son, if you want to make money, study business and economics." "Thanks, Pop."

It was all so appealing to our hormone-induced, ignorance-is-bliss modus operandi, especially among young men. Econ 101 presented a world order with a singular objective: Consume. The individual was king, and money was the object of our desire. The rules were laid out in straightforward equations. At the intersection of the "laws" of supply and demand, X always marked the spot.

Economics also fit an American patriotism under which we were raised: our pledge of allegiance to free markets to win the Cold War. Throughout our childhood, we imagined long bread lines behind a mysterious Berlin Wall. Doctors and janitors working for the same menial wages. A Soviet Union draped in gray and black. In America, you could buy anything, anywhere, at any time. Our duty to country was to be good consumers. Gone were motivations beyond the self. Community was a marketplace, and votes were in dollars. My high school army recruiter's pitch comes to mind, as I was implored to join the military not to serve my country but to earn some money to "buy a black Trans Am."

Principles of economics were seen as foundational to ordered, logical, rational thinking. For the business student, micro and macro was the prerequisite to marketing, accounting, and finance. How do we get more people to consume? Marketing. How do we tally our efforts? Accounting. How do we pay for it all? Finance. And for the English or biology or political science or any other liberal arts and science major, economics became the social science elective to make sense of our side in the Cold War.

Econ 101 tells a story of the unlimited wants of individuals, in a world of limited means owned by the same. On the supply side, people are atomized as production units (L for labor), and all other means of production are reduced to capital (K, a never spoken tribute to *Das Kapital* by Marx). L and K combine in a mathematical equation to produce Q (output). Simple. On the demand side, what is produced is unimportant as long as it meets demand and provides an amorphous pleasure called "utility." Because we can't measure utility directly, it's equated with consumption of all that Q, weighted by market prices (P). The joy of consumption does not distinguish between needs and wants. We need only concern ourselves with anonymous Qs, produced by Ls and Ks, valued by Ps, by the owners of the Ls and Ks.

This circular economics worldview was built on a persona that has come to be known as *Homo economicus*, a caricature of human behavior that describes a self-maximizing, isolated individual at a point in time—what Thorstein Veblen described in 1898 as a "homogeneous globule of desire." In a free society, the globules own their own L. In a capitalist society, some also own their own K. The consumption choices of one globule aren't to be compared with those of another. And because the wants of each glob are assumed insatiable, the world will always need more Q (at least for those with the willingness and ability to pay the P).

To make more Q, we'd better have more L and K, or, better yet, squeeze every last drop of Q from our resources through technology. If K can do it better than L, so be it. After all, K doesn't demand raises, sleep at night, get a virus, or whine about healthcare. K can also be hired and fired without a hint of guilty conscience. To keep this system growing only requires new investment in K (L sold separately). Where does investment come from? Savings. Who saves the most? Rich people. The conclusion: We'd better make sure the wealthy globules keep those hard-won dollars, especially the ones who own the K.

In the education of the economist, each step of abstraction into a world of Ps, Qs, Ls, and Ks removes us further and further from the context of societies of people, cooperating under mutual interest, entirely dependent on each other and our environment. In an economic worldview, the social and eco spheres are deemphasized with the goal—to quote Grover Norquist, one of the architects of today's conservative movement—to shrink government "down to a size where we can drown it in a bathtub." Who knows better what to do with your labor and capital: you or the government?

So the logical conclusion is to shrink government and cut taxes, especially on the wealthy capital owners (a.k.a. the job creators). As the story goes, it's the rich who will take care of everyone—not out of any benevolence for the commoners but simply as a side effect of pursuing their own self-interest. As Adam Smith put it, "It is not from the benevolence of the butcher, the brewer, or the baker that we expect our dinner, but from their regard to their own interest."

In the go-go '80s, the baker became the banker, and we were told that cutting taxes on capital gains would bring a rising tide to lift all boats (fortified yachts and leaky life rafts alike). It was Smith's 1776 *Wealth of Nations* on steroids, without the ethical constraint of his forgotten 1759 *Theory of Moral Sentiments*. Gone was the inspiration of my parents' youth, when President Kennedy was inaugurated on a call to "ask not what your country can do for you; ask what you can do for your country." As we went off to college in the Year of the Gekko, the Reagan revolution told us, "Government is not the solution to our problem; government is the problem."

$\sim$

What about ethics? Law? Science? Surely my generation learned more than economics, marketing, and finance. Surely other disciplines challenged economic hegemony. Surely institutions of "higher" learning were chartered to do more than produce new consumers. All true, but a truly "world" view accounts for all challengers.

With ethics, an economic worldview provides an internal framework where it's ethical to be greedy. After all, one person's greed to consume is another's paycheck to produce. Prosperity for all, by posterity of none. Under an ethic of avarice, any restriction on the right to more stuff was an assault on our basic liberties. Citizen was consumer. Obligation was to self. Laws in defense of our constitutional right to private property were tolerated. Others were branded "regulations" to be drowned in Norquist's bathtub. If consumers want clean air and clear water, fine, let them demand it in the marketplace. Producers will follow the dollar. Entrepreneurs will save the world.

There could be no losers in a truly free market because everyone was permitted to vote with their wallet. No bread lines because the natural state of free markets was equilibrium. The part of the demand curve where people couldn't afford to buy was never discussed. The quite explicit assumption was that free markets lead to lopsided outcomes only because of lopsided effort. Gekko's "greed for life, for money, for love" was what our founding fathers must have meant by "life, liberty, and the pursuit of happiness." Democratic freedom was code for free markets, and the price of entry was hard work and entrepreneurship by red-blooded, self-made Americans.

With an internal ethic and legal scaffolding that feigned first principles of constitutional democracy, economics departments and business programs could elbow out any dissent from other "humanistic" pursuits of knowledge. But the success of economics also lay in its claim to be the "most scientific of the social sciences," to quote the majority view of a survey of economics graduate students.[2] An economic worldview could beat back competition from ethics, law, and political science through a game of "my theory is more popular than yours." However, to take on the sciences would require camouflage, not competition.

And so economics draped itself in mathematics, claiming an adherence to the scientific method through elegant proofs. The education of the economist is a journey into the depths of abstraction. It starts in such innocence, with linear graphs of demand and supply curves settling into predictable market equilibrium. After Econ 101, add a little calculus to get your smart on. Same story, but now we can solve for X in what seems more and more like hard science.

The ultimate prize for the professional economist is the PhD, where only the most mathematically dogmatic ascend to the heights of abstraction. Qualifying examinations in graduate school are like Catholic catechism: Memorize, regurgitate, repeat. Only the faithful shall pass and ultimately defend dissertations judged by the high priests of the Econ tribe. Intelligence is measured by publishing proofs with the full force of the Greek alphabet, backed by the faith in market equilibrium sketched by hand on the very first quiz in Econ 101.

The education of an economist is soup to nuts, and the PhD degree is the key to power and glory. Since 1946, it has been credentialed economists who sit at the right hand of the US president on the Council of Economic Advisers. Since 1969, credentialed economists have been given Nobel prizes (well, sort of), a "memorial" prize added outside the 1895 will of Alfred Nobel, bought and paid for by the central bank of Sweden.[3] And since the Reagan revolution, economics as a worldview has dominated our politics, our communities, and our sense of self.

Stanford economist Edward Lazear, chairman of George W. Bush's Council of Economic Advisers at the onset of the Great Recession, concluded in his article "Economic Imperialism" that economics is "not only a social science, it is a genuine science."[4] Professor Lazear finds his brethren's use of the "construct of rational individuals who engage in maximizing behavior," models that "adhere strictly to the importance of equilibrium," and a "focus on efficiency" to be the "ingredients" that "have allowed economics to invade intellectual territory that was previously deemed to be outside the discipline's realm." Translation: Greed is good, markets are the path to societal perfection, and economists have an objective truth rule of efficiency by which *all* decisions can be judged.

This "Superiority of Economists," as described with tongue in cheek by Berkeley sociologist Marion Fourcade, who has studied our academic species, is reinforced by established hierarchy within the field and a "high market demand for services, particularly from powerful and wealthy parties."[5] Fourcade points to evidence that 40 percent of the income of economists publishing in finance and industrial organizations comes from consulting activities with business and government.[6] To defend this privileged position in society, the caretakers of the field come largely from the top-ranked economics departments (based on citations of each other's work), where they vote themselves onto boards of academic journals and associations and hire each other's graduate students.[7]

This study of economists explains much of what I experienced in my graduate economics classes at Cornell University, an Ivy League department with the big five (Harvard, MIT, Princeton, Chicago, and Stanford) in its crosshairs. This position of superiority was clear from the swagger and contempt from my professors for competing views of the world, fostering an isolationism unlike any other field. In a survey of "The Social and Political Views of American Professors," economics stands out as the only field where a majority (57.3 percent) *disagree* with the statement, "In general, interdisciplinary knowledge is better than knowledge obtained by a single discipline."[8]

We were taught not to question authority, which for a field built on the ideology of "free" markets is more than a bit ironic. Acceptance was the secret to passing economics examinations. Classes in history, ethics, and (especially) natural science were often at odds with economic theory, so we were taught to not bother with collaboration because we are the superior race. More than in any other field, economists largely cite other economists.[9] Authors in prestigious journals (measured by the number of citations) cite articles from the same prestigious journals. Any cross-disciplinary research is inevitably dominated by the "superior" view of the "collaborating" economist; otherwise, it wouldn't get published and cited in a prestigious journal (with an editorial board culled from the top few departments). In economics, academic incest is always and everywhere rewarded.

Our elite forces of PhD-wielding economists are then taught to spread the love. Parts of sociology, political science, and psychology have been colonized by economics, especially through rational choice theory. How should we model the sociology of family relations, child rearing, or marriage choice? Utility maximization. How should we judge the merits of political structures, rules, and regulations? Cost–benefit analysis. How do individuals behave when faced with choices? Rationally, weighing the next cost with the next benefit of each action.

Even fields outside the social sciences have succumbed to this economic worldview. Today a conservation biologist is likely to argue for species and habitat protection in terms of dollars and cents rather than endangerment and extinction. To be taken seriously, a climate scientist must make the economic case for reducing greenhouse gas emissions alongside physical models of the Earth system. Economics can even tally what the Earth is worth to humans: $33 trillion and change according to a 1997 study published in the leading science journal *Nature*.[10]

There really is no boundary recognized by economists to "thinking like an economist." The discipline's self-confidence hit new highs in 1992 when the University of Chicago's Gary Becker landed a Nobel "for having extended the domain of microeconomic analysis to a wide range of human behavior and interaction, including nonmarket behavior."[11] Professor Becker pushed the rational actor model into inquiry on discrimination, family organization, crime, and drug addiction. Popular trade books followed, from *The Armchair Economist* (1993) to *Freakonomics* (2005), promoting economic puzzle solving from the ordinary to the outrageous. Best-selling textbooks for Econ 101 promoted "economic naturalism" to explain the world.[12] As the freakonomists claim, "If morality represents how people would like the world to work, then economics shows how it actually does work."[13]

When any decision can be lumped into costs and benefits, measured by dollars and cents, there's no stopping economic logic. The Earth is K, people are L, and making more Q is the game. As Frank Ackerman and Lisa Heinzerling describe in a law review article on "Pricing the Priceless," the extension of economic cost–benefit analysis into public policy undermines "the fundamental equality of all citizens."[14] They cite a study on "Cigarette Taxation and the Social Consequences of Smoking," by Harvard professor Kip Viscusi, that concludes smoking will save states money because smokers die younger, suggesting that "cigarette smoking should be subsidized rather than taxed." Considering the high cost of caring for an aging population, the "economic" logic is impeccable.

Why stop with valuing the life of a smoker? In a study published in the *Southern Economic Journal*, economists Paul Carlin and Robert Sandy use estimates of time saved by mothers when improperly fastening their children into car seats for "Estimating the Implicit Value of a Young Child's Life."[15] Time saved multiplied by a mother's presumed wage rate yields a "willingness to pay" estimate of a "statistical child's life" of about $500,000 at the time. Other economists have asked similar questions, using the cost of raising a child or discounted lifetime earnings to measure the economic benefits of regulating air pollution to reduce deaths from asthma or banning lead in our water to protect against mental retardation.

In the end, the education of the economist is complete when all ethical or scientific qualms are set aside. What's left is a carefully molded, rational, dispassionate, objective truth seeker to rationally appraise the economic costs and benefits of each new action (the past is of no consequence), to dispassionately consider the preferences of each individual as worthy and right (no judgment on necessity vs. luxury allowed), and to objectively seek the preordained truth that only markets can allocate resources efficiently (those without buying power need only work harder).

This is what generations of economists have preached and practiced, reinforced by a self-confidence that echoes throughout our consumer society. Most PhDs, are men, shaping collaborations that are inevitably influenced by patterns of gender difference and power relations in society.[16] White men in black suits line the halls of Congress, forge political campaigns, direct public policy decisions, advise titans of industry, expound opinions on editorial pages, parachute into the Global South to spread the good word, and teach the next generation of followers. Thousands of credentialed economists, lording over millions inoculated with Econ 101, build global acceptance of a singular worldview.

The deeper I dug, the more I questioned, pushed back, and felt like a round peg in a square hole. Although my father's seemingly practical advice to go forth and make money certainly fit the world around me, in my heart of hearts I was my mother's child. My mom raised my two younger brothers and me in a single-parent home on a preschool teacher's salary. My sense of justice came from watching her struggle to make ends meet while always looking out for those less fortunate. Our social circle included families living in economic chaos, including abused women sleeping on our couch and childhood friends born into generational poverty. Struggling families were some of the hardest-working people I knew, but the promise of economic freedom through the "just work harder" motto always seemed to be out of reach.

My mother also nurtured a deep reverence for our natural world. We fished, hiked, biked, sledded, skied, and otherwise spent our lives outdoors. My boyhood was spent building forts in the forest and fields known as "the trails" at the edge of our working-class suburb. Boy Scouts followed Cub Scouts. Summer weeks at YMCA camp. Winter months skiing on local hills. My brothers and I learned that we were not separate from the natural world but born of the very soil, rock, water, and air around us. These lessons from my mother haunted me during the economics classes recommended by my father.

I remember distinctly, as a junior at Cornell, sitting in Professor Will Provine's evolutionary biology class in the afternoon, trying to come to terms with Professor Robert Frank's microeconomics theory class from that morning. Over breakfast, I flexed my math muscles, assuming the role of Veblen's unhuman "lightning calculator of pleasures and pains, who oscillates like a homogeneous globule of desire of happiness under the impulse of stimuli that shift about the area, but leave him intact." After lunch, I was confronted with a rich history of humanity rooted in biology, interacting with other species, and dependent on the environment and each other, our morality evolving through the social interactions of our primate branch of the family tree.

In Professor Provine's class I learned that Charles Darwin was a contemporary of the "classical" economists (men like Malthus, Mill, and Ricardo), and they borrowed ideas from one another back in the day. The only economist we ever heard of across campus was a prophet named Adam Smith who published the biblical *Wealth of Nations* in 1776, the same year our founding fathers (who must have been economists, right?) signed the Declaration of Independence. It turns out Smith wasn't called an "economist" in his day. He was a "moral philosopher." Blasphemy.

I didn't learn this in my economics classes because much of economics was taught ahistorically. Why learn about past ideas, debates, or schools of thought when the mathematical perfection of the neoclassical model was before us? But Professor Provine, teaching with joint appointments in history and ecology, got me thinking. When I stumbled across John

Kenneth Galbraith's *Economics in Perspective* in a used-book sale, I couldn't resist. Here was a Harvard professor and advisor to presidents Roosevelt, Truman, Kennedy, and Johnson, who outright rejected the abstraction from reality of his profession. As I thumbed through his work, I read that "economic ideas are always and intimately a product of their own time and place; they cannot be seen apart from the world they interpret."

Hmmm. Perhaps economic theory in an age of cheap and abundant fossil fuels need not concern itself with the environment. Perhaps a model that atomized people would predictably promote policies that, well, atomized people. Perhaps a society with an ethic of consumption would grow to accept a measure of a statistical life as the hypothetical wage of a mother's saved time while improperly buckling up her kid.

In reading economic history, I discovered that the classical economists of the 1700s and 1800s were careful to separate out land in their production function, alongside capital and labor. In the time and place of cleric-turned-economist Thomas Malthus, economic value was thought to come *from* labor working the land *with* capital. Inputs into a production process were viewed as complements to one another, always and everywhere used together. Sure, better technology could substitute for land and labor, but only to a point. Smith's baker could bake more bread with a better oven, but he'd always need more wheat for flour and fuel for heat. It was the agricultural surplus—all the extra food from farmers—that made all other economic activity and trade possible. In his 1798 "Essay on the Principle of Population," Malthus lamented, "The power of population is so superior to the power in the earth to produce subsistence for man, that premature death must in some shape or other visit the human race."

Hmmm. The core of "neo"-classical economics had stripped out land as a factor of production. A Malthusian tragedy simply wasn't possible on paper. At the heights of the US environmental movement, the

American Economic Association's 1969 reader on welfare economics by Stanford professors Kenneth Arrow and Tibor Scitovsky had no reference to the environment or the capacity of the Earth "to produce subsistence for man." As the Cuyahoga River in Ohio caught fire (again) in 1969, economists pointed to side notes in textbooks that recognized "Pigouvian externalities," exceptions to the rule of market efficiency that could be "corrected" in supply curves through technology or demand curves through changing consumer tastes. In the 1973 Ely Lecture of the American Economic Association, Nobel laureate and MIT growth theorist Robert Solow, speaking a bit tongue-in-cheek about the power of technical substitution in the neoclassical model, noted, "The world can, in effect, get along without natural resources, so exhaustion is just an event, not a catastrophe."

By the 1970s, labor was also hard pressed for attention as a capital theory of growth prevailed. Even the focus on capital diminished into the '80s under the Chicago School. Attention was turned instead to getting the conditions right for a general equilibrium model: a web of markets all brought into balance through rational actors reacting to free-floating prices. University of Chicago economists asked, "How do we get the real world to match the conditions of our models?" Stripped away from regulations and government, free markets could take care of themselves. And what's true in the physical realm of widgets must hold for the financial realm of money. By 1990, the Nobel prize was shared by three financial economists: Professor Markowitz on "micro theory of portfolio management for individual wealth holders," Professor Miller on "contributions in the field of corporate finance," and Professor Sharpe on "a general theory for the pricing of financial assets."

The econ superheroes had figured out how to make something from nothing—financial asset valuation—and the class of '87 from the Year of the Gekko took notice. I enrolled in finance classes at Cornell and played stock trading games with real-time tickers from Wall Street, just like in the movie. We were bused from College Street to Wall Street to take in the full majesty of the trading floor. I wiggled my way into MBA classes and learned to write business plans and compete in case competitions. I watched graduating seniors land six-figure offers. Go forth, young man, study economics, major in business, make lots of money. My dad was right.

Yet my mom's voice lingered in my subconscious, and that damn evolutionary biology class gnawed at my sense of a real world out of reach of economists. I couldn't help but wonder who else was thinking about the implications of magical production functions with no matter and no energy to run the economy. Easy-bake cash ovens with no resources and no waste. An economy sketched as a circular flow diagram with firms on one side, households on the other, and the sum of exchange in dollars as the goal. An isolated economic system with its own set of rules in direct conflict with the biophysical world and outright hostile to the social.

At Cornell, economic education was everywhere. Consumer economics in the College of Human Ecology, labor economics in the School of Industrial and Labor Relations, business economics in the School of Business Administration, agricultural economics in the College of Agriculture and Life Sciences, and, of course, straight-up economics in the College of Arts and Sciences. No matter the subdiscipline, we were inoculated with economic theory in the economics department, but there were many choices of subject matter to which to apply our new craft.

Back when I applied to Cornell, the decision of which economics flavor to study had been easy. The Department of Agricultural Economics was housed on the public side of the university and so was much, much cheaper. Sold. So when I found myself struggling to build bridges between the life sciences and social sciences, I had a somewhat sympathetic support group in my home department. These were economists who had to at least consider soil and water. Some actually grew up on farms and now shared a corner of campus with plant scientists, forest ecologists, and climatologists. And there was even a class called "natural resource and environmental economics," which seemed to be just the bridge I was searching for.

~

Professor Duane Chapman didn't look like an economist. Unkempt hair, untrimmed beard, and a quiet demeanor that conveyed anything but the "superiority of economists" I had experienced across campus. His research and writing centered on problems, not theories, such as air pollution, acid rain legislation, nuclear waste management, mining impacts, and oil depletion. Economics was presented more as a tool and less a worldview. Insights from economic models were held up against physics, chemistry, and biology. The influence of power, politics, and privilege on economic function and form were the undertones of the world according to Duane. He had studied economics at Berkeley in the '60s, and his inner hippie often shone through.

Dispassionate reason was still an aspiration in Duane's world, but the boundaries were expanded beyond the circular flow diagram of dollars for widgets. In natural resource economics, I discovered a line of inquiry that reached back to classical economics, reinserting land into the production function, along with coal, oil, minerals, timber, fish, crops, and other natural resources that fed the economic machine. The economy was sustained by flows from the Earth and sun, and the resource economist's job was to keep the engine tuned and well fed.

At the other end was the tailpipe, and in "environmental" economics I found a newer focus on the externalities of the free market system. Economists had dusted off Arthur Pigou's *Economics of Welfare*, first published in 1920, to make the obvious case that markets left unchecked would consider only *private* costs and benefits. Costs such as pollution were imposed on the public at large, not tallied in the ledgers of a company, and should therefore be estimated and included in the price of goods and services through—dare I say it—government regulation. Environmental economics was born on the heels of the first Earth Day, April 22, 1970, and scrambled to catch up with new laws to clean our water and air, protect endangered species, and balance development with conservation.

Duane's class situated the economy as an intermediary between resource extraction and pollution emission, a bridge I sought between the natural sciences and social sciences. Questions over limits to growth now arose as we read reports from the Club of Rome and ran simulations with the World3 computer model. We learned of long-held criticisms of gross domestic product as a measure of society's welfare (the holy grail in our macroeconomics classes). We were introduced to the Brundtland Report, the 1987 publication of the World Commission on Environment and Development that popularized the concept "sustainable development."

Most classes left me with more questions than answers. A sustainable economy, designed with the UN Commission's goal to "meet the needs of the present without compromising the ability of future generations to meet their own needs," called into question an allegiance to consumption, a morality of greed, and a limitless frontier. Shit, now what? I could feel my teenage dreams of a career in high finance slip away.

I must have made an impression through my endless questions. Duane asked if I ever thought about graduate school, probably just to get me out the door one day. Sure, I'd work a few years after graduation, get some business chops, then do my MBA and head to Wall Street— my go-to answer since high school. Had I thought about a master's of science instead, a degree with a research thesis that would pay my way? My thought process went something like this: "Go to school for free, are you kidding me? Where do I sign up?"

The summer between BS and MS I was hired to read, think, and write—the first time I had earned a paycheck outside flipping burgers or mowing laws. My research project was the economics of climate change. This was the perfect project for a morally conflicted twenty-one-year-old: a charge to unpack the mysterious equations under the hood of coupled climate–economy models. The central conclusion of economists studying climate change in the '80s and '90s was that global warming was good (or at least not too bad) for the economy. Unlike my economics courses to date, Duane coached me to accept nothing at face value, especially from economists.

So I set aside *Liar's Poker* and dove into *The End of Nature*, the first book by a Harvard-educated twenty-something named Bill McKibben who was all the rage. Writing for a general audience, McKibben made the eye-popping claim that nature was dead. With the pen of a poet and insight of an atmospheric scientist, he argued that nature as pristine, separate from human interference, no longer existed on a planet where we were transforming the global climate system. The world was indeed our oyster, and we were boiling it.

McKibben had authored my generation's *Silent Spring*, a renewed call to pay attention to science and act with haste. Rachel Carson's writing ushered in a decade of sweeping environmental policy, from the 1963 Clean Air Act to the 1973 Endangered Species Act. The environmental movement for McKibben was now global, and NASA's James Hansen had rung the alarm bells in his historic testimony to the US Senate in 1988. By the 1992 publication of Senator Al Gore's *Earth in the Balance*, politics was catching up to science, and twelve years of profits over planet under Reaganomics was under assault. In a heated presidential election year, the Bush administration had just exempted itself from our Endangered Species Act in the notorious "God Squad" hearings over spotted owl habitat, and a US delegation was met with global disdain at the 1992 Earth Summit in Rio de Janeiro.

As I peeled back the layers of how economists were considering climate change, the disconnect between the science of Earth systems and a religion of economic systems came into focus. Economists such as Yale

University's William Nordhaus treated climate change as a cost–benefit analysis at a global scale. His Dynamic Integrated Climate-Economy model (a.k.a. DICE) was a simple utility maximization problem centered around a representative agent, a single human representing the consumer preferences for all humanity. This particular homogenous globule got pleasure from consumption and pain from paying to reduce greenhouse gases. A perfectly predictable warming climate system hurt the global production of more things to consume. Technology was modeled as manna from Heaven, an automatic bonus of a growing economy that would make more and more stuff with less and less waste. To "optimize" pollution reduction, the hypothetical utility maximizer evaluated sacrificing more consumption today against an investment that might pay off tomorrow, all assuming an annual "discount rate" that made the future much, much less valuable than the present.

The conclusion from "rolling the DICE," as Nordhaus was apt to describe model runs, was simple: Reducing greenhouse gas emissions had known costs today and unknown benefits in the future. If industrialized countries were to do anything, it should be small reductions that made sense for other reasons, such as saving money on your energy bill (what came to be known as a "no regrets" climate change policy under the Bush administration). And most of the smoothly increasing, perfectly predictable impacts were assumed to happen to agriculture. In a National Academy of Sciences study, Professor Nordhaus concluded, "Agriculture, the part of the economy that is sensitive to climate change, accounts for just 3 percent of national output. This means there is no way to get a very large effect on the US economy."[17] As with any other economic output, food was valued at the margin. The United States could just substitute less food for more of something else, or perhaps import food in trade for something else. This sort of economic logic could get you a Nobel! In fact, it did in 2018.

The superiority of economists was at play, and their political advisees liked what they heard. Scientists were deemed "irrational" under an economic worldview. They didn't account for faith in markets to forever improve technology, belief in human ingenuity to adapt to a changing climate, and reliance on infinite economic growth to pay for it all. Economic models included clairvoyant farmers who would adopt new cultivars, shift crop mixes, or simply sell the farm and do something else with their L and K under a new climate. And the representative utility maximizer averaged out the Manhattanites safe behind a new seawall with the Bangladeshi refugees fleeing a flooded nation.

My master's thesis research ended up challenging this reigning economic dogma on climate change on both scientific and ethical fronts. I worked with plant scientists to call into question climate–economy models that assumed higher levels of carbon dioxide would accelerate plant growth, so-called CO_2 fertilization. This was certainly true in controlled greenhouse experiments, behind the glass where water, nutrients, and temperature were optimized. However, take away these assumptions under in-field conditions of drought, pests, heat, and weather variability, and model outputs turn from pretty good to really bad for agriculture.

Certainly more honest science could build more realistic models to inform better decisions. Climate–economy models were improving all the time, but there was a party line that seemed baked into model conclusions. Statistician George Box was often quoted in my modeling classes: "All models are wrong, but some are useful." But I started to ask, "Useful for whom, and for what purpose?"

I published "From Ecology to Economics: The Case against CO_2 Fertilization," in an up-and-coming journal called *Ecological Economics*, my first publication.[18] The first sentence of the conclusion laid out my chicken-and-egg hypothesis: "Funding from the US Environmental Protection Agency, Department of Agriculture, and Department of Energy has clearly pushed for modeling the maximum benefits from CO_2 fertilization." Then I got a bit snarky further down the page: "Relying on CO_2 fertilization to fertilize the world's agriculture is analogous to relying on your car's exhaust to fertilize your home garden." Why weren't the confounding factors of pests, water and nutrient availability, and the plant-killing pollutants that came along with CO_2 considered? My concluding paragraph was completely off script from the economist-in-training handbook:

> Concluding on a moral note, CO_2 fertilization is more of a justification for fossil fuel dependence than an interpretation of ecological reality. The profile of this dependence reveals one-fourth of the world's population consuming three-fourths of the world's energy. The fires of fossil fuels have left the few with the riches of industrialization, and the many with the externalities of their use. Glorifying the emissions of CO_2 as benefiting the world's agriculture supports the status quo of vast inequalities between nations, avoids pertinent policy decisions on mitigation and adaptation, and hampers efforts for global commitment to preservation and sustainability. Misinterpreting the risks of tomorrow can only devalue the prevention efforts of today.

A peer-reviewed journal with "economics" in its title actually published this drivel. Who were these peers? I didn't know it at the time, but I had discovered a like-minded community of economists who didn't let their training get in the way of science fact and moral reason.

~

I defended my master's thesis the month the Clinton/Gore team won the White House. My foray into climate–economy models left me disenchanted with all flavors of economics, environmental or otherwise. Integration of the environment *into* economics had seemed promising. But the dominant economic worldview still, well, dominated. Economy was the mother, environment the daughter. All seemed upside down. How could environment be born of—embedded within—economy?

Shouldn't it be the other way around? Was anyone thinking about economics as a life science, built on an edifice of physics, chemistry, and biology? Was an economic worldview somehow more deeply flawed, not to be rescued by simply drawing boundaries around the system a bit wider? Now what?

Duane offered me a shot at redemption: funding for a PhD in . . . more economics. My wife had just been accepted into Cornell's veterinary college (yes, I was married with kids at twenty-one), and we were committed to Ithaca for another four years. She had a plan. I had Duane. Get paid to learn and defer my student loans a bit longer. Sure, where do I sign up?

The PhD was a different animal all together. The first year was pure economic theory and abstract mathematics in the economics department, followed by a comprehensive examination. The prize for passing was to continue in your home department. Fail, and a master's degree was the end of the road. In my crop, half got the booby prize.

I survived through a newfound talent: a photographic memory. Not perfect, but enough to memorize math proofs and regurgitate equations to mind-numbing questions. If you imagined real people with real struggles behind the alphas and betas, symbols and signs, you wouldn't survive. Abstraction was both the tool and goal of the education of an economist. In hindsight, we were dumbed down by being made to feel brilliant.

The grand plan had the opposite effect on me. The more mathematics I mastered, the more stupid I felt. I went in search of ammunition, not from without but from within. Many had attacked the economics armada from outside the profession, including scientists such as Stanford's Paul Ehrlich, Dartmouth's Donella Meadows, and Cornell's David Pimentel, to name a few. But who was mounting a mutiny from onboard?

With eyes wide open, it's amazing what you find. In a free book pile in Warren Hall, I stumbled across *Economics, Ecology, Ethics: Essays Toward a Steady-State Economy*, edited by Herman Daly. Working from within the heart of the mainstream, a senior economist at the World Bank had published a collection of essays pushing for a properly sized and justly shared economy. The laws of physics were cast as central to the economic problem. Theologians framed economic choice with moral ends. And Daly himself made the case for "Economics as a Life Science" in a reprint from his *Journal of Political Economy* article from 1968. Apparently, he had been inciting the mutiny for some time.

In Daly, I discovered a member of the high priesthood turned mutineer. He had studied with Romanian economist Nicholas Georgescu-Roegen, whose 1971 magnum opus *The Entropy Law and the Economic Process* was heralded as a masterpiece by apostles and traitors alike. With theologian John Cobb, Daly wrote *For the Common Good* in 1989, a book that helped frame an "ecological" economics formalized with colleagues that same year through a new professional society and academic journal. His stint at the World Bank from 1988 to 1994 helped institutionalize sustainability and began to wean the development agenda away from GDP growth as the singular metric of success.

In a fit of rebellion, I declared myself an ecological economist. Academics like to split hairs over names, but the significance of an "ecological" economics to me was its overt challenge to the mainstream. My graduate classes in environmental and natural resource economics seemed like mere servants to the master, where the market could be fixed simply by getting the prices right. With ecological economics, it felt like I was joining an insurgence that was finally coming of age.

As good mentors are apt to do, Duane insisted I make the case. He was writing a new textbook on environmental economics and challenged me to write a concluding chapter that would cast doubt on the previous eighteen. I accepted, and my doctoral dissertation was now teed up, as were my job talks for the interviews to come. When I saw an ad recruiting an ecological economist in the Department of Economics at Rensselaer Polytechnic Institute (RPI), perhaps the first such opening at a university anywhere in the world, the door opened wide for me to join fellow conscientious objectors to economic rule.

At RPI we set out to build the world's first doctoral program in the field. I joined John Gowdy (also a student of Georgescu-Roegen) and Sabine O'Hara (a German economist with roots in the growing European ecological economics movement). Our aim was to topple the mainstream from the halls of America's oldest engineering college. In subsequent years I helped found the US Society for Ecological Economics; served on the board of our international society; authored and co-authored the requisite number of papers and books to get tenure and then a full professorship; worked with some of the pioneers in our field, including Herman Daly; and went on to manage the Gund Institute for Ecological Economics at the University of Vermont.

Mine is not an extraordinary career by any stretch of the imagination but rather the intentional outcome of renegades who seeded a new path for the education of an economist. When ecological economics was formalized, new grads like me were supposed to be hatched. This book is ultimately a reflection on my own successes and failures during this stage of a broader movement to educate a new generation of economists. Like others before me, I followed the bandwagon at the advice of my father but got disillusioned along the way with the good sense of my mother. A teenager of the '80s, student of the '90s, and teacher of millennials today, I'm of a generation now coming to terms with the mantra of "greed is good" in our family, work, community, and political lives.

We were not an aberration in our faith in economics to illuminate the way but the beginning of a current wave. The power and stature of economics have only grown, particularly as the dominant worldview of a growing financial sector. By 2006, the size of the financial industry as a share of the US economy had more than doubled since the Year of the Gekko, hitting the too-big-to-fail heights of over 8 percent just before the Great Recession. The sector's share of all US profits grew to as high as 40 percent—yes, 40 percent of all profits from 8 percent of the economy. Between 1980 and 2006, the US GDP increased fivefold while financial sector profits increased sixteen times over.[19]

The higher education boot camp was all too happy to produce soldiers of finance. The Ivy League to Wall Street pipeline grew leaps and bounds. By 2006, 46 percent of jobs landed by Princeton grads were in the financial services. Yale and Harvard placed one in four of their 2006 class in finance.[20] By 2012, the most popular bachelor's degree nationwide was business, more than twice the number of graduates in the other social sciences and humanities combined, each with Econ 101 at the base of their learning pyramid.[21] Business is now the most popular master's degree in the United States, surpassing education for the title.[22]

Millions of magical thinkers, wielding business and economics degrees, are now among us. And Econ 101 features prominently on the freshman transcripts of millions more. In *USA Today*'s June 2014 "Surviving College" section, the headline read, "5 classes every college student should take (no matter what your major)." At the top of the list is the finance–accounting–business management triad, with principles of economics serving as the prerequisite gatekeeper. Surviving college for many, now, requires an economics inoculation.

Today I see the conflict in my own students' eyes, a struggle similar to my own with social norms of consumer over citizen, market over community, growth over development, and discipline over unity. Our entire consumer society has come of age in the Anthropocene, the term many scientists now call our human-dominated geological epoch. Naming the Anthropocene could be yet another sign of human hubris, a false sense of planetary domination achieved by destroying the only home we've ever known. Or this could be the beginning of a grand reconciliation project, between each other and all forms of life with whom we share the Earth.

I'm convinced that economics as currently taught and practiced throughout the world is a planetary path to ruin, but there are obvious cracks in the castle walls. I'm certainly not the first to see the economic fortress straining under its own weight and delusions, and I won't be the last. But perhaps my own awakening to the tragic myths of economics can deliver on the promise of my mentors and obligation to my children to be good ancestors and leave the world a bit better than we found it.

CHAPTER 2

Ascension of the Queen

> The ideas of economists and political philosophers, both
> when they are right and when they are wrong, are more
> powerful than is commonly understood. Indeed, the
> world is ruled by little else. Practical men, who believe
> themselves to be quite exempt from any intellectual
> influences, are usually slaves of some defunct economist.[1]
>
> —John Maynard Keynes

It was just another September weekend in New York City. Hot summer days were giving way to cool fall nights. The Yankees were a few wins shy of a trip to the playoffs. And more than 8 million people went about their busy lives. But against the constant noise from the city that never sleeps, a simple call to action managed to escape:

OccupyWallStreet. September 17. Bring Tent.

By weekend's end, Zuccotti Park, a few blocks from the New York Stock Exchange, was a full-on encampment. In the weeks and months to come, sleeping bags and coolers led to tents and electric generators.

A General Assembly convened to make decisions by consensus, volunteers staffed a makeshift kitchen, and donations poured in from around the world to support a 24/7 occupation. A People's Library took hold of the northeast corner, workshops and discussion forums bubbled up throughout lower Manhattan, and teach-ins began in the city's universities and colleges. Anyone could join a conversation on topics ranging from Palestinian rights and nuclear disarmament to healthcare and climate change, but the common threads were growing social and economic inequality and solutions to take back democracy.

Zuccotti Park was private property, and absent any directive from the owner, initially the police let it all unfold. Without a city permit to use amplified sound, a human microphone was born. Daily crowds shouted in unison, one soundbite at a time, from announcements to debates to full lectures. When the fire department removed gas-powered generators, protesters switched over to bicycle-powered batteries to charge cellphones, laptops, and Wi-Fi to keep stoking the social media fire.

What began as an image of contradiction in *Adbusters* magazine—a dancer atop Wall Street's charging bull—quickly grew to a global rally against corporate greed and government austerity. A month after Occupy Wall Street jammed up lower Manhattan and lit up Twitter and Facebook, all fifty states had their own protests and occupations in nearly four hundred cities.[2] There were over fifty Occupy groups in California alone.[3] On October 15, this growing network joined global protests from Spain to Iceland to Greece under the slogan "United for #GlobalChange." Marches and encampments surged, by one count, in 951 cities across eighty-two countries.[4] Thousands marched on New York's Times Square to chants of "We are the 99%," and hundreds of thousands nicknamed "the indignant" took to the streets of European cities.

Occupy, initially ignored by city mayors and corporate media alike as a moment, had turned into a movement. By GDP standards, the US economy had fully recovered from the Great Recession, but data on employment and household income told a different story. Throughout 2011, US unemployment rates hovered around 9 percent, but underemployment, including skilled workers looking for better jobs and part-timers looking for full-time work, was over 16 percent. Youth unemployment hit forty-year highs across the United States and Europe, with one in five under age twenty-five looking for work in the richest nations in the world.[5] Median household income in the United States had fallen $5,000 from 1999 highs, more than a month's pay lost to a household in the middle of the US income distribution.[6]

The 2008–2009 Great Recession also punctuated more than thirty years of a great "regression," where middle-class America was falling further and further behind the nation's top earners. An average middle-class household had nearly $18,000 less income in 2007 due to nearly thirty years of growing income inequality.[7] Labor's share of the GDP pie had fallen precipitously from 1970 highs to all-time lows, despite the fact that the average American worker was producing more per hour than ever before.[8] Between 1979 and 2013, labor productivity grew by nearly 65 percent, while hourly pay of 80 percent of the private-sector workforce grew by a little over 8 percent. However, the top 1 percent of earners were doing phenomenally well, with cumulative gains in annual wages topping 153 percent over the same period.[9]

Two weeks before Occupy began, former labor secretary Robert Reich published a *New York Times* op-ed on the causes and consequences of "The Limping Middle Class" in America.[10] Since the late 1970s, politicians nationwide had deregulated and privatized the economy, cut spending on public infrastructure and education, weakened social safety nets such as unemployment insurance, and withered unions to less than 8 percent of private-sector workers. Taxes on capital gains and wealth inheritance were cut, while sales and payroll taxes increased. Reich argued that the consequence was unprecedented inequality that destabilized both democracy and the economy by putting too much wealth and earnings into the hands of too few. It was no coincidence that the top earners' share of the nation's income peaked in 1928 and 2007, the two years before the two biggest economic crashes the world had ever known.

In Zuccotti Park, these economic stats and stories found their way into speeches through the human microphone, slogans on cardboard signs, and manifestos in paper leaflets. When the nonpartisan Congressional Budget Office released their October "Trends in the Distribution of Household Income between 1979 and 2007," a snoozer in a typical year was circulated like a bestselling spy novel from the People's Library. The human mic, armed with facts and figures about growing inequality and a lopsided economic recovery, was echoing around the world, "We will limp no more."

Not surprisingly, the political pundits and economic establishment either ignored the movement or later claimed it was all for nothing. However, an undeniable narrative was born that helped shape the 2012 elections and fed a growing antiestablishment sentiment among the electorate on both the right and left. Four years later, a billionaire nationalist from the 1 percent and a democratic socialist against the 1 percent rode a wave of economic populism into the 2016 presidential race. All the while, a new generation of voters, activists, and citizens found their voice among the hashtags and YouTube videos that questioned the basic assumptions of society, including a seemingly out-of-touch economics discipline postulated in the classroom and propagated in policy.

It was here, on college campuses throughout the United States, where Occupy Wall Street found a sympathetic audience. Notably at Ivy League schools, Occupy cast a shadow of doubt on an employment pipeline that kept investment banks flush with talent. In the years preceding the Great Recession, universities like Princeton, Harvard, and Yale sent between 20 and 40 percent of their graduating classes to the financial sector—as high as 46 percent from Princeton in 2006 at the height of Wall Street excess.[11] By the end of November 2011, a *New York Times* headline said it all: "At Top Colleges, Anti–Wall St. Fervor Complicates Recruiting."[12]

I remember when the recruitment craze from investment bankers was just getting started during my Cornell days, but the pressure on millennials to choose finance careers was extraordinary. And it worked. As math professor Chris Wiggins from Columbia University explained to the *New York Times*, "Zero percent of people show up at the Ivy League saying they want to be an I-banker, but 25 and 30 percent leave thinking that it's their calling. The banks have really perfected, over the last three decades, these large recruitment machines."

But Occupy helped tap the brakes. A new narrative reverberating just blocks from Wall Street not-so-subtly suggested to students that a finance career, while lucrative, lacked meaning, and that a dominant economic worldview espoused in their classrooms was no longer beyond question. Student newspapers at Cornell, Dartmouth, and Harvard featured columns that urged their peers to look beyond the financial sector for work. Stanford students launched an online campaign to "Stop the Brain Drain."[13] And for the first time in decades, students joined together in protest of power, with one particular target in their crosshairs: Econ 101.

~

Perhaps no student protest received greater attention than the November 2 walkout of professor Greg Mankiw's principles of economics class, the largest class at Harvard University. An open letter from the student organizers declared a resolve "to express our discontent with the bias inherent in this introductory economics course" and deep concern "about the way that this bias affects students, the University, and our greater society."[14] The bias was identified as a specific, limited view of economics that they believed "perpetuates problematic and inefficient systems of economic inequality in our society today."

The students took aim, in part, at Professor Mankiw himself. As chairman of the Council of Economic Advisors during president George W. Bush's first term, Mankiw was a symbol of a conservative brand of economics that Occupy blamed for the Great Recession. As one first-year student told the *Harvard Crimson*, "His conservative views are the kind that created the collapse of 2008."[15]

But in the larger economics profession Mankiw was caretaker of the faith, and so students also walked out on the discipline. As author of the best-selling principles textbook, the wunderkind groomed at prep school and Princeton had become king of the self-proclaimed queen of the social sciences. By 2015, in its seventh edition, *Principles of Economics* sold for $280, with more than one million copies in circulation and an estimated $42 million in royalties paid to Professor Mankiw.[16]

At the heart of *Principles* is an argument for laissez-faire economics, a deep faith in free markets to efficiently allocate private resources for private gain. Income inequality is simply a natural outcome of an efficient labor market that rewards some more than others based on contribution to the economy. As Mankiw made clear in his peer-reviewed response to Occupy, a 2013 paper titled "Defending the One Percent," labor productivity varies within a society, as do tastes for consumption, leisure, and job attributes.[17] Unequal distribution is simply a product of uneven marginal products of labor (your contribution to the economy with each new hour of effort) and varying marginal utilities of income (your pleasure from each new dollar of spending).

In the world according to Mankiw, the 1 percent had the talent, effort, and taste to merit their "just deserts." To redistribute their "earnings" to others would violate the most sacred principle of economics: the Pareto efficiency criterion. Italian economist Vilfredo Pareto outlined this idea in 1906, during the early years of the neoclassical revolution, and it has been economic dogma ever since.

In a perfectly competitive economy, so the century-old story goes, everyone will work, spend, and consume until all "Pareto improvements" are exhausted, a point of market equilibrium where no one can be made better off without making someone else worse off. This maximizes consumption and production and thus creates the biggest economic pie for all to share. The size of your slice is worked out in a system of free exchange, with no one forced to produce or consume. This conception of fairness precludes value judgments. Comparing the most frivolous desires of the rich with the most basic needs of the poor is not allowed. Nor is judging the worth of a hedge fund manager's contribution to society against that of a preschool teacher.

In "Defending the One Percent," Mankiw went on to compare a hypothetical law that forces kidney donations from the healthy to the sick with redistribution of income from the wealthy to the poor. If a society couldn't tolerate the former, so the logic goes, how could it endorse the latter? In the analogy, a million dollars of discretionary income that could have been spent on a rich man's third or fourth home is equivalent to an organ. The million dollars instead taxed and redistributed to thousands of homeless in soup kitchens is the transplant.

At the heart of Occupy was an outright rejection of this chain of logic, including market efficiency as the primary organizing principle of society. Age-old questions were back on the table. What resources were being allocated and for whose gain? Where was the dividing line between private and public? Was private gain even possible without public support? What should be counted as earned from private effort versus taken from the public commons? Were public institutions serving all the people or just the privileged few?

In Zuccotti Park, the narrative was, "The game is rigged." Inequality was seen as a function of the structure and rules of the game, not only the talent of the players. The idealistic assumptions of the core economic model didn't hold. Imperfect information, environmental externalities, and monopoly power were all discussed in Econ 101 as market failures—exceptions to the rule of market efficiency. But nationwide occupations, university teach-ins, class walkouts, and a global wave of civil disobedience in the months and years ahead cried in unison: Market. failure is the rule, not the exception.

In a rigged economy, benefits flow to the powerful and costs to the powerless, inequality widens as wealth begets wealth, and prosperity grows alongside rising despair. Economic recessions tend to shine bright lights on the trends of status quo systems. The powerless, with nothing left to lose, rise up as a last resort and demand change. The gap between theory and reality becomes too large to ignore. Growing inequality in a nation of plenty comes into focus.

For students of economics, the questions never asked include, How did the queen of the social sciences ascend to a throne that justified prosperity for the few while forsaking poverty of the many? Why does a narrative of progress that rose to prominence in the nineteenth century persist today alongside so much evidence of its inadequacy? What competing narratives were lost or silenced along the way?

My generation learned to sweep such questions under the rug, but. millennials wanted answers. Since the Harvard walkout, student protests have emerged at other prominent universities around the world. In the United Kingdom, University of Manchester students formed the Post-Crash Economics Society to campaign for pluralism in economics, including a report on the failings of economics education and a roadmap for reform.[18] Protest groups followed at campuses throughout England and Scotland, from Cambridge and London to Leeds and Glasgow.

By 2014, economics students from forty-one groups in nineteen countries formed the International Student Initiative for Pluralist Economics.[19] In a letter to the profession they declared, "The lack of intellectual diversity does not only restrain education and research. It limits our ability to contend with the multidimensional challenges of the twenty-first century—from financial stability to food security and climate change."[20] And some of their teachers were writing letters of their own, criticizing an "intellectual monoculture which is reinforced by a system of public university funding, based on journal rankings that are heavily biased in favour of orthodoxy and against intellectual diversity."[21]

The queen was under fire, but she would not go down without a fight.

～

The worldview in the crosshairs—neoclassical economics—has dominated economic teaching, research, and policy for well over 100 years. Its roots can be traced to the late nineteenth century, when a new breed of economists as mathematicians imagined a new social order. "Classical" economics based on moral philosophy was left behind in favor of an idealized system of equations that assumed away any ethical qualms to pure self-interest. The system was set up so that only the next decision mattered to each individual consumer or producer. If the next benefit was bigger than the next cost, then consume or produce more. If not, then stop. The sum of all these individual decisions would then be what's best for society.

French mathematical economist Léon Walras (1834–1910) is most often credited with developing the core of today's neoclassical model, what came to be known as the "marginalist revolution."[22] In 1874, Walras pulled together the first comprehensive mathematical description of the small, individual, incremental decisions that, left alone, could bring the entire economy into balance. Economic historian Joseph Schumpeter later called Walras's Éléments d'Économie Politique Pure the "Magna Carta of Economics."[23]

Walras's "general equilibrium" theory was built on the inquiries of classical economics, but he proposed that the purity of mathematics would break economics free from philosophy to become a truly scientific social science. In the tradition of Rene Descartes and the French rationalists, Walras set out to find a "scientific solution" to "the Problem of Distribution of Wealth," which would be "for social science what the laws of Kepler have been for astronomy."[24]

Economists have always had physics envy, but Walras was one of the first to act on the impulse. Looking for first principles to define economic life, Walras drew from a Cartesian brand of physics to construct a purely mechanistic world of economic exchange. He crafted careful assumptions about consumer and producer preferences that would then "naturally" lead all markets to simultaneous (a.k.a. "general") equilibrium. A perfect social order would result where—you guessed it—no one could be made better off without making someone else worse off.

A purely mathematical approach to a "theory of social wealth"—the subtitle to his *Elements of Pure Economics*—could evade both politics and morality. Economists of the classical era, beginning with Adam Smith and continuing through David Ricardo, Thomas Malthus, and John Stuart Mill, had made the case that individual well-being was critical to the wealth of nations. Their political motivations were to wrangle power from church and state. However, they never fully abandoned the constraints of a moral person with social obligations to their brethren (and God). Economic value to the classical economists was still bound to moral codes of religion and physical transformation of the land by capital and labor.

Through mathematics, Walras was able to sidestep observation and moral persuasion with a purely deductive rationale for free markets. He need only assume people were self-interested and rational, producers were competitive and plentiful, information was free and complete, capital and labor were substitutable, and all change was smooth and continuous. Walras was Smith on steroids with the newfound power of Cartesian mathematics and the cover of untestable assumptions.

Adam Smith's invisible hand was now in full view, sketched on graph paper with precise Cartesian coordinates. Many efficient outcomes were possible depending on the initial allocation of resources, differing consumer tastes, and variability of production technology. But any equilibrium reached through private, uncoerced, unregulated exchange was assumed better than the centrally planned alternative.

In Walrasian economics, the burden of proof was on others, not economists, to argue that the starting point for free exchange was unjust. With a focus on efficient outcomes, mathematical economists could disregard the influence of inheritance on intergenerational wealth transfer, the impact of discrimination on bolstering a privileged race, or the power over labor that came from enclosing the commons through private ownership. The model was only forward looking, asking, What are the possibilities along a frontier of efficient outcomes given an initial distribution of resources? A science of choice at the margin need only allow for incremental improvements to anyone, rich or poor, to make the case for maximizing social welfare for everyone.

This marginalist revolution set a course for economics different from all other social sciences and humanities for the next century. Mathematics and deductive logic laid the groundwork for the twentieth-century textbooks to follow. The lineage started with Alfred Marshall's *Principles of Economics* (1890), extended to Paul Samuelson's synthesis of microeconomics and a postwar macroeconomics in *Foundations of Economic Analysis* (1947), and continues today in *Principles of Economics* by Gregory Mankiw, leading a parade of textbooks in the lucrative Econ 101 market. Generations of students have learned the same basic story of the primacy of efficiency, the purity of perfect competition, and the claim of mathematical deduction as scientific proof.

However, deductive reasoning has always had a debilitating weakness. If an assumption is untrue, the conclusion is suspect, if not dead wrong. Through *in*ductive reasoning—observe, hypothesize, test, repeat—assumptions of the Walrasian model have been proven wrong year after year, economist after economist, and even Nobel after Nobel in recent years. For example, when sellers know more than buyers, information is asymmetric, which breaks an essential free market rule. Also, markets concentrate ownership and power over time through positive feedbacks baked into capitalist systems, overturning the benevolent assumptions of an impartial invisible hand. Modeling the economy as a whole based on the actions of individuals has failed even the most basic tests of predictive power. And in more recent years, economists working with the behavioral sciences have found people largely to be irrational, cooperative, and even moral, surprising no one except perhaps narrowly trained economists.

Time and again, the neoclassical model has been challenged and found wanting. Granted, some accommodations have been made along the way, particularly for a truly "macro" economics that emerged from the Great Depression, where savings, investment, money, and interest rates could steer the economy, not just the sum of hapless individual decisions. The development of any thought system is a dance between the deductive and the inductive. But in mainstream economics, by and large, deductive reasoning has won out. The core nineteenth-century principles persist today, especially in the more conservative wings of the discipline where even the lessons of the 1930s have been lost to history. Why?

The short answer: A wealthy elite has always liked this model—a *lot*. Neoclassical economics presents a world order in which the ups and downs of the business cycle are deemed natural. Ever since Walras, any distribution of wealth and income in society is easily justified as an efficient outcome of a natural process of economic exchange. Any government meddling, especially redistribution of wealth or income, so the story goes, moves the private market away from where it naturally wants to go. Free markets in the model self-correct, so downs will always be followed by ups, and recessions are assumed to be few and far between, a little friction in the gears of the machine.

As true then as today, the general equilibrium model of the economy didn't match up with everyday experience of the everyday person. The industrializing countries of the 1800s experienced a degree of economic instability never seen before. A growing free market society produced extraordinary levels of income and wealth but equally astonishing swings between boom and bust. When Walras published *Elements of Pure Economics* in 1874, the world was in the beginning of what was then called the Great Depression (later renamed the Long Depression when an even greater one hit in the 1930s). After the bank panic of 1873, the first truly international economic crisis hit the British and American economies particularly hard.

But the leading economists of the late 1800s, especially in the United Kingdom and United States, did not experience the economy like everyday people. The neoclassical model was forged during the heights of a depressed global economy by college-educated men of relative privilege. Alfred Marshall, easily the most influential economist emerging from the neoclassical revolution, was educated in the Cambridge system, ascended to the rank of professor of political economy, and founded a Cambridge School of Economics that defined the field in the first half of the twentieth century. His concerns for improving the material conditions of society were no doubt genuine, but his cure was to double down on the free market logic based on a stylized mathematical model, not firsthand experience with poverty or the toils of hard labor.

However, there was one economist who broke the mold, a contemporary of Marshall and Walras who experienced economics not through indoctrination but as a student of life. He challenged the power of the neoclassical model with both critique and alternative but took it a step further to seed a political movement. His story illustrates both the built-in biases of today's dominant model and the power of the status quo to never let it go.

Henry George was born into a middle-class family in a row house in Philadelphia in 1839. He was the second of ten children to Catherine Pratt and Richard George, a publisher of religious texts who encouraged his son's voracious appetite for reading. In an act of early defiance of

Episcopal and school doctrine alike, George quit the seventh grade and found work as a cabin boy, sailing around the world to Australia and India and back again. After a second voyage around Cape Horn to San Francisco, George was swept up in the get-rich-quick craze of the western Gold Rush. He quickly lost what little he had prospecting for gold in British Columbia and eventually found work as a typesetter in San Francisco at nineteen years old.[25]

San Francisco was the definition of a boom town. The California Gold Rush of 1849 had brought an estimated 300,000 forty-niners to the west coast of the Mexican Cession, the major prize of the Mexican–American War. Statehood followed in 1850 in the great political compromise between the slave and free states, and by the time George printed his first newspaper the spoils of the Gold Rush and land claims of early settlers had turned Mexico's Yerba Buena into the first American city west of the Mississippi.

By 1865, Henry George had failed in his initial newspaper endeavors, was married with four children, and was forced to beg in the streets to feed his family. He experienced firsthand the deprivation of poverty amid a growing city that was quite literally the golden gate to the fortunes of prospectors, land speculators, bankers, and trade merchants. He eventually found steady work with the *San Francisco Times* as a printer and quickly rose through the ranks from news and editorial writer to managing editor. Journalism would be his profession, with economics his principal focus.

Unencumbered by formal education, Henry George set out to explain the world around him. The rapid economic transformation of San Francisco was his laboratory. The Gold Rush was only the first wave, and with the transcontinental railroad in sight, George speculated on the next. Writing "What the Railroad Will Bring Us" in 1868, the year before the completion of the Central Pacific Railroad, George concluded that the "California of the new era will be greater, richer, more powerful than the California of the past" but that the coming economic growth "will not be benefit to all of us, but only to a portion."[26] While others saw the material advance of society as progress, George saw a great contradiction between an increasing concentration of wealth among the new industrialists and the growing struggles of the landless poor to compete for lower and lower wages while paying higher and higher rents.

He saw the locomotive as the "great centralizer" in that "it kills little towns and builds up great cities, and in the same way kills little businesses and builds up great ones." He looked to the great cities of the eastern states and Europe for lessons on so-called progress of the past. When George traveled back east later that year, he found the inspiration for what would become his life's work. His son, Henry George, Jr., reflected years later on the "burning thought, a call, a vision" that occurred to his father as he wandered the streets of New York City "filled with wonder at the manifestations of vast wealth" alongside a "poverty and degradation, a want and shame, such as made the young man from the open West sick at heart."[27]

Henry George was a man awakened. He became politically active, using his editorials to argue for tax reform and the end of railroad subsidies, rubbing elbows with like-minded California governor Henry Haught throughout the next decade, and ultimately running (albeit unsuccessfully) for the California legislature. In 1871, he published a forty-eight-page pamphlet on "Our Land and Land Policy, National and State."[28] Selling for 25 cents apiece in the shops of San Francisco, it laid the foundation for his evolving inquiry into the causes and consequences of economic depressions and his "burning thought" that the privatization of land was at the root of "deepening poverty amid advancing wealth."

George was an eyewitness to the closing of the American frontier through the near extermination of Native Americans and the massive land monopolies granted in the wake of colonialization. The west was won at gunpoint but more fundamentally by a belief in manifest destiny: that a United States forged by individual liberty would stretch from coast to coast. Behind the moral justification of western expansion lay a deeply held belief in the sanctity of private property as core to American values, institutions, and democracy. When George lashed out against private property, he struck at the very heart of American exceptionalism and the core teachings of economics ever since Smith.

George pored over the works of the classical economists Smith, Ricardo, and Malthus, asking age-old questions of the source of economic value. The writings of Karl Marx were not yet translated to English; otherwise, he would have found a sympathetic assessment of the interplay between capital ownership and social inequality. Instead of a broad critique of all capital, George followed the tradition of David Ricardo and homed in on the special attributes of land. A bare lot in the middle of a thriving metropolis was valuable because of its proximity to streets, shops, buildings, and other public and private investments, not the effort of the individual landowner. Land value came from location, location, location. Agricultural land was valuable because of the hard work of laborers—plowing the soil, sowing the seed, and harvesting the bounty—and not through any inherent characteristics of ownership. And unimproved land in the vicinity of the coming railroad was ripe for the biggest windfall profits of all.

As he noted in the first sentence of his pamphlet, "The public domain not yet disposed of amounted on the 30th of June, 1870, to 1,387,732,209 acres." That's a lot of land, more than six times the size of the original thirteen states and three times the size of all of Europe at the time. About 200,000,000 acres had already been "granted, but not yet patented, to railroad and other corporations," a privatization of public land unprecedented in the history of civilization. England had privatized the commons during the eighteenth- and nineteenth-century shift from feudalism to capitalism through a legal process known as "enclosure." But that was kid's stuff compared to the closing of the western frontier.

George witnessed the rise of a new American empire, born from massive public land grants to private railroad companies. Millions of acres were granted to a new breed of western industrialists. Men such as Leland Stanford, president of Central Pacific Railroad, who drove the ceremonial final, golden spike in the transcontinental railroad in Promontory, Utah, on May 10, 1869. Christened by the Gold Rush and baptized by rail, Stanford was part of the original American 1 percent, coined the "robber barons" by social critics of the day. Joining the likes of Vanderbilt, Rockefeller, and Carnegie—still ranked today as the wealthiest Americans in history—a rising industrialist class amassed fortunes by privatizing the commons by any means necessary (above *and* below ground in the case of John D. Rockefeller and Standard Oil).

George saw clearly the ties between an American aristocracy and the land. Land for rail was the means for barons of the old east to supply untapped demands of the new west. Land near rail was the source of the demand, the space for new towns, farms, and markets to emerge. Homesteaders arrived on trains by the thousands to settle and work the land, manifest destiny by wagon no more. The new world would be privatized and grew smaller every day.

What followed was a period of unprecedented land speculation, inevitably contributing to the bank panic of 1873. The original "great depression" ensued and spread throughout the world. The spread of misery in a land of plenty ultimately framed Henry George's magnum opus. But no publisher was interested in a book on the economy from an uneducated, little-known, brash reporter from San Francisco. Economics texts were authored by the academic giants of Cambridge—Mill, Ricardo, Marshall—not obscure social critics working nights and weekends. So George put his skills as a typesetter to work, and in 1879 he set the print to his own book, *Progress and Poverty: An Inquiry into the Cause of Industrial Depressions and the Increase of Want with Increase of Wealth, the Remedy.*[29]

With great skepticism over its sales potential, and with Henry George himself obliged to pay the cost of the printing plates, the next year D. Appleton and Co. of New York printed the first market edition.[30] To the surprise of everyone, except perhaps Henry George, by the end of the century *Progress and Poverty* sold several million copies, second only to the Bible in the 1890s. His work marked the beginning of the Progressive Era of American politics. By the 1930s, John Dewey estimated that the best-seller, translated into at least thirteen languages, "had a wider distribution than almost all other books on political economy put together."[31]

The "inquiry" part of his subtitle was the diagnosis of the booms and, especially, busts of the industrial era. The largely unregulated, unstable economy of the post–Civil War era was, quite literally, the wild, wild west. His eloquent, no-nonsense prose grabbed the attention of the commoner and public intellectual alike. From Leo Tolstoy and George Bernard Shaw to Alfred Russel Wallace and Helen Keller, those who listed George as an influence on their own thinking was broad and diverse. Albert Einstein wrote in a 1933 letter to Henry George's daughter, "One cannot imagine a more beautiful combination of intellectual keenness, artistic form and fervent love of justice."[32]

It was this "love of justice" that set George apart. He didn't set out to merely describe the economic system. He wanted to change it, and the end of the subtitle hinted at an argument that would rattle the status quo. The "Remedy" struck at the age-old source of power of monarchs and capitalists alike: private land. By "land," George meant all that nature provided on which the economy was built, fueled, and fed. Neither the space above nor the soil, minerals, and oil below was created by any person, and therefore returns from the land should not be wholly captured by any owner. The unearned income, created simply from a government-assigned right to own property, should therefore be taxed as part of our common wealth.

To be a "Georgist" became synonymous with a movement for a single land tax. The logic followed that taxing income from labor or capital investment was taxing earned earnings. To tax this "true" income would discourage work, investment, and entrepreneurship. The sanctity of an individual's rights to an individual's earnings was paramount to George and thus not far from the moral positioning of classical economics. A single tax on land was, instead, a charge to use a resource that we all hold in common. To George, land taxes would discourage speculation and encourage investment, especially on land within cities made valuable by infrastructure. Shifting the tax base from labor to the landowner would steer progress toward ending poverty. Industrializing societies had a choice: progress for all or poverty for many.

Henry George hit a nerve both at home and abroad. *Progress and Poverty* immediately fanned the fire of the Irish Land War of 1879–1882. When sent to Ireland to cover the growing conflict between rural tenants and landlords for *The Irish World* newspaper, George had the occasion to speak publicly to groups such as the Political Prisoners' Aid Society. His popularity soared in Ireland, as well as back home among Irish Americans, especially after he was arrested in an apparent act of intimidation by the Royal Irish Constabulary.[33] His fame grew as a public speaker, and in 1884 Britain's Radical Liberals sponsored a lecture tour that included seventy-five speeches in thirty-five cities throughout Ireland, Scotland, and England.[34]

Try as they might, even the Cambridge economists couldn't ignore the growing populist appeal of Henry George. In 1883, Alfred Marshall devoted three of his Bristol lectures to a critique of *Progress and Poverty*, arguing from the outset that Henry George was "by nature a poet, not a scientific thinker."[35] While admitting that poverty persisted in the industrial era, Marshall proposed a solution similar to those of conservative economists today, an appeal to hard work and family values. He ended his final lecture with this: "If the men and women of England set themselves with holy purpose to make the next generation stronger in body and mind and spirit than this is, and if our children do the same by their children, the pauper will disappear." The magic of a free market would make things right—just give it time. When Henry George's speaking tour landed in Oxford, Alfred Marshall was the first to rise during Q&A, setting, by all accounts, a tone of disrespect and hostility toward the "rhetorician" whose ideas "instilled poison" in the minds of his listeners.[36]

Although the backlash from the economic elite was considerable, then and for years to come, the ideas of Henry George reached deep into society. *Progress and Poverty* provided an intellectual foundation for the original progressive movement, bubbling up in village squares and city halls across the United States. Republican reformist Theodore Roosevelt experienced George's politics firsthand in 1886 when the two ran against each other for mayor of New York City; both were defeated by the Tammany Hall Democrat, but George finished well ahead of the future president. In addition to a land tax, the Liberty Union platform of Henry George included support for government ownership of railroads and telegraphs, better working conditions, and an end to police obstruction with peaceful assemblies.[37]

The great American experiment with democratic governance of a capitalist economy was pushing back on the excesses of the Gilded Age, the corruptive influence of the robber barons, and the laissez-faire philosophy of a budding neoclassical economics. By the end of the 1890s, the official Progressive Era was in full swing, landing in the White House with the election of Roosevelt in 1901 and defining reformist agendas of both the Democratic and Republican parties for the next two decades. George missed the crest of the progressive wave he helped start, dying suddenly in 1897 at the age of fifty-eight, just four days short of election day during his second run for mayor of New York City. Over 100,000 people joined the procession to his burial in Brooklyn, one of the largest American funerals of the nineteenth century.

George's popularity left an indelible mark on the masses, but his influence on the economics profession never got past the neoclassical guard. Besides Alfred Marshall in England, the list of notable economists who opposed George stretched from east to west. In *The Corruption of Economics*, the University of California's Mason Gaffney and Fred Harrison from London's Land Research Trust document the rise of early-twentieth-century economics departments with a clear anti-Georgist mission, each financed by the deeply compromised interests of the industrialists.[38] Cornelius Vanderbilt and Vanderbilt University. Leland Stanford and Stanford University. John D. Rockefeller and the University of Chicago. Andrew Carnegie and the Carnegie Institute. J. P. Morgan and Columbia University. University benefactors were a who's who list of nineteenth-century robber barons.

Gaffney and Harrison note that the industrialist's attack on populism, with George as an early figurehead, marked a period of secularization of higher education where "businessmen were replacing clergyman on boards" and academics were expected to "placate or perish." Nowhere was this more apparent than at Columbia University, where Wall Street bankrolled a full assault on Henry George on his home turf. The economics department swelled in ranks with some of the most resolute anti-Georgists in the academy, including, most notably, John Bates Clark. Clark was among the early neoclassicals who helped erase the distinction between capital and land. If land was reduced to the characteristics of any other machine, then economics need only concern itself with a generic, homogenized capital. If the economy was free from the land, then capitalists need not pay rents back to society for unearned income. The windfall profits of the barons of rail, oil, and real estate, plus the banks to pay for it all, would be protected under neoclassical economics. Land, and all its natural resources, would be struck from the economics texts of the twentieth century. Henry George, and anyone else not singing the neoclassical party line, would be relegated to the footnotes of economic history.

~

Students are now digging through these footnotes, demanding a more historical, diverse, and introspective economics, and their patience is growing thin. On the eve of the 2015 annual meeting of the American Economic Association (AEA)—the caretaker of the neoclassical faith for well over a century—a group of students gathered around a projector outside the Sheraton Boston Hotel.[39] Above the entrance to the conference they beamed a quote in 6-foot capital letters from economic historian Robert Heilbroner: BEFORE ECONOMICS CAN PROGRESS, IT MUST ABANDON ITS SUICIDAL FORMALISM.

As the conference got under way, student protesters demonstrated during panel discussions, rose to ask critical questions, and beamed more quotes with pocket projectors on ballroom walls. At a session with their favorite target on the stage they projected, GREGORY MANKIW'S DEFENSE OF THE 1% CONTAINS "UNSTATED PREMISES, DUBIOUS ASSUMPTIONS, AND OMITTED FACTS." The quote, from Nobel laureate Robert Solow, showed that even the old guard had lowered their defenses of ideology with no foundation.

The protesters interviewed by the *Washington Post* included Keith Harrington, a climate activist who realized that progress on climate change policy would be fleeting "without system change." He helped launch Kick It Over in partnership with *Adbusters* to reform how economics is taught. Occupy Wall Street had been the proving ground for progressive economic messaging; now kickitover.org was promoting campus meme wars and arming students with pointed questions to ask their professors, such as these:

If the rational, selfish "economic man" of mainstream theory does not exist in the real world, why do we study that model at all? After all, would it make sense for medical students to study unrealistic models of the human body for their training in anatomy?

Should the financial system serve as an engine for speculative profits, or should it serve as a well-regulated public utility whose end is
to promote the economy's productive capacity?

If it is true that capitalism cannot solve and in fact is worsening
intractable global problems like poverty, inequality, ecological decline,
armed conflicts, and financial instability, why don't we spend any
time learning about systemic alternatives beyond capitalism and
state socialism?

In leaflets circulated throughout the AEA conference they made their
broader aim clear:

On campus after campus, we will chase you old goats out of power.
Then, in the months and years that follow, we will begin the work
of reprogramming the doomsday machine.

The reprogramming need not start from scratch, but it does require
turning away from the march of the mainstream. Henry George was
one of many who confronted the rise of a well-financed neoclassical
revolution, what today is called "conventional" economics when "radical" might be more accurate. Many would challenge the mathematical
abstraction, lack of institutional context, and laissez-faire philosophy of
a rising neoclassical economics. Keith Harrington and his fellow protesters had tapped a historic vein of discontent that dated to the original Progressive Era, waxed and waned over the last century, and always
seemed to find voice in times of economic turmoil.

Harrington got a taste for alternative approaches to economics while
studying at the New School in New York City. Founded in 1919 as the
New School for Social Research by progressive academics and intellectuals, it has long been a sanctuary to those outside the mainstream.

Among the founders, economist Thorstein Veblen had bounced from oil-financed Chicago to rail-financed Stanford before deciding that a new university model, where faculty would control its own membership, was necessary to save academic freedom. His life's work called for an evolutionary economics, drawing on the new science of anthropology to provide cultural context to economic institutions.

Other founders included historian Charles Beard, who had resigned from Wall Street–financed Columbia in protest of a university that, in his words, "is really under the control of a small and active group of trustees who have no standing in the world of education, who are reactionary and visionless in politics, narrow and medieval in religion."[40] His controversial reinterpretation of American history—including questioning the economic motivations of the drafters of the US Constitution—fit right in at the antiestablishment New School. And the best-known founder of all (as with Veblen, also a University of Chicago refugee) was philosopher and education reformer John Dewey, who brought to the New School a pragmatism that said, "Education is not preparation for life; education is life itself."

These were the post–World War I years, and the founding of the New School is one of many examples of academic sanctuaries springing up in a country reeling from the first Red Scare. A mass hysteria was sweeping the nation, fearful of anything that hinted of communism, including labor unions, socialist parties, and left-leaning academics. Many progressive economists touched or built on the work of German philosopher and economist Karl Marx, who challenged the very power structure of capitalism, which neoclassical economics was designed to support. But the war brought an end to the Progressive Era and an abrupt return to free market economics. The emotional, patriotic Roaring Twenties were not kind to economists with socialist leanings.

The polite word for economists who didn't fall in line was *heterodox*, to emphasize their existence outside the "orthodox" mainstream. But the labels that stuck on many who questioned capitalism included *Marxist,* *socialist,* or, the most damning, *communist.* On the heels of the Bolshevik revolution in Russia, the rise of Lenin, and the formation of the Soviet Union, pure unadulterated capitalism was framed as the only alternative to communism. Dissent was deemed un-American. Academics were told to fall in line, to march to a drum beat directed by an ever-concentrating capitalist class.

A critique of the postwar education system was published in Upton Sinclair's 1923 exposé *The Goose Step,* a provocative reference to the German soldiers' obedient, single-file march with straight legs kicked high. The muckraking journalist (himself a disgruntled Columbia alumnus) had traveled the country visiting campuses in twenty-five cities and talking with over one thousand teachers, pupils, parents, board members, deans, presidents, trustees, and anyone interested in the state and fate of American education. His conclusion: "Our educational system is not a public service, but an instrument of special privilege; its purpose is not to further the welfare of mankind, but merely to keep America capitalist."[41]

Neoclassical economics was perfectly situated to bolster capitalism as the ideal form of economic organization. From the ashes of the Progressive Era, the queen of the social sciences ascended to her throne, rarely to reexamine her own contentious beginnings. In his 2002 book *How Economics Forgot History,* institutional economist Geoffrey Hodgson quotes economic theorist Frank Hahn on a common sentiment that could have been spoken by my own economics professors: "What the dead had to say, when of value, has long since been absorbed, and when we need to say it again we can generally say it much better."[42] History lost meant the queen's rule could be absolute.

But the occupation of Zuccotti Park renewed age-old calls for economic justice to preempt economic efficiency. The walkout on Professor Mankiw's Econ 101 demanded that the discipline be open to broader, historical, heterodox views of the economy. A growing network of student-led organizations and sympathetic faculty are calling for a reexamination of the foundation and motivation of neoclassical economics. An economics taught as if history mattered would investigate the early challenges to the neoclassical model, discuss their strengths and weaknesses, debate the relevance of the critiques today, and adjust or overturn accordingly.

The work of Henry George—linking the concentration of land ownership with the creation of poverty—is one historical example more relevant than ever. Look no further than Adam Smith's birthplace of Scotland for a modern-day story of the growing landless poor toiling for the concentrating landed rich. More than half of Scotland is owned by fewer than five hundred people, by one estimate, "the most concentrated pattern of land ownership in the developed world."[43] All the while, one in ten Scots lived in "severe poverty" in the 2010s, trapped in a vicious cycle of low-wage work, high rent payments, and slashed social programs under the austerity advice of free market economists.[44] And in an age of globalization, with fewer and fewer restrictions on the flow of foreign capital investment, the wild, wild west of George's life and times is now planet-wide. Growing evidence points to a global land rush that is under way, pushing the most vulnerable in society to the very edge of existence while borderless multinational corporations consolidate land holdings worldwide.[45]

Over 130 years ago, Henry George wrote, "Everywhere, in all times, among all peoples, the possession of land is the base of aristocracy, the foundation of great fortunes, the source of power." Students should wrestle with such claims and form testable hypotheses of their own on the source and consequence of growing, unprecedented inequality today. They should question the wisdom of an ahistorical, unscientific, ideological model that has never fit the realities of the real world. And they should explore the broad range of heterodox schools that have developed since the split between classical and neoclassical economics. Different strands are named for people (Ricardian, Marxian, Georgist), places (Austrian, German historical, Stockholm), and focus (institutional, evolutionary, social, feminist, behavioral, and ecological), but they all have common concerns over the narrowness and unjustness of the mainstream.

As I found in my own wanderings off the beaten path, students of school and life alike who dare to venture outside the orthodoxy will find a new economic story, one that puts care, community, and common-wealth ahead of plunder, person, and profit.

CHAPTER 3

Growing a Market Society

For years, I thought what was good for our country was good for General Motors, and vice versa.[1]

—Charles Wilson

During the 1953 senate hearings for President-Elect Eisenhower's nomination to secretary of defense, the chief executive officer of General Motors, Charles Wilson, was asked whether he could make a decision for the nation that might harm his company. GM was the largest supplier to the Department of Defense, receiving 12 to 18 cents of each defense budget dollar.[2] The CEO of America's biggest corporation at the time argued his holdings of GM stock presented no inherent conflict of interest with running the defense department. The Senate worked to change federal ethics laws to accommodate him but eventually buckled under public protest. Wilson ceded, cashed in his stocks, and was appointed to the new president's cabinet.

The front-page controversy came to symbolize a postwar period when the lines were blurred between service to state and service to economy. To Wilson, building industry and employing people was good for country and corporation alike. Profitability need not be at odds with patriotism, especially in the interest of national defense. What was being produced, or whose stock was being affected by cabinet-level decisions, mattered little compared to production. Wilson's response, often quoted today, underlined eroding twentieth-century distinctions between a market economy and a democratic society. A nation reeling from two world wars and the economic roller coaster in between was questioning its ongoing transformation into a "market society."

The causes and consequences of becoming a market society, a nation-state run largely by private market rules and interests, was the central theme of Karl Polanyi's 1944 book a decade earlier on *The Great Transformation*. The Austro-Hungarian political economist had studied England's radical transformation from eighteenth-century mercantilism to nineteenth-century capitalism. The shift from state protection of domestic industry to full-blown international competition was a case study in widespread social disruption. Polanyi took an anthropological approach to his work, concluding that the increasing reliance on competitive markets to allocate resources, distribute rewards, and arbitrate value was changing people's mentality. The obligation to self had become preeminent in service to society.

At the time of Charlie Wilson's testimony, the great transformation was in its third century. The eighteenth- and nineteenth-century classical economists had argued that a nation's wealth should be built by empowering consumer and producer choice, reducing barriers to trade, breaking from traditions of feudal states, and leveling the playing field between the working and merchant classes. Cause had consequence in the old world; interpersonal relationships were governed by social norms and strict rules. Markets were a minor part of daily life. But in the new world, free markets were preached as the natural state of affairs: self-organizing entities adjusting to resource constraints, technical change, and people's tastes through freely moving prices. Booms would be followed by busts, to be followed by booms, and so on. As long as prices and wages were allowed to increase when demand exceeded supply and decrease when supply exceeded demand, all would eventually settle to equilibrium. Government tinkering was generally thought to do more harm than good.

As industrializing nations embraced free markets, the rise of late-nineteenth-century neoclassical economics doubled down on individualism, abstracting from real people embedded in real cultures with real institutions. Organizing society around markets required a degree of anonymity and separation between responsibility and action. A belief system crafted around atomized, rational, self-interested individuals supported the rising political philosophy of laissez-faire, French for "leave alone." Democratic freedom began to be equated with market freedom.

Polanyi followed in the tradition of the institutional economists such as Veblen, who first challenged a myopic belief in self-organizing markets. He argued that a market society was anything but a magical, invisible hand. For markets to dictate social arrangements required a sea change in political support, including carefully crafted market-friendly institutions (an invisible handshake) and legal frameworks of private property (an invisible foot).[3]

The US Constitution is a case in point. Written by slave owners, land speculators, and a rising American aristocracy, it set the property and participation rules of the new world economy to benefit White men of relative privilege. Freedom had self-made boundary conditions. It took seventy-six years and a civil war to amend the constitution and abolish slavery (Thirteenth Amendment, 1865). It took another fifty-five years for women to have the nationwide right to vote (Nineteenth Amendment, 1920). It was the mass movements behind abolitionism and women's suffrage that were self-organizing, not the narrow economic interests protected by property and voting rights they sought to reform.

The turn-of-the-century progressive movement was similarly self-organized by everyday people pushing back against the recklessness of a

market society, particularly the lopsided benefits to landowners, industrialists, and a new merchant class of rail, oil, and banking monopolists.
They formed labor unions to fight for fair pay and safe working conditions. They elevated women's voices in the fight for equal rights, public
health, and children's education. They launched a Progressive Party with
trust-buster Teddy Roosevelt himself at the helm. And they helped pass
legislation to regulate many aspects of the economy, from banking and
railroads to food and medicine. The Progressive Era reforms worked to
rein in the worst of the corporate and political abuses of power, recognized that markets always and everywhere have social and cultural context, and reminded the citizenry that it's the *people* of a democracy (all
the people) who should ultimately have the *power* over the economy (all
the power).

But World War I put the brakes on the movement to keep markets in
check. What emerged in the aftermath was a Western economy tooled
for growth and led by a fear of government planning and regulation (lest
we slip into communist rule). The political winds shifted, and unfet-
tered markets would sail free again. In the United States, Ohio newspaper man Warren G. Harding won the 1920 election in a landslide
against progressive Democrat James Cox (and his running mate Franklin
D. Roosevelt) and socialist labor organizer Eugene Debs (in his fifth run
for president, this time campaigning from a prison cell). Recognized as
one of the most corrupt presidents in history,[4] Harding set into motion
an era of unprecedented deregulation, speculation, and inequality. After
Harding's sudden death in office, VP Calvin Coolidge took the reins of
the growing conservative movement. The Vermont lawyer was elected
for his own term in 1924, a race that represented by some accounts the
"high tide of American conservatism," with both major parties embrac-
ing limited government, reduced taxes, and less regulation.[5]

What came to be known as the Roaring Twenties helped restore
prominence to laissez-faire philosophy and the neoclassical revolution

firmly entrenched in economics departments on both sides of the Atlantic. However, there was dissension in the ranks, this time from within the mainstream. The publication of *The Economics of Welfare* in 1920 by Arthur C. Pigou, the successor to Alfred Marshall at Cambridge, marked a notable departure from Walras's original ideas about equilibrium analysis. Pigou set out to broaden the scope of economics to encompass human welfare. He aimed not only to *describe* the economy but to *prescribe* how to change the world.

The Economics of Welfare preserved marginal analysis as the foundation of neoclassical economics. However, Pigou asked whether all costs and benefits were actually reflected in the price of goods and services. In Pigou's words, "It might happen, for example . . . that costs are thrown upon people not directly concerned, through, say, uncompensated damage done to surrounding woods by sparks from railway engines."[6] These costs did not directly affect producer or consumer decisions and were external to market prices. Pigou argued, therefore, that a *private* market equilibrium was not the same as a *social* optimum.

In order for markets to maximize welfare, Pigou reasoned, "All such effects must be included—some of them will be positive, others negative elements—in reckoning up the social net product of the marginal increment of any volume of resources turned into any use or place." Translation: Governments should intervene in the market to discourage negative external costs (with Pigouvian taxes) and incentivize positive external benefits (with Pigouvian subsidies). The punchline: In a world increasingly run by markets, governments should legitimize social concerns by making them economic.

Similar logic would make the case for redistribution of income through a progressive tax system. Economists assume income gains follow a path of diminishing returns where each new dollar spent provides less new utility than the last dollar spent. Diminishing marginal returns to income, consumption, and production are what make general equilibrium possible in the neoclassical model. With increasing returns, we'd never stop doing one thing in only one market. Therefore, deductive reasoning dictates that the total welfare of society would be maximized by putting more money in the hands of those with the highest marginal utility available: those who need a buck the most. The economic logic is impeccable. The additional value of an extra dollar to a poor person is greater than that to a rich person, and therefore society's total welfare increases with redistribution.

Pigou had established an economic argument for governments to steer private markets toward more efficient and fair outcomes, building the foundation for a truly *macro*economics in the process. A new generation of economists, including many of Pigou's students, broke from strict interpretation of laissez-faire and opened up questions on the role of government regulation of the money supply, currency exchange, labor standards, infrastructure investment, environmental conservation, and, in general, the *macro*economy. The Progressive Era left a legacy of public intervention in the private marketplace, and the Great War showed the power of government spending to steer the economy. The pendulum between hands-off and hands-on economics was to swing again.

Those questioning laissez-faire now asked whether central planning of a wartime economy could keep the boom alive during peace. What role could fiscal (spending money) and monetary policy (managing money) play in controlling the business cycle? Could government interventions counteract both the deep busts and speculative booms that had inflicted industrialized economies since the freeing of markets? Was there a middle ground, running on a free market engine with democracy at the wheel, that could create and sustain broad prosperity?

~

One student of Arthur Pigou raised his hand high to these questions. He answered with a new economic story. One of compromise between unadulterated market freedom and unyielding government control. One that would steer the economy toward higher social purpose. One that would set the goalposts for the discipline of economics in the next century.

Born in Cambridge at the dawn of the neoclassical era, John Maynard Keynes seemed to live a preordained life, scripted by an earlier generation of economists-as-moral-philosophers. His father, John Neville Keynes, was a philosopher and economist at the University of Cambridge. His mother, Florence Ada Keynes, was a social reformer and first female councillor of Cambridge Borough. By the time Maynard, as he was known by his friends and family, drew the attention of Professor Pigou, he was well on his way to economics royalty.

Keynes had a combination of scholarly intellect and bureaucratic pragmatism that provided a bridge between economics and government. His credentials were impeccable: top of his class at boarding school, scholarship to King's College at Cambridge, bachelor of arts in mathematics. Upon return from civil service in economic statistics in India, Neville Keynes and Arthur Pigou (by then the chair of the economics department) joined forces to privately fund young Keynes's dissertation on probability at Cambridge. His work led to his election as a Fellow of King's College and a lectureship on money, credit, and prices. His first book, *Indian Currency and Finance*, turned a small profit, and by the outbreak of the Great War, Keynes's reputation as editor, author, and analyst was second to none.

During the war, he put his penchant for public finance to good use, rising through the ranks of the Treasury Department to help guide the financing and economic coordination of the Allied front. But the war's devastating aftermath left a mark on Keynes, and he turned his intellect and civil service reputation toward making the case for peace through economic relief to central Europe. As a delegate of the British Treasury, Keynes participated in the Paris Peace Conference, advocating for debt forgiveness between allies and economic investment with foes. Woodrow Wilson, the last of the American progressive presidents, similarly argued for greater economic integration to craft a "just and secure peace" in his Fourteen Points speech.

The Allied powers opted instead for revenge. The resulting Treaty of Versailles forced Germany to disarm, cede land, and pay reparations. Germany, Austria, and the whole of central Europe plunged into misery under the weight of economic sanctions. In his bestselling 1919 book *The Economic Consequences of the Peace*, Keynes described the deepening impoverishment of the German people, particularly the condition of its children, criticizing his own country "in whose opinion justice requires that such beings should pay tribute until they are forty or fifty years of age in relief of the British taxpayer."[7]

A Cambridge pedigree and high-level Treasury experience would have led many to fall in line and cash in with a lucrative career in banking. However, Keynes returned to King's College, leveraged his academic freedom, and took to the news columns of the *Manchester Guardian* and the *Nation* to plead the case for reducing German reparations. Government bookkeeping and applied statistics were his munitions for peace and prosperity. As with his mentor Pigou, Keynes saw economics as an instrument to improve social welfare, not merely as a lens through which to watch the world go by, trusting that free markets would save us in the end.

Keynes looked past the ideological positions of his generation and made the case for policy to steer the economy toward prosperity. To Keynes, a prosperous world had less incentive to go to war. By 1924, the title of his Sidney Ball lecture at Oxford University, "The End of Laissez-Faire," made clear his maturing views on the reigning orthodoxy. Keynes lamented, "The political philosophy, which the seventeenth and eighteenth centuries had forged in order to throw down kings and prelates, had been made milk for babes, and had literally entered the nursery." In his view, "the dogma had got hold of the educational machine" despite evidence from Alfred Marshall himself of "leading cases in which private interest and social interest are *not* harmonious."[8]

In search of a "wisely managed" capitalism, Keynes argued for a role of the state to control money and credit, provide economic data, direct savings and investment, and even control population size. The British economy stagnated throughout the 1920s, but the Keynesian prescription for stimulus would need another patient. Across the Atlantic, the US economy was booming, and laissez-faire was all the rage. But as so often happens in the field of economics, it would take unprecedented crisis to surface unorthodox views.

When the Roaring Twenties came to a screaming halt on October 29, 1929, John Maynard Keynes was ready with the alternative. The US stock market lost nearly one-quarter of its value in two short days, and the world's economy followed. The slide continued for the next three years, hitting bottom at 20 percent of the value of 1929 highs. By 1933, nearly half of US banks had closed their doors and a third of the labor force couldn't find even part-time work (among those still looking). Historians later renamed the 1870s depression of Henry George's time as merely the "long" depression. The 1930s would be forever remembered as the Great Depression.

∼

The 1930s mainstream of economics—lacking any deliberate, empirical, policy-oriented study of the macroeconomy—was still clinging to Say's Law of markets from the early 1800s. French economist and businessman Jean-Baptiste Say had popularized the idea that demand is created by production in an economy. The logic was that the act of production would create the income that would purchase said production. In *A Treatise on Political Economy* (1803), he deduced "that in reality we do not buy articles of consumption with money, the circulating medium with which we pay for them. We must in the first instance have bought this money itself by the sale of our produce."[9]

If supply creates its own demand, as Say's Law came to be understood, then a truly free market system would be immune from recessions and depressions. The market wheel left free to spin would forever turn around and around and around. In good times, leave markets alone. In bad times, leave markets alone. The money-making motives of the supply side would take care of us all. This logic became the prevailing principle of the macroeconomy throughout all the booms and busts of industrializing economies of the nineteenth century. Recessions were blamed on excessive restraints on business (a.k.a., the job creators), and so Say's advice was to reduce the size and oversight of government. Producers would respond, and demand would follow, in the nineteenth-century version of "What's good for General Motors is good for the country."

The postwar, anti-communist, free market philosophy of the Roaring Twenties doubled down on Say's Law. None other than robber baron Andrew Mellon was appointed as secretary of the treasury, serving Republican presidents Harding, Coolidge, and Hoover from 1921 to 1932. Mellon orchestrated steep tax cuts through the Revenue Acts of 1921, 1924, and 1926, repealing wartime rates that had topped out at 73 percent.[10] The highest marginal tax rates were cut and cut and cut again, bottoming out at 24 percent by the end of the decade. And the size of the federal government was accordingly cut and cut and cut again from wartime highs of over 20 percent[11] to just below 3 percent of the national economy by 1929.[12]

Small government, low taxes, balanced budget, growing economy—the 1920s conservative agenda was all the rage. The private sector saw unprecedented growth, but so did the gap between the rich and poor. By the dawn of the Great Depression, an estimated 17 percent of the nation's annual income flowed to the richest 1 percent, the most lopsided US economy at the time and ever since.[13] Although comprehensive national income statistics had yet to be invented, let alone reported on a quarterly basis as today, the contrast of opulence beside squalor recalled images of a not-too-distant time in America. Mark Twain's 1873 novel *The Gilded Age* saw a resurgence in popularity as a satire of a similar time in recent history, where social ills were masked by a thin layer of gold. With so much of the economy controlled by so few interests, the new proletariat class of 1920s America grew to resent the rise of the 1 percent, yet they knew their own livelihood depended on not rocking the boat.

But the persistence of long economic slumps had always challenged the status quo, and the Great Depression presented the strongest evidence to date that markets can be slow, if not downright obstinate, to self-correct. With new construction nearly ground to a halt and factories and farms idle, how long should a nation wait for supply to rebound and create its own demand? Income tax rates couldn't be cut much more without completely starving what little government was left. Even free marketeers such as President Hoover began to increase government spending to help stimulate recovery, rising to about 8 percent of the economy by 1932. But support was focused on the sectors where the nation's wealth was already concentrated: banking and railroads. Direct aid to the unemployed was a philosophical no-no for fear of government interference with "rugged individualism," Hoover's caricature of American exceptionalism at the heart of the conservative agenda.

But by the 1932 election, a less rugged and more haggard electorate had lost faith in pep talks on how hard work and faith in free enterprise would ultimately prevail. A desperate nation went to the polls and dared to challenge the conservative agenda that had held the White House ever since Wilson. At the depths of the Depression, a new economic story emerged that found unprecedented market freedom as the cause of, not the solution to, unprecedented market collapse. A new chapter in American democracy arose that promised to employ the unemployed, aid the poor, plan for retirement, subsidize home ownership, protect banking deposits, and make public investments in public goods with public money. This new narrative rallied around a democratic candidate with the progressive pedigree and name recognition to try a new approach; indeed, a New Deal.

Franklin Delano Roosevelt's full cabinet was sworn in together just hours after his March 4 inauguration.[14] Within the first hundred days of the new administration, fifteen major bills were passed and ninety-nine executive orders were signed by a busy president.[15] The philosophical shift was clear from the beginning. Economic advisors such as Stuart Chase, credited with coining "The New Deal," were influenced by the writings of Henry George and Thorstein Veblen and didn't shy away from recommendations for government planning and direct intervention in the economy.[16] Secretary of Labor Frances Perkins, the very first woman cabinet member and "moral conscience" of the Roosevelt administration, advocated for a forty-hour work week, minimum wage, unemployment compensation, abolition of child labor, Social Security, federal employment service, and universal health insurance.[17] Roosevelt took on nearly wartime powers through regulating prices, issuing new debt, and broadly stimulating the economy through the government's ability to borrow and spend. It was all very Keynesian.

Keynes watched the early days of the New Deal experiment take shape as Roosevelt sought to balance the necessity of immediate recovery with a strategy for long term reform. Government expenditures pushed toward 10 percent of the economy but were constrained by falling prices and meager tax receipts. Congress gave the president a lot of latitude in his first hundred days, especially on levels of deficit spending not seen since the Great War. But conservative fears of government control loomed large. Keynes was convinced that initial New Deal spending would need to grow further in order to foster a US-led global economic recovery. To Keynes, the war against the Great Depression, like the Great

War he helped win behind a desk at the British Treasury, would be won through government spending and coordination.

Contrary to the mainstream of his profession, Keynes had come to reject Say's Law, arguing instead that the ups and downs of the business cycle were largely a function of demand, not supply. If people stopped spending because they lost their jobs, saved too much for a rainy day, or simply lacked confidence in the future, then waiting for falling wages to stimulate supply could have long lag times. With lower and lower incomes buying fewer and fewer goods and services, businesses would have to make further and further cuts in employment, which would lower incomes further still. A multiplier effect could ensue, bringing the economy away from its presumed full employment level. To stop the downward spiral, households would need to be induced to spend, not by waiting for workers to find a low-wage job but by directly increasing their purchasing power through government programs. Business spending through new investments would also need to be stimulated by lowering interest rates through the government's ability to control the money supply.

Under Keynesian logic, the key to fighting recessions and depressions was government spending (fiscal policy) and money creation (monetary policy) to generate new economic demand. His own nation did just the opposite by cutting government spending to balance budgets. Keynes argued that austerity was not wise in bad times. Instead, deficit spending should be directed to stimulate consumer demand. Additionally, the deficits themselves would push bond prices up and thus interest rates down, creating further stimulus by incentivizing business borrowing and investment. Frustrated with his own country—and sensing a weakening resolve for New Deal spending across the Atlantic—Keynes took to the pages of the Sunday *New York Times* on New Year's Eve, 1933, to make his case to President Roosevelt.[18]

He began the "open letter" by fully admitting the political costs of his advice. Keynes then emphasized immediate action to further stimulate short-term recovery while pleading for more patience in sowing the seeds for long-term economic reforms. He included a wonky critique of the National Industrial Recovery Act, but its real punch was an argument for the moral authority of the United States to borrow, spend, and grow the world economy out of the Depression. As Keynes implored, "In the past orthodox finance has regarded a war as the only legitimate excuse for creating employment by governmental expenditure. You, Mr. President, having cast off such fetters, are free to engage in the interests of peace and prosperity the technique which hitherto has only been allowed to serve the purposes of war and destruction."

Keynes provided the intellectual horsepower for a new "mixed" economy story that Roosevelt and his political allies came to embrace. The US economy grew out of the Depression, led by New Deal spending. Although the recovery was broad-based, with income inequality falling sharply throughout the 1930s, it took another war to grow the economy to its full potential, with government spending surpassing 40 percent of US output at the height of World War II. By the time of Germany's surrender on V-E Day, May 8, 1945, Keynes was an international economic superhero. The Japanese surrender followed three months later, and by the end of the year a new economic order was ratified by Allied powers with Keynes as a principal architect. Keynes found redemption since the last German surrender, setting out to craft a more stable, more integrated, more global, and more peaceful version of a market society. The post–World War II economy was to be powered by a private enterprise engine, but Keynesian economics was clearly at the wheel.

~

Keynes's major work—*The General Theory of Employment, Interest, and Money*, published in 1936—became the missing foundation to a truly macro economics.[19] In the world according to Keynes, markets should not be free to oscillate on their own in search of a full employment equilibrium. Markets should instead be purposively steered to keep economies growing, inflation in check, and unemployment as low as possible. In Keynes's world, new economic data would be needed to guide fiscal and monetary policy, gauge economic outcomes, and coordinate national economies. New economic institutions would be required to stabilize currencies, regulate trade, and finance development. And new economists would be educated to advise decision makers in a new economic story of global peace through economic integration and growth.

The demand for economic data had a headwind of its own. Presidents Hoover and Roosevelt were largely flying blind during the Great Depression, using fragmented and incomplete stock market indices, price data, and freight car loadings to gauge economic production.[20] So in 1932, a Senate resolution directed the commerce secretary to develop economy-wide income statistics for the period 1929 to 1931: a postmortem analysis of the depth and extent of the Depression. Noted economic growth theorist and statistician Simon Kuznets from the National Bureau of Economic Research was tapped to lead the study, and in January 1934 he reported the first public estimates of national income. Kuznets found that US national income—the net value of all economic goods produced by the nation—had fallen by more than 50 percent between 1929 and 1932, with incomes from mining, manufacturing, and agricultural sectors each falling by more than 70 percent and construction by more than 80 percent.[21]

The study also pointed to the distributional consequences of the Depression, with wage earners hit harder than salaried workers and small business entrepreneurs losing ground relative to property owners. Roosevelt capitalized on the findings to lambast big business for their greed and to side with labor in making the case for government work relief programs. The politics of quantifying the complexity of the economy into a simple income statistic was not lost on Kuznets. He noted in the original Senate report that "the definiteness of the results suggests, often misleadingly, a precision and simplicity in the outlines of the object measured" and that measurements of national income "deal with matters that are the center of conflict of opposing social groups where the effectiveness of an argument is often contingent upon oversimplification."

Roosevelt, and certainly every president since, staked his political life on the "effectiveness of an argument" to grow the economy. National income statistics, reported on a monthly basis by 1938, became the centerpiece to New Deal legislation. And as the prospect of American engagement in another world war became more and more likely, the need for more detailed, sector-by-sector estimates of national production (the mirror image of national income) came into focus. In January 1940, just four months after Great Britain declared war on Germany, President Roosevelt asked Congress to increase defense spending to a little over $1 billion, or 14 percent of the federal budget. A year later, the defense budget request grew 25-fold, and by 1942 defense expenditures were up to $53 billion, or 90 percent of total government expenditures.

This unprecedented military spending pushed the economy to heights not seen since before the Great Depression. As government spending grew toward half of national income, policymakers feared both inflation and the crowding out of consumer goods and services. Extraordinary coordination was needed to steer national production from peacetime to wartime to peacetime again while keeping prices stable, workers employed, and the economy growing to pay back all the new debt. Politicians framed a "guns and butter" debate of military versus consumer spending, including Roosevelt's New Deal programs. Could a nation at war overseas afford the social programs that fought back poverty at home? National income statistics were now a mainstay of post-Depression policies designed to stimulate consumer demand, but World War II required new numbers—a gross national product—to answer such questions and better steer production.

Help came again from abroad. Working for the British cabinet under the direction of Keynes himself, Cambridge economist Richard Stone produced the first comprehensive national income *and* product accounts for Great Britain in 1941. The accounting framework, data collection, and publication of the GNP was the culmination of what the US Department of Commerce has called "one of the great inventions of the 20th century."[22] Stone is credited for developing the "double-entry accounting" system still in use today to estimate gross domestic product (GDP, the cousin to GNP) for nearly every national economy on the planet. The values of all goods and services produced make up one side of the macroeconomic ledger, with the income sources to pay for it all on the other.

By early 1942 the United States released its own GNP, just months after declarations of war on the Axis powers of Germany, Italy, and Japan. Sector-by-sector details provided the basis for wartime planning, including rationing between private- and public-sector expenditures and financing through expanding income taxes. The tax base grew intently from 4 million individuals in 1939 to 44 million by 1944,[23] and to encourage payment of taxes the government promoted a new brand of economic patriotism through radio, newspaper, and film. Roosevelt's Office of War Information even recruited Donald Duck and friends to champion the "duty" and "privilege" of paying "taxes for guns, taxes for ships, taxes for democracy, taxes to beat the Axis."[24]

Duty to country was duty to economy, and GNP became the idol of economic growth. And grow the economy did. The wartime boom produced 17 million new civilian jobs, each producing twice as much output per hour as before the war.[25] Higher wages, expanded savings, new technologies, and broader workforce participation by women and African Americans built a new economy seemingly overnight. As Allied troops came home to victory parades, a new allegiance to GNP helped pivot economies from wartime production to peacetime consumption.

~

With the gauge of a new economics taking hold, Keynes could next turn his attention to the engine—money, finance, and trade—and a second chance to forge an integrated global economy that could keep the peace. In July 1944, more than a year before the end of World War II, delegates from all 44 Allied nations met at the Mount Washington Hotel in Bretton Woods, New Hampshire, to craft a new economic world order. Keynes led the UK delegation as advisor to the British Treasury, providing the intellectual architecture for negotiations. And his American counterpart, Harry Dexter White, special assistant to the US secretary of the treasury, leveraged the stability of the US dollar—backed by over three-quarters of the world's gold deposits—to pay for it all.

Keynes set his sights on breaking the corrosive forces of all forms of economic nationalism, particularly currency manipulation and trade protectionism. The Bretton Woods meeting, officially the United Nations Monetary and Financial Conference, was a culmination of two years of proposals and counterproposals between Keynes and White on the structure and function of global institutions that could stabilize exchange rates, finance reconstruction of war-torn Europe, and reduce barriers to trade. The main result was an agreement to peg global currencies to the US dollar and the dollar to a fixed exchange rate with gold (the US Federal Reserve price of $35 per ounce, to be exact). The fixed exchange regime would be managed through the International Monetary Fund (IMF), headquartered in Washington, DC, and designed to facilitate short-term financial assistance to correct any balance-of-payments deficits.

Keynes had argued instead for a supranational currency, the bancor, with a multilateral clearing system independent from the US dollar. But stacks of gold at Fort Knox won the day, the result of the US Gold Reserve Act from a decade earlier, a prohibition against private ownership and export of gold. In the depths of the Great Depression, US citizens were forced to cash in gold for a fixed price, foreign gold further flooded the safe haven, and Roosevelt effectively devalued the dollar by 60 percent.[26] This was the real secret sauce of the US recovery, a recipe for guns *and* butter. US exports would become very cheap—great for supplying European allies with guns—and imports to the United States would become very expensive—great for protecting homegrown butter. By Bretton Woods, the United States had huge trade surpluses, and the dollar was the most secure currency in the world.

The second Bretton Wood institution was the International Bank for Reconstruction and Development (a.k.a. the World Bank). The bank was initially charged with financing the reconstruction of Europe, and together with the IMF they officially opened for business two days after Christmas in 1945. Both were headquartered in Washington, DC, just a stone's throw from the US Treasury. The bank quickly got to work, approving its first reconstruction loan to France of $250 million in May 1947.[27] Loans to the Netherlands, Denmark, and Luxembourg followed, paving the way for the US Foreign Assistance Act of 1948 (a.k.a. the Marshall Plan) to the tune of nearly $13 billion in loans and direct aid to eighteen European allies (roughly $140 billion in today's dollars).

The "reconstruction" part of the World Bank was good business, so it didn't take long to move to the "development" part, focused squarely on the so-called developing world. By 1948, the bank's membership had grown to forty-seven nations with the addition of Austria, was tentatively building missions in war-torn Asia, and began shifting attention from the colonizers to the colonized (all strings attached). The development agenda was cloaked in Western liberal values of freedom and prosperity for all, but as Polanyi had warned in 1944 in *The Great Transformation*, the very year of Bretton Woods, the private interests of a market economy were too powerful to be constrained by the public interests of a social democracy. Bank leaders from the beginning were hand-picked from Wall Street, and market fundamentalism arising from the unholy trinity of the IMF, World Bank, and US Treasury came to be known as the Washington Consensus.

The third ingredient to a new world order took a more torturous path. Bretton Woods agreed in principle to reduce trade barriers, but it took nearly four years to arrive at the "Havana Charter," a plan to complement the IMF and World Bank with an International Trade Organization (ITO). However, the ITO ultimately died in the hands of President Truman in 1950 after several unsuccessful attempts at treaty ratification in the US Senate. The 1947 General Agreement on Tariffs and Trade (GATT) became the de facto trade institution, a nearly toothless vehicle to pursue so-called free trade. However, without a counterbalance to the IMF and World Bank, international financing—and especially bilateral loans and grants stemming from the Marshall Plan—had plenty of not-so-free-trade strings attached to keep colonial powers in a strong bargaining position.

On trade, the new economic order was as old as time. Cheap natural resources flowed from the global South to North in exchange for military arms and bases to keep any communist aspirations in check. Nearly five decades and eight rounds of multilateral negotiations eventually led to replacing GATT with the World Trade Organization (WTO) in 1994. But by then any Keynesian dream of world peace through free and fair economic alliances had long been replaced by Eisenhower's warning of "unwarranted influence" of the "military–industrial complex." The "economic consequences of the peace" this time around was a forty-five-year Cold War between East and West, and the real thing in Korea, Vietnam, and countless civil wars and rebellions throughout Southeast Asia, Latin America, the Middle East, Central Europe, and Africa. US military expenditures during the Cold War years approached perhaps $8 trillion,[28] peaking at 10 percent of GDP, while by some estimates the Soviet Union annually spent upwards of 20 percent of GDP on the Red Army.[29] On April 16, 1953, shortly after the death of Soviet premier Joseph Stalin, President Eisenhower lamented, "Every gun that is made, every warship launched, every rocket fired signifies, in the final sense, a theft from those who hunger and are not fed, those who are cold and not clothed."[30]

Despite Keynes's best efforts, punctuated by a heart attack at Bretton Woods that nearly took his life, an international version of "wisely managed" capitalism outlined in the *General Theory* fell short. The controls put on currency manipulation came the closest, though guided largely by the interests of the US Treasury. Before Bretton Woods, countries free from fixed exchange rates could devalue their currency to make imports expensive and exports cheap, protecting national interests at the expense of larger goals of economic stability. After Bretton Woods, those who signed on to the IMF committed to pegging their currency to a gold-backed US dollar, giving up a key lever of protectionism.

This was a tough pill to swallow for the United Kingdom, in tatters after the war and slowly losing its grip on the Sterling Area, a greatly weakened confederation of states backed by the British pound (sterling). Returning to a more rigid, pre–Depression era gold standard was also an affront to free-floating rates argued for under laissez-faire economics. A familiar tune of "Let the market figure things out, national interests be damned" was alive and well again, despite Keynes's best efforts. When *The Road to Serfdom* was published just four months before Bretton Woods by Austrian-British economist Friedrich August von Hayek (1899–1992), Keynes again needed to defend the virtues of managed capitalism in the court of public opinion. Hayek's treatise was the latest case against socialism, especially state-controlled socialism, yet was used as an argument against all forms of economic planning, especially any international control. The University of Chicago published a US version later in 1944, followed by an abridged version in *Reader's Digest* in 1945. As Western bloc nations worked to ratify Bretton Woods agreements in domestic legislatures, Hayek became fodder for libertarian soundbites on "individual liberty," "free society," and "limited government."

Against this familiar drumbeat, and with the entire Bretton Woods agreement in the balance, on December 18, 1945, Keynes took to the floor of the House of Lords (now a lord himself) to argue that the United Kingdom accept the United States' terms. He spoke frankly against British nationalism on one extreme and unchecked markets at the other, arguing that "the outstanding characteristic of the plans is that they represent the first elaborate and comprehensive attempt to combine the advantages of freedom of commerce with safeguards against the disastrous consequences of a laissez-faire."[31] Casting aside the fears of planning, the bogeyman of economics, Keynes made the case for "attempting a great step forwards towards the goal of international economic order amidst national diversities of policies."

The agreement was ratified five hours later, Western allies fell in line in the days to follow, and by New Year's Day 1946, the Bretton Woods era had officially begun.

~

With GNP as the gauge and international finance the engine, economists were clearly in the driver's seat of the new market society. Keynes never had the opportunity to shape what he helped create, succumbing to heart disease on Easter Sunday, April 21, 1946, just weeks after returning from the inaugural meetings of the IMF and the World Bank in Savannah, Georgia. But he did leave behind a blueprint. In a 1924 obituary essay honoring his teacher, Alfred Marshall, he wrote,

> The master-economist must possess a rare combination of gifts. . . .
> He must be mathematician, historian, statesman, philosopher—in
> some degree. He must understand symbols and speak in words. He
> must contemplate the particular in terms of the general, and touch
> abstract and concrete in the same flight of thought. He must study
> the present in the light of the past for the purposes of the future.

No part of man's nature or his institutions must be entirely outside his regard. He must be purposeful and disinterested in a simultaneous mood; as aloof and incorruptible as an artist, yet sometimes as near to earth as a politician.[32]

Not exactly a modest charge, but no one ever accused Keynes of thinking small. Indeed, in the decades to follow, generals sat at the left hand of world leaders, with economists on the right. The United States didn't waste any time. A White House Council of Economic Advisers was anointed by late 1946 "to develop and recommend to the President national economic policies to foster and promote free competitive enterprise, to avoid economic fluctuations or to diminish the effects thereof, and to maintain employment, production, and purchasing power."[33] As Mr. Laissez-Faire himself, Milton Friedman, lamented over a decade later, "We are all Keynesians now." Unlike in the 1920s, the Keynesian prescription for government's role in the market could no longer be put back in the bottle. Friedman's oft-quoted saying captured the sentiment of most economists in the 1950s and 1960s for some degree of macroeconomic planning, but the "we" generally fell into two camps.

In one corner were the post-Keynesians, who generally argued for a heterodox approach to economics, rejecting the individualistic core of the neoclassical model. These included contemporaries of Keynes, the so-called Cambridge Keynesians, who believed in a strong role of government to seek full employment, low inflation, and steady growth by fighting the inherent tendency of capitalist economies toward wild boom–bust cycles, especially over the long run as the rich got richer and the poor got poorer. They recognized that wealth and power are self-reinforcing, leading to highly uneven development both within and between nations; that the concentrating forces of monopolies (one seller), monopsonies (one buyer), and oligopolies (colluding sellers) were the natural tendencies of markets; and that the predominance of "nonrational expectations" of the future quite predictably led to economic instability and crises. They brought the full human animal into the realm of economic decision-making, emotions and all, by emphasizing what Keynes had referred to as our "animal spirits."

The post-Keynesians included economists whose own lives had been shaped by the push and pull between capitalism and socialism, including Michal Kalecki (1899–1970) from Poland, Nicholas Kaldor (1908–1986) from Hungary, and Piero Sraffa (1898–1983) from Italy. They included a British economist, Joan Robinson (yes, a woman!), who deftly said, "The purpose of studying economics is not to acquire a set of ready-made answers to economic questions, but to learn how to avoid being deceived by economists."[34] And they included skeptics of the growing application of statistical methods to economic data (i.e., econometrics), what Keynes described as being "like those puzzles for children where you write down your age, multiply, add this and that, subtract something else, and eventually end up with the number of the Beast in Revelation." Burn!

In the other corner were the neo-Keynesians, responsible for the "neo-classical synthesis," an appropriation of Keynes into the orthodoxy of mathematical economics. The mathematization of *The General Theory* started right away with the investment/savings–liquidity/money (IS-LM) model, first proposed in 1937 by British economist John Hicks (1904–1989). The model superimposed the price versus quantity equilibrium obsession of microeconomics to an interest rate versus national income relationship for macroeconomics. The macroeconomy, so the story goes, would naturally move toward an equilibrium level of income and interest rates, supporting an equilibrium level of employment. If economic output was deemed too low by the political powers, then fiscal stimulus could push national incomes higher, but at the expense of higher interest rates (good for savers but not for borrowers). Alternatively, a monetary stimulus could boost the economy but with lower interest rates resulting (good for borrowers but not for savers). All sorts of tradeoffs of macroeconomic policy became mathematized, painting an illusion of equilibrium as the natural state of affairs, with only mild course corrections needed by the monetary or fiscal powers that be.

The work of Hicks was extended by Alvin Hansen (1887–1975), one of the drafters of the US Employment Act of 1946 that created the Council of Economic Advisers. It also influenced Franco Modigliani (1918–2003), the originator of the "non-accelerating inflationary rate of unemployment" (a.k.a. NAIRU), a theoretically tolerable level of unemployment that won't cause too much inflation. These neo-Keynesians got the party started, but the chief architect of the largely American-led neoclassical synthesis was MIT's Paul Samuelson (1915–2009). He published his Harvard PhD dissertation in 1947 as the *Foundations of Economic Analysis*, followed in 1948 by *Economics*, which became one of the best-selling Econ 101 textbooks of all time.[35] Samuelson was a self-proclaimed "cafeteria Keynesian," picking and choosing what worked within the confines of a neoclassical tradition.[36] By the nineteenth edition of *Economics*, published with Yale University's William Nordhaus in 2009, the synthesis was six decades in the making, built on the story of a "mixed economy—an economy that combines the tough discipline of the market with fair-minded governmental oversight."

By the 1970s, and by any measure—textbook sales, economic department heads, White House appointments—the neo-Keynesians had won the hearts and minds of the economic establishment. When the Central Bank of Sweden established the Sveriges Riksbank Prize in Economic Sciences in Memory of Alfred Nobel, it was the architects of the neoclassical–Keynesian synthesis who got the early nod. Ragnar Frisch and Jan Tinbergen, whose research was the object of Keynes's "puzzles for children" quip, were awarded the first memorial prize in 1969 for their foundational work in econometrics. Paul Samuelson was up next in 1970, followed by Simon Kuznets in 1971 for developing national income accounting, without which there would be no macroeconomics. By 1972, the prize went to John Hicks for the IS-LM model and to

Kenneth Arrow, brother-in-law and Columbia/Stanford/Harvard counterpart to Samuelson. Wassily Leontief, doctoral advisor to Samuelson, received the 1973 prize for his work on input–output analysis, the gold standard of macroeconomic statistics and modeling.

These first five years of the memorial Nobel recognized seven of the early architects of the neoclassical synthesis. But by 1974 a Swedish economist from the post-Keynesian tribe, Gunnar Myrdal, snuck into the club for his work on monetary theory and the tendency of economies to get stuck in low-income and high-unemployment ruts, so-called disequilibrium traps. Myrdal reluctantly shared the spotlight with Friedrich Hayek, the first from the counter-Keynesian movement of libertarianism to win, a sign of the post–Bretton Woods era under way. True to form of the heretics of post-Keynesians, and following widespread criticism of the award two years later to University of Chicago economist Milton Friedman, Myrdal called for the abolition of the memorial Nobel to the "soft" science of economics because of its "unsophisticated approach and the confused admixture of science and politics."[37]

~

Economics has always been political. Despite claims of positivism championed by Samuelson—and taught to millions of students through nineteen editions of *Economics* published in forty-one languages for over sixty years—the act of deciding on what, how, and for whom resources should be allocated is at its core a value decision. Even the very first decision to name and claim nature as "natural resources" for all humanity reflects a certain set of values, namely the Judeo-Christian dominion over all creation that undergirds Western economics, law, ethics, and the entire worldview of a market society.

By the 1970s, both the values and the worldview of economics were again at a crossroads. When the United States abandoned the gold standard, Bretton Woods came to an unceremonious end. This fueled ongoing debates between different flavors of Keynesianism but also about whether Keynes should be abandoned altogether. Alternating columns between Milton Friedman and Paul Samuelson in *Newsweek* magazine from the late '60s into the early '80s not only put Keynes on trial but also caricatured the battle over the mainstream. Samuelson had brought the center of economics from Cambridge, England, to Cambridge, Massachusetts. But Friedman and the "Chicago School" were pulling the mainstream further west, arguing that government was doing more harm than good in shaping a market society. By one count, today thirty-three of the eighty-four Nobel laureates in economics have been affiliated with the University of Chicago as alumni, faculty members, or researchers, one less than MIT and one more than Harvard (with plenty of double-counting as graduates or faculty at one of the big three become visiting researchers or faculty at an another).[38]

Despite retreating to flexible exchange rates, by 1975 the United States was experiencing 9 percent unemployment, alongside an inflation rate over 12 percent—the dreaded double-whammy of stagflation in economists' nightmares.[39] The conventional wisdom that inflation could be tolerated as long as the economy was growing came under fire, compounded by the Arab oil embargo, debt from a nearly trillion-dollar Vietnam War (in today's dollars),[40] and the mounting cost of new mandatory government spending on healthcare, Social Security, and other social safety nets. Monetarists such as Friedman blamed inflationary monetary policy but also the general philosophy of government steering the macroeconomy, government financing of so-called welfare capitalism, and government regulations in general. The free market pendulum was swinging back again, wedded to a libertarian movement that had been simmering since the New Deal, was bubbling by President Kennedy's 1960 New Frontier speech, and was at full boil when President Johnson launched the Great Society in 1964.

The free marketeers used "freedom" in John Locke's 1690 sense of individual liberty where "persons have a right or liberty to (1) follow their own will in all things that the law has not prohibited and (2) not be subject to the inconstant, uncertain, unknown, and arbitrary wills of others."[41] The Kennedy and Johnson administrations made the case for freedom in a different sense, calling for more freedom *from* and less freedom *to*. Freedom *from* economic oppression, the aim of the Equal Opportunity Act of 1964 and forty programs at the center of Johnson's "war on poverty." Freedom *from* discrimination based on race, color, religion, sex, or national origin, the core of the Civil Rights Act of 1964 and signature of a "great society" for all. Freedom *from* pollution, with a wave of new environmental laws including the Clean Air Act, Water Quality Act, Solid Waste Disposal Act, and Motor Vehicle Air Pollution Control Act.

The Great Society also expanded human rights to include the right to healthcare for the most vulnerable through Medicare and Medicaid. The right to education through federal funding of Head Start, a National Teacher Corps, bilingual education, and grants to schools serving low-income populations. The right to safe roads and cars through the Motor Vehicle Safety Act, to consumer product information through the Fair Package and Labeling Act, and to full disclosure from banks through the Truth in Lending Act. The right to lands set aside in the Wilderness Act, "where the earth and its community of life are untrammeled by man," and to free-flowing rivers designated under the Wild and Scenic Rivers Act, with "outstandingly remarkable scenic, recreational, geologic, fish and wildlife, historic, cultural or other similar values." The domain of legislated rights even expanded beyond the human community with the passage of the Endangered Species Preservation Act of 1966, precursor to the 1973 Endangered Species Act, conveying unprecedented protections from extinction due to the "consequence of economic growth and development untempered by adequate concern and conservation."

The Great Society agenda was a new high water mark of American progressivism, taking aim at many of the social injustices that persisted after the New Deal era. Whereas President Kennedy had defeated Richard Nixon in one of the closest elections in US history, by 1964 Lyndon

Johnson defeated Barry Goldwater in one of the most lopsided, winning all but six states. Democrats took enough seats in both the House and Senate to hold more than a two-thirds majority in the 89th Congress, and the progressive legislative achievements were unparalleled. Johnson signed into law eighty-four of the eighty-seven bills his administration sent to Congress in 1965 and 1966.[42]

But this much success this fast was perhaps bound to be short-lived. This was a different time from the long Roosevelt years, whose triumph in building a New Deal coalition was bolstered by a country united in fighting a "just" world war. In contrast, the Johnson administration faced a political left crying hypocrisy over the false promise of a "great society" engaged in secret wars in Southeast Asia. And on the political right, a conservative counter movement had a rising tide of its own.

Riding the opposition wave was none other than Roosevelt-Democrat-turned-Republican Ronald Reagan. As an aging, out-of-work Hollywood actor, in 1964 he took to the stage at Goldwater campaign events to perform his now infamous "A Time for Choosing" speech, later dubbed simply "The Speech." Reagan framed America's choice as no longer "between a left or right" but instead as "up to man's age-old dream—the maximum of individual freedom consistent with law and order—or down to the ant heap of totalitarianism."[43] The future governor of California and president of the United States built his new career on tapping into the communism paranoia of the Cold War: the "red scare" he experienced firsthand in Hollywood as one of the high-profile "friendly witnesses" during the 1947 hearings of the House Un-American Activities Committee.[44]

By the 1968 election, the Great Society was unraveling, as was the thirty-six-year-old New Deal coalition of labor unions, blue-collar workers, minorities, farmers, White southerners, intellectuals, and state party bosses. The primary season was chaotic, to put it mildly. Alabama governor and segregationist George Wallace was first to break ranks, deciding to run for the White House his fourth time around under the newly formed American Independent Party. President Johnson campaigned in the early primary states, but in the face of growing antiwar protests and surging challengers, he dropped out on March 31. Civil rights leader Martin Luther King, Jr. was assassinated on April 4, shaking the country's pursuit of racial justice at its core. Next the late entrant to the race, Senator Robert F. Kennedy, was assassinated on June 5, just hours after winning the California primary, and any shred of Great Society optimism all but vanished. By late August at a highly fractured Democratic National Convention in Chicago, vice president Hubert Humphrey was the last man standing. Outside, over 10,000 protesters violently clashed with over 23,000 police and National Guard members.

The Republican Party had chosen their own candidate with far less acrimony earlier that month in Miami, Florida. Richard Nixon, Eisenhower's vice president, was back again, winning the nomination over New York governor Nelson Rockefeller and California governor Ronald Reagan. The "New Nixon" went on to win the general election on promises to end the Vietnam War overseas, uphold law and order back home, and support the "silent majority," a term he resurrected from the 1920s that became synonymous with a growing conservatism of White, blue-collar voters from suburban, exurban, and rural communities.

The Nixon White House was the beginning of the end of the New Deal coalition, Bretton Woods, and the Great Society. The neoliberal turn had begun—predicted by Karl Polanyi's *Great Transformation* twenty-five years before—and the door of the White House was kicked wide open to a more conservative brand of economics that would not only reshape American politics but also the values, ethics, and course of humanity worldwide. A market society was now in full bloom, and Polanyi's diagnosis that "human society had become an accessory of the economic system" seemed vindicated.

CHAPTER 4

Coming of Age in the Econocene

Economics are the method; the object is to change the heart and soul.[1]

—Margaret Thatcher

I was born November 20, 1969, ten months after the inauguration of Richard Nixon as the thirty-seventh president of the United States. The day Apollo 12 headed home after humanity's second walk on the moon. Just six weeks shy of a new decade, into the front end of a rootless Generation X. Growing up in the '70s, my generation clung to the promises of the '60s—to JFK's inaugural charge to our parents to "ask what you can do for your country." In another universe, his brother Bobby would have turned forty-four on my birthday, perhaps ten months into a presidency built on the hopes of the Great Society. But the 1970s and 1980s shaped a different story: the third act of the cultural epoch of the Econocene.

Act 1 concluded as my great-grandparents—first- and second-generation immigrants from Sweden, Ireland, Germany, and the Netherlands—were having kids of their own. At the turn of the nineteenth century, the commons of the old world were enclosed, and a new wave of colonizers were after what remained. The evolution from an agricultural to industrial economy was inevitable, led by a new world empire growing from the fires of fossil fuels. Slaves were emancipated, but African Americans were segregated. Women entered the workforce but didn't have the right to vote. Labor unionized, progressives trust-busted, and mainstream economics fractured in two.

Economics as moral philosophy (classical) gave way to economics as market fundamentalism (neoclassical). Privatization of the inputs, industrialization of the outputs, and marginalization of the working class were key ingredients to a society built on economism. First named by Russian revolutionary Vladimir Lenin in 1899,[2] economism is the main storyline of the Econocene, what ecological economist Richard Norgaard defines today as "the reduction of all social relations to market logic."[3]

My grandparents were born between 1904 and 1914, at the beginning of Act 2 of the Econocene. They were the children of immigrants who fled European enclosure with dreams of fencing in a new frontier of their own. The Ericksons, Doughertys, LaBodas, and Terwilligers never got farther than the farmland and small towns of New York's Hudson River Valley, coming of age in the Roaring Twenties under the full expression of market logic, only to be whiplashed by the Great Depression.

I knew my maternal grandfather, John LaBoda, as the essence of rugged individualism. His older brother, Gus, left home to fight in the Great War, and my grandpa left school after the sixth grade to help his mother and father on the farm. They were a family of three brothers and six sisters. Days were long and living was lean. A childhood friend recalled that when my great-grandfather Johann slaughtered a pig, "he used everything but the squeal." At eighteen, Gus landed my grandfather and his brother Louie jobs with room and board at the Poughkeepsie State Hospital. Starting as a kitchen attendant, he worked his way up to become a steamfitter within a few years. I knew him as a blue-collar guy with callused hands and a faint smile, forging a middle-class life in Middletown, New York, my grandmother's birthplace.

Margaret Dougherty was raised on the Irish side of town with five brothers and two sisters. She studied hard in school and broke free from her family's immigrant story by earning a teaching degree at a coed college in Pennsylvania. She went on to take summer graduate classes at the University of Virginia, which allowed women students but not women graduates. My aunt described her as a flapper, one of the short-skirted, jazz-listening, hair-bobbed independent women and cultural icons of the Roaring Twenties. She met John LaBoda in 1933 on an ice-skating pond. They fell in love, saved for a house, got married in the Catholic Church, and started a family at the tail end of the ten-year Depression. She taught for years in a one-room schoolhouse on the outskirts of town, and my grandfather worked until he retired as a steamfitter at the Middletown State Hospital.

As young adults during the Great Depression, with ethnic identities still rooted in German and Irish ancestry, they must have felt their belief in the American Dream shaken. When the Roaring Twenties came to an end on October 29, 1929, a culture built to glorify economism was again questioned. The shared promise of a New Deal, and shared sacrifice of another world war, raised societal values above economic ones, especially for the White working class. Historians later described them as the "greatest generation," one balancing allegiance to country and economy. A generation who knew the follies of excess, the face of poverty, the costs of war, and the privilege of European roots.

But the reins on economism were short-lived. My parents were born in 1943 and 1944, at the height of the Second World War, and on the cusp of a new allegiance to gross national product. War was good business, and Middletown factories were bustling in the 1940s. The troops came home to a new American optimism that, together with the forces of globalization, consumerism, and a nuclear arms race, injected steroids into the economy. My parents witnessed the "Great Acceleration" over their lifetimes as global population more than tripled from 1950 to 2010, global GDP grew twelvefold, and foreign direct investment expanded a mind-boggling 18,000+ times over.[4] More stuff for everyone. Global finance to pay for it all. Guns and butter all around, charged to a global credit card that the International Monetary Fund (IMF) estimated at $184 trillion by 2017, or more than twice the size of the world economy.[5]

As with the New Deal generation before, when my parents came of age in the 1960s economism again came under fire. The civil rights movement asked just exactly whose freedoms earlier generations had defended. The antiwar movement asked whether the postwar boom was a perpetual war economy in disguise. The environmental movement asked whether the well-tallied benefits of economic growth outweighed the uncounted costs of depletion, pollution, and extinction. Ultimately the Great Society asked whether capitalism served democracy, or was it the other way around?

For my grandparents, Franklin Delano Roosevelt helped shaped a worldview that countered the forces of greed and individualism. For my parents, it was the Kennedys. When John F. Kennedy was assassinated on that fateful day in Dallas, Texas, November 22, 1963, the unfilled promise of a New Deal for all—no matter your color, gender, or inheritance—seemed shattered. But national mourning quickly turned to a political mandate not seen since the depths of the Great Depression. Lyndon Johnson capitalized and signed long-stalled civil rights legislation into law on July 2, 1964. The momentum continued into his first term as the duly elected president submitted eighty-seven bills to the 89th Congress and signed all but three into law within his first nine months.[6]

The secret to success of the Great Society agenda was more than political leadership or public pressure. It passed because of the growth of the very economic system it sought to change. The US economy grew at annual rates north of 4 percent from 1961 through 1966. When 1965 hit 8.5 percent—a rate not since surpassed—the White House could push through nearly any law with an open checkbook to cover the charges. A growing consumer base with growing consumer appetites was the secret sauce to growing government revenues and growing social programs.

However, as the economic euphoria started to fade toward the end of Johnson's first full term, another Kennedy took another swipe at economism, this time at the very core of its ideology. On March 18, 1968, just two days after he formally announced his candidacy for president, senator Robert Kennedy questioned the nation's blind faith in economic growth. It's worth quoting at length from his immortal speech at the University of Kansas:

> Too much and for too long, we seemed to have surrendered personal excellence and community values in the mere accumulation of material things. Our Gross National Product, now, is over $800 billion dollars a year, but that Gross National Product . . . counts air pollution and cigarette advertising, and ambulances to clear our highways of carnage. It counts special locks for our doors and the jails for the people who break them. It counts the destruction of the redwood and the loss of our natural wonder in chaotic sprawl. It counts napalm and counts nuclear warheads and armored cars for the police to fight the riots in our cities. It counts Whitman's rifle and Speck's knife, and the television programs which glorify violence in order to sell toys to our children. Yet the Gross National Product does not allow for the health of our children, the quality of their education or the joy of their play. It does not include the beauty of our poetry or the strength of our marriages, the intelligence of our public debate or the integrity of our public officials. It measures neither our wit nor our courage, neither our wisdom

nor our learning, neither our compassion nor our devotion to our country, it measures everything in short, except that which makes life worthwhile.[7]

Kennedy foresaw the dangers of an economic system built on "false hopes or illusions." He laid bare the folly of a system built on perpetual growth. And he outlined the unfinished agenda of the Great Society that ultimately influenced Nixon's first term, especially on the environmental front. When the first Earth Day was observed on April 22, 1970, the conservative president had to take notice. The nationwide teach-in— organized at over two thousand colleges and universities, over ten thousand primary and secondary schools, and hundreds of communities across the United States—prompted executive action that December to create the Environmental Protection Agency (EPA). Democratic majorities in the House and Senate also sent bills to Nixon's desk that came to define US environmental law, including the National Environmental Policy Act of 1969, amendments to the Federal Water Pollution Control Act in 1970 (later amended to be the Clean Water Act), and the momentous Endangered Species Act of 1973.

Although the civil rights movement, environmental movement, and war on poverty partially counterbalanced Nixon's new conservatism, a swing back to laissez-faire economics had been under construction ever since Keynes. Nixon appointed the University of Michigan's Paul McCracken as chair of the Council of Economic Advisers, the first card-carrying member of the Mont Pelerin Society to serve a US president.[8] As a free market counterweight to Bretton Woods, the society was first organized in 1947 at its namesake Swiss resort by Friedrich Hayek. Founding members included leading libertarian intellectuals such as Hayek's mentor Ludwig von Mises, philosopher Karl Popper, and the principal architects of the Chicago School: Frank Knight, George Stigler, and Milton Friedman. McCracken joined in 1968, a rite of passage for the *new* liberal movement of neoliberalism that would take 1600 Pennsylvania Avenue and every White House since.

~

The term *neoliberalism* was proposed at the 1938 Walter Lippmann Colloquium to signal a break from the past.[9] Lippmann was a prominent American journalist, credited as "the most influential" of the twentieth century by some accounts,[10] and the Paris gathering of European intellectuals explored his book *An Inquiry into the Principles of the Good Society*, published the previous year. The fear of rising fascism in Europe was front and center, as were the failures of "classical liberalism," especially the extremes of laissez-faire ideology that brought the world to the depths of the Great Depression. Discussions of a new liberalism wrestled with competing visions of liberty and the role of the state in a market economy.

Friedrich Hayek featured among the attendees and found inspiration for his life's work. Although the defeat of fascism and the rise of Keynesianism would sideline the neoliberal project after the war, Hayek and other participants in the Paris meeting waited patiently for their opening. The Mont Pelerin Society helped nurture a small but well-funded group of conservative economists who eventually seized the moment of a Nixon presidency and ultimately seeded the Reagan revolution. *Guardian* columnist George Monbiot describes the neoliberalism that reemerged in the 1970s and 1980s as a political movement where citizens were cast as consumers "whose democratic choices are best exercised by buying and selling, a process that rewards merit and punishes inefficiency," and where society is organized around a competitive market that "ensures that everyone gets what they deserve."[11]

Neoliberalism is often conflated with other terms such as *neoconservativism*, *libertarianism*, *laissez-faire*, and *market fundamentalism*. Its distinguishing feature is the essence of economism: the reduction of all social relations to market logic. The neoliberal turn of the 1970s fused libertarian politics and free market economics into one. We all know the master narrative. Freedom is market choice. Free enterprise creates jobs. Regulations reduce choice and kill jobs. Government is inefficient and incompetent. Millionaires and billionaires earned what *they* get. The poor and unemployed are lazy and deserve what *they* get.

Its modern version came in the form of Reaganomics, a full merger of you-get-what-you-deserve politics with a vote-with-your-dollars economics. Tax cuts for the wealthy, deregulation of business and banks, and slashes to social programs were the policy principles of Reaganomics. "Reaganisms" became the economisms of my generation. "As government expands, liberty contracts." "Unemployment insurance is a pre-paid vacation for freeloaders." "The most terrifying words in the English language are: I'm from the government and I'm here to help." And perhaps Reagan's most ironic quote: "The best minds are not in government. If any were, business would steal them away."

Reagan's oratory was a product of the slow burn of a neoliberal movement in America. Well-funded, pro-business advocacy groups and think tanks had patiently cultivated and promulgated a focused narrative. Some of the most influential included the US Chamber of Commerce (founded in 1912), American Enterprise Institute (1938), Institute of Economic Affairs (1955), Heritage Foundation (1973), and Cato Institute (1974). Each has a rolodex of all-star neoliberal thinkers and funders, with multi-million-dollar budgets and extensive networks of political commenters, expert witnesses, editorial writers, and academic researchers. They routinely top lists of the highest-spending DC lobbyists and in any given year put out hundreds of policy briefs, media advisories, and research reports. And they have been doing this day in and day out for years and years.

Consider the power and influence of the US Chamber of Commerce, in recent decades the highest-spending lobbyist in Washington by far.[12] Originally founded to consolidate a pro-business voice against the rising labor and consumer protection movements of Teddy Roosevelt's time, the chamber evolved into a political influence machine representing the interests of legacy industries such as oil, tobacco, banks, and their family wealth.[13] The foundations of their current strategies are outlined in the infamous Powell Memo, a confidential memorandum written on August 23, 1971, by Lewis Powell to the chamber's education director.[14] A corporate lawyer, Philip Morris board member, and soon-to-be Nixon appointee to the Supreme Court, Powell provided a litany of examples from college campuses, the media, and other "new leftists" as proof of what he called an "Attack on the American Free Enterprise System." The call to arms outlined a blueprint for the chamber and the broader pro-business lobby, grounded in "careful long-range planning and implementation, in consistency of action over an indefinite period of years, in the scale of financing available only through joint effort, and in the political power available only through united action and national organizations."

Powell's multipronged strategy included building an army of conservative intellectuals to be deployed on college campuses as a counterbalance to left-leaning academics. He recommended an evaluation of social science textbooks by "eminent scholars who believe in the American system," development of "attractive, articulate, well-informed speakers" who would advocate for "equal time on the college speaking circuit," and targeted outreach to graduate schools of business in particular. In the media, Powell's strategies similarly called for a deployment of scholars and speakers, monitoring of any criticism of the free enterprise system, and financial incentives to publish across a full spectrum of magazines, newspapers, books, and scholarly journals. To round things out, both political action and judicial influence were called upon to defend business interests, with no "reluctance to penalize politically those who oppose it."

The Powell Memo is one example of setting a targeted agenda for a coordinated neoliberal turn. The resulting organized and well-funded strategies led to political, media, and academic capacity and influence. Corporate public affairs offices in DC grew from 100 in 1968 to over 500 by 1978, registered corporate lobbyists from 175 firms in 1971 to 2,500 by 1982, and corporate political action committees from under 300 in 1976 to over 1,200 by 1980.[15] A wave of new conservative think tanks such as the Heritage Foundation produced reams of policy papers to arm their hand-picked political candidates. Their *Mandate for Leadership*, released in January 1981, included more than two thousand recommendations in what United Press International called "a blueprint for grabbing the government by its frayed New Deal lapels and shaking out 48 years of liberal policy."[16] What became known as the "manifesto of the Reagan revolution"[17] was circulated at his very first cabinet meeting, and an estimated 60 percent of the individual suggestions were implemented or initiated by the end of Reagan's first year in office.[18]

The ideological shift in America was purposeful and profound. A 1997 study commissioned by the National Committee for Responsible Philanthropy investigated the grant-making strategies of conservative foundations in their pursuit of an "overtly ideological agenda based on industrial and environmental deregulation, the privatization of government services, deep reductions in federal anti-poverty spending, and the transfer of authority and responsibility for social welfare from the national government to the charitable sector and state and local government."[19] Grants from the top twelve conservative foundations—with names largely unrecognizable to the general public, barring the now-infamous Koch brothers—were investigated over a 1992 to 1994 study period. Funding prioritized first and foremost college campuses and education networks with 42 percent of all "charitable giving," followed by national think tanks (38 percent), media groups (7.8 percent), legal organizations (5 percent), state and regional think tanks (4.4 percent), and religious and other philanthropic institutions (2.6 percent).

The academic grants to endow professorships, write new curricula, fund public policy centers, and underwrite research all shared one aim: spread the gospel of free market economics and limited government. Number one on the list of 145 academic grantees was the University of Chicago, receiving nearly 12 percent of all funding during the study period, followed closely by Harvard at 11 percent. Highlights included support of the growing popularity of law and economics programs and their influence on deregulation, conservative leadership training in public policy schools and centers, and efforts to resist multiculturalism in favor of the "universal culture" of Western civilization (to quote Boston University's president at the time).[20]

Beyond universities and colleges, education funding also went to networking organizations such as the Intercollegiate Studies Institute (ISI), a free market group founded in 1953 with broad and sustained presence on college campuses to prepare students "to defend and advance the principles that made America free and prosperous."[21] In a 1989 speech to the Heritage Foundation, ISI president Kenneth Cribb made clear that the higher education strategy was to "provide resources and guidance to an elite which can take up anew the task of enculturation" and that this "coming age of such elites has provided the current leadership of the conservative revival."

The chorus of the revival was simple and effective. Public is bad; private is good. Government is inept; business is brilliant. The poor are freeloaders; the rich are hard workers. Planning is inefficient and political; markets are efficient and fair. Cooperation is for losers; competition is for winners. These were the stark contrasts of an all-encompassing worldview, resurrected from my grandparents' youth and questioned by the baby boomers, that ultimately paved Reagan's and Thatcher's path to "change the heart and soul."

And it worked.

Generation X was rootless no more. When the Clinton campaign wrote "The economy, stupid" on the strategy board of their war room, we nodded our heads in unison. When George W. Bush responded to the 9/11 terrorist attacks with a plea to go shopping to save the economy, we pulled out our Mastercards and got to work.[22] When big-oil-funded climate economists preached "the market will innovate and adapt," we kept driving, flying, and burning in the hopes of a technological savior.

With nearly all human values reduced to economic logic, the dream of the Econocene was in reach.

~

I remember when the Econocene hit its peak. To be dramatic, I'll give it a date: May 15, 1997. The cover of *Nature* read "Pricing the Planet." The lead paper in the leading science journal was by University of Maryland ecologist Robert Costanza and a multidisciplinary team of economists, geographers, and environmental scientists. In the culmination of a week-long meeting in Santa Barbara, California, they workshopped the economic value of "the entire biosphere." The price tag: 33 trillion US dollars.

This was a big number, which was the point of the exercise. The team had combed through a growing literature on the economic valuation of ecosystem services but emphasized that "because of the nature of uncertainties, this must be considered a minimum estimate." Figure 1 illustrated the final frontier of the neoclassical synthesis: the familiar supply–demand curves of freshman economics. X marked the spot at the intersection of the limited means of the entire planet and the unlimited wants of one all-powerful resident. Price times quantity for seventeen ecosystem services, tallied across five marine and seven terrestrial biomes, all added up to a number $15 trillion bigger than the gross national product of the entire world economy at the time (desert, tundra, ice, and rock sold separately).

"The *Nature* paper," as it's often referred to by economists who study the environment, was inevitable. The specialization of environmental economics was formalized twenty-five years earlier to ask these sorts of valuation questions, albeit at more modest scales. Economists in the 1970s had rediscovered Pigou's *Economics of Welfare* from fifty years past and asked whether negative externalities—costs imposed on others and not reflected in individual consumer and producer decisions—were perhaps the rule, not the exception, to a growing economy. Pesticides poisoning our lands and waters in Rachel Carson's *Silent Spring* were labeled a "market failure." The Cuyahoga River fires were simply the unpaid costs of doing business in Ohio. America's very symbol of freedom, the bald eagle, just needed to be commodified and assigned as someone's property right to save it from extinction. In the environmental economics storyline, the market engine of society was sound; prices just needed to be "corrected."

Environmental economics was, at first, perceived as a challenge to the mainstream. The neoclassical synthesis was hesitant to elevate Pigou from historical footnote to a central feature of the market model. The fear was that depletion, pollution, and extinction were not simply market *failures* but rather market *features*. Could the neoclassical synthesis hold together if both private and social costs were included? Samuelson's eighth edition of *Economics*, published in 1970, the year of his memorial Nobel, made scant reference to "external diseconomies" of smoke from a factory chimney as a special case for "justifiable" government activities on page 151. In a later chapter on "Analysis of Costs and Long-Run Supply" there was an obligatory footnote to Pigou in reference to "sound economics [that] would suggest some limitations on individual freedom in the interest of all." Two paragraphs on two pages of an 868-page best-selling textbook in economics.

Despite mainstream resistance, environmental concerns had featured in several well-known economic research programs at the time.

For example, the DC-based think tank Resources for the Future was founded by economists in response to a 1952 presidential commission on natural resource scarcity. There was also a legacy of natural resource economics on which to build, with roots in Harold Hoteling's *Economics of Exhaustible Resources* (1931), Siegfried von Ciriacy-Wantrup's *Resource Conservation: Economics and Policy* (1952), H. Scott Gordon's "The Economic Theory of a Common Property Resource" (1954), and Ronald Coase's "The Problem of Social Cost" (1960). The idea of putting a price tag on the environment was there all along; it just needed to be expanded from resources that were sold (e.g., oil, land, lumber) to things not priced at all (smog, PCBs, bald eagles). Under the wave of 1970s environmental legislation, scientists provided x-axis quantities in parts per million of pollution, species at risk of extinction, or human health casualties. To make economics relevant, environmental economists just needed to conjure up the y-axis prices.

Without real markets with real prices, economists devised clever ways to fake it. The general approach was to extend people's "stated preferences" in surveys or "revealed preferences" in market decisions to value a unit less of a pollutant, a unit more of an endangered animal, or another year of a statistical human life. Surveys were developed to measure "contingent values" of people's willingness to pay for something gained or willingness to accept something lost. Travel costs of actual money spent on actual visits to a public park, sightings of a wild animal, or scenery of an undeveloped beach were tallied to reveal preferences for wilderness, species, or views. Statistical techniques were designed to "assign" value to the environment through choice experiments: hypothetical exercises to measure tradeoffs between things we buy in markets and things we value in society. And because studies were expensive and time consuming, environmental economists developed "value transfer" methods to take results from one survey of one population at one location in one context at one moment and use them to infer values in all others.

Armed with nonmarket prices, a new generation of environmental economists was ready to serve the new wave of environmental policies. My doctoral advisor was one of them. Duane Chapman finished his PhD at Berkeley in 1969 under the tutelage of Siegfried von Ciriacy-Wantrup, a German-born economist who helped develop the related subdiscipline of natural resource economics. After a brief stint as an energy economist at Oak Ridge National Laboratories in Tennessee, he landed a tenure-track position in the Department of Agricultural Economics at Cornell University. Applied economics departments in agricultural colleges were some of the first to teach environmental economics. They need only shift from studying the use of natural resources toward the environmental impacts of that use. Environmental economics simply expanded the human household to include the source and sink of producing and consuming things.

This new frontier of economism produced a new generation of economists, but demand for their talents was initially lacking. The amendments to the Clean Air Act in 1970 and the Clean Water Act in 1972 explicitly prohibited economic considerations in setting environmental standards.[23] Air pollution limits were set based on public health criteria, and clean water goals called for the "elimination of the discharge of all pollutants into the navigable waters by 1985," no matter the economic costs or benefits. The Endangered Species Act of 1973 similarly avoided any economic considerations in the listing and protection of threatened or endangered species. These were policies built on societal demands from a surging environmental movement. Regulations were meant to be developed by science-informed bureaucracies, not ideologically constrained economists.

However, as the influence of economics rose under neoliberalism, so did its role in environmental policy. In the "environmental decade" of the 1970s, presidents Nixon, Ford, and Carter all issued executive orders to slip limited economic analysis into regulatory review.[24] The Office of Management and Budget (OMB), sitting in the executive office of the president, effectively became what President Johnson's OMB director later called the "lobby for economic efficiency."[25] As progress on signature environmental laws came into conflict with powerful economic interests, Congress also took steps to relax regulations and add more flexible market-based options to compliance. The EPA was sued by the auto industry, electric utilities, and a range of businesses in danger of being shut down for noncompliance with new air pollution standards. So the Clean Air Act amendments of 1977 extended deadlines, provided industry waivers, and allowed regulatory flexibility through pollution offsets,[26] the precursor to tradable permits, a favorite market-based approach to pollution control advanced by environmental economics.

Amendments to the Endangered Species Act in 1978 also backpedaled on original intent. Earlier that year, in *Tennessee Valley Authority v. Hill*, the Supreme Court upheld the law and suspended the $120 million Tellico Dam Project to protect a small endangered fish, the legendary snail darter.[27] The court ruled that the act lacked any "balancing test" to consider costs and benefits of listings. In response, the congressional amendments added an exemption process through a new Endangered Species Committee, an appointed body that could exempt any economic activity that was "in the public interest and is of national or regional significance."[28] The so-called God Squad was convened, held hearings, and sided with the fish. But the legislative branch had the last word, authorizing construction of the dam in an unrelated bill. Although the exemption amendment got the most press, the new law also added critical habitat designation with requirements to use "the best scientific data available and after taking into consideration the economic impact, the impact on national security, and any other relevant impact."

With a growing focus on the costs of environmental regulations, economists got their foot in the policy analysis door. When Ronald Reagan won the 1980 presidential race in all but six states, a new neoliberal mandate kicked the door wide open. Just four weeks into his first term, Reagan issued an executive order mandating that "regulatory action shall not be undertaken unless the potential benefits to society from the regulation outweigh the potential costs to society." In a special to the *New York Times* later that year, the "dean of environmental journalism," Philip Shabecoff, wrote that with Executive Order 12291 Reagan had "transformed with a stroke of his pen what had been a useful economic tool into an imperative of Federal decision making."[29] The "intense economic, political and philosophical debate" that ensued came to define the neoliberal approach to environmental policy, especially "assigning dollar values to things that are essentially not quantifiable: human life and health, the beauty of a forest, the clarity of the air at the rim of the Grand Canyon."

Henry Waxman, US representative from California, worried at the time about the political use of "cost–benefit analysis to reach decisions that will favor business and industry in this country rather than the public." Although many environmental regulations would survive a cost–benefit analysis (CBA) test, many more were not pursued under a pro-business CBA culture. Economists grew in number and influence at the EPA, Fish and Wildlife Service, and other federal agencies, tasked with controlling the costs of implementation and justifying the benefits of regulations. Where environmental laws explicitly forbid economic analysis they could be amended, as with the 1996 CBA amendment to the Safe Water Drinking Act. When amendments got hung up on philosophical differences over CBA, bureaucracy was used to block or underfund implementation. Most notably, reauthorization of the Endangered Species Act was politicized during the second convening of the God Squad in 1992 over the northern spotted owl. Calls for CBA held up reauthorization (then and ever since), and today the United States' signature environmental law limps along as an unfunded mandate subject to the whims of general government appropriations.

The neoliberal yardstick of CBA was tweaked by presidents Clinton, Bush, and Obama, but the focus on economic efficiency has remained true to Reagan's original intent. In 2017, Executive Order 12291 was rated by *Time Magazine* as one of the "9 Executive Orders That Changed History,"[30] not just for the actions it mandated but for the cultural shift it foretold. Worldwide, the privileging of economic analysis of environmental protection has become so pervasive that it's no wonder scientists, health professionals, and nearly anyone from any field has yielded to economic reason under a banner of "environmental pragmatism."[31] It's no longer sufficient to argue for environmental policy on scientific or ethical grounds. Decades of economism have reduced nearly all values to dollars and all choices to the margin.

In my circles, the subtext of the 1997 *Nature* paper was clear: "If you can't beat 'em, join 'em." Global assessments of climate change, biodiversity loss, and land conversion have since been dominated by economic valuation. Many, such as the UN's Millennium Ecosystem Assessment, take a broad view of the constituents of human well-being, but when presented in class, statehouses, or the media, it's the economic numbers that grab attention. The universality of the dollar makes everything comparable: All things are open to tradeoffs and all decisions subject to the logic of marginal costs and benefits. Today, climate scientists, conservation biologists, and environmentalists can have a seat at the neoliberal table if they learn the language of the economist. Seated all around are the corporate executives and their economist consultants, who have been fluent for decades, well schooled in the rules of the game.

As an environmental advocate once advised me on how to win in the Econocene, "I don't care how you get the number, just as long as it's big."

꙳

I didn't realize the significance of the 1997 *Nature* paper until November of the following year. The fifth meeting of the International Society for Ecological Economics (ISEE) had convened in Santiago, Chile, and "pricing the planet" was at the center of a debate that was pulling our new field apart.

Ecological economics had been formally named and established just ten years before as a distinctly different approach to economics, not just a newer version of environmental economics with new tricks to value nature. From the vantage point of ecology—the science of interactions between organisms and their biophysical environment—the economy was fundamentally embedded in and interdependent on the web of life. Economic growth had both benefits and costs as the human-defined subsystem grew into a biophysically determined whole system. Finding the right size of the economy was prioritized over the efficiency of internal exchange between consumers and producers, as was the distribution of the economy's benefits and burdens. If we could no longer count on growing the size of the pie to avoid comparing each other's share, then simply voting with our dollars wasn't going to suffice.

On one side of the pricing debate were pragmatists such as Bob Costanza, who had worked tirelessly to build the professional society, launch a peer-reviewed journal, and grab the attention of the international development profession. Sessions on "Valuing Environmental Assets" easily had the most presentations, and mainstream economics had a visible influence on a conference program co-sponsored by the World Bank. In the pragmatist view, all were welcome at the table, especially those in positions of power and influence. Maurice Strong, one of the world's most established environmental diplomats, gave the opening keynote address. Strong was the founding director of the UN Environment Programme in 1972 and secretary general of the UN Conference on Environment and Development (a.k.a. The Earth Summit) twenty years later, a clear signal that ecological economics had arrived.

On the other side, ecological economics was held up as a movement to topple the mainstream, take the "science" in social science seriously, deemphasize money in all aspects of our lives, and enable the next phase of human development based on balance and resilience, not growth and greed. Some conference participants were asking whether ecological economics had succumbed to the very worldview it set out to challenge. A European contingent had formed a regional society of their own to resist, in part, the growing influence of valuation on mainstreaming the field. They asked whether ecological economics had become just a small improvement on environmental economics—another step down the well-worn road of economism—or whether the field represented a genuine countermovement to the neoliberal agenda to reduce all social *and* ecological relations to market logic. Perhaps Maurice Strong's presence—the oil-executive-turned-global-diplomat—signaled surrender, not victory.

This was my first international conference as a newly christened assistant professor of ecological economics, the first such named in the world. Fresh out of grad school, I had joined John Gowdy and Sabine O'Hara at Rensselaer Polytechnic Institute (RPI) the previous year to help launch the world's first PhD program in ecological economics from the halls of America's oldest engineering college. The city of Troy sat at the crosswaters of the Hudson River and the Erie Canal in New York State—the very heart of America's industrial revolution—the perfect place to take on the full history and momentum of the economic orthodoxy. We saw our mission as tearing down the hyper-individualism and market fundamentalism of neoliberalism, and with an international group of new students in tow, Santiago provided a daily reminder of what was at stake both in and outside the capital's convention center.

While conference participants debated the future of economics, the city streets swelled with daily marches and protests over the future of a nation. Just the month before, long-time Chilean dictator General Augusto Pinochet had been apprehended on human rights violations during a medical visit to London. Pinochet came to power in a brutal US-backed military coup in 1973, ruling for seventeen years by detaining, torturing, and executing leftists, socialists, and political critics.[32] Earlier that year the eighty-two-year old had stepped down as commander-in-chief of the Chilean army and became a constitutionally protected senator-for-life with full immunity from prosecution. However, his trip abroad put him in the crosshairs of extradition proceedings for long-standing charges of murdering Spanish citizens.

Pinochet's shadow loomed large on a conference whose theme of "Beyond Growth: Policies and Institutions for Sustainability" was antithetical to our host's decades-long experiment with neoliberalism. At the behest of the "Chicago Boys," Pinochet had instituted deep monetarist reforms to beat back 1970s inflation, including severe government budget cuts, widespread deregulation of the financial sector, unrestricted free trade, and privatization of anything with a pulse.[33] His economic advisors were selected from among the dozens of Chilean economists trained at the University of Chicago between 1956 and 1964 under Project Chile, part of the US Point Four Program of technical assistance and economic aid to "underdeveloped" countries. Chile had been cultivated ever since as a "laboratory" for economic and social engineering by Theodore Schultz, Chicago's renowned economics department chair and development economist.

After the coup, the Chicago Boys looked past the brutality of Pinochet's military junta for the unbridled opportunity to unleash full-scale economic liberalization. Milton Friedman himself visited Pinochet in 1974, followed by a series of personal letters recommending an immediate "shock treatment" to fight inflation and grow the economy, with "a very difficult transitional period" in between.[34] Members of the Mont Pelerin Society (including Hayek) also lectured, consulted, and even held a regional 1981 conference at the Chilean seaside town of Viña del Mar. Full praise of neoliberalism was on display, including a presentation by Virginia Tech's James Buchanan on public choice theory that was interpreted as a rationale "to limit democracy and to depoliticize the state in order to enable unconstrained market forces to guide human interaction."[35] What Friedman called "the miracle of Chile" forged a neoliberal brand of development economics and political theory that spread throughout Latin America, garnering Schultz a memorial Nobel in 1979 and Buchanan one in 1986.

The Chicago Boys also greased the wheels with foreign banks and the IMF on a promise of capitalizing the miracle. Chile and much of Latin America borrowed heavily from the North to finance market liberalization. With the global South open for business, imports flooded in and outcompeted domestic industry. Newly privatized industry couldn't defend against the economic imperialism that followed. The promise of free trade, private enterprise, and small government built an overleveraged house of cards. When Mexico defaulted on debt payments in 1982, a financial contagion spread, and it all came tumbling down. Structural adjustment ensued throughout the global South with even bigger cuts to government programs than the original neoliberal reforms. Friedman's prediction of a "very difficult transition period" would later be called the "lost decade."

By the 1990s, Chile and all of Latin America were still recovering from the debt crisis, and very thick strings were attached to widespread loan forgiveness initiated by US secretary of the treasury Nicholas Brady (the so-called Brady Plan). The institutional trilogy of the Washington consensus—IMF, World Bank, US Treasury—was now fully in control of a new world order. Chile's economic miracle was praised by the Mont Pelerin Society and multinational corporations alike for opening markets and liberalizing financial capital flows, but the general population saw only foreign control over domestic austerity. Healthcare, education, social services, and other previously public systems were in shambles, and a decades-long economic recovery stole the future from children of the lost decade.

At our 1998 conference, the exuberant extension of market principles to price nature poured salt in the open wounds of this Northern-imposed, neoliberal assault on human life and dignity. Not surprisingly, the World Bank's interest in a Southern ecological economics conference was met with skepticism, as was an expanding Northern-led research agenda on Southern ecosystem valuation. Presentations such as "North–South trade in carbon emissions," "environmental services of Brazil's Amazon forest as a potential source of monetary flows," and "valuing biodiversity—insights from the pharmaceutical industry" were viewed by some as neoliberalism in disguise. Those not bound by the economic faith were asking, Who was pricing the planet and for what purposes? Was ecological economics simply another justification for privatizing the commons, exploiting the poor, and reducing social relations to market transactions? Was the "science and management of sustainability" narrative, the theme of earlier meetings of ecological economics, yet another wolf in sheep's clothing?

~

My own questions about the state and fate of ecological economics led me back to the future, as it were, in search of foundational principles for the study of the economy rooted in ecology and ethics. At RPI, I was struggling to break free from my own economics training in service of a new generation of students looking for strategies to exit the Econocene, not double down on its core market logic. The first batch came to our fledgling PhD program from Europe and "alternative" US schools, where the neoliberal brainwashing of undergraduate education had yet to run its course. Some had science backgrounds, such as Evelyn Wright, my first doctoral student with a master's in physics from Harvard, approaching the isolated discipline of economics from a fresh perspective. All took a chance on RPI with a purpose of studying economics in some part, as Keynes's star student Joan Robinson famously said, "not to acquire a set of ready-made answers to economic questions, but to learn how to avoid being deceived by economists."

I had only started to unravel the deception a few years earlier through the writings of an earlier generation. Herman Daly's 1973 collection of essays, *Toward a Steady-State Economy*, gave me a roadmap to "both physical and ethical first principles" for economics. The eclectic group of authors included biologists such as Stanford's Paul Ehrlich, who had made waves in 1968 with the best-seller *The Population Bomb*; theologians such as John Cobb, who expanded ethics to the nonhuman community of life; and systems modelers such as Donella Meadows and Jørgen Randers, whose *The Limits to Growth* study released the year before sent shockwaves around a world coming to terms with the specter of an OPEC oil embargo.

Daly's fellow economists such as Kenneth Boulding, E. F. Schumacher, and Nicholas Georgescu-Roegen were also in the mix. Boulding's 1966 essay "The Economics of the Coming Spaceship Earth" provided the goalposts for a new economics, Schumacher's 1968 essay on "Buddhist Economics" opened the door to non-Western systems of thought, and an excerpt from Georgescu's 1971 masterpiece on *The Entropy Law and the Economic Process* turned the entire edifice of equilibrium economics on its head. A section of *The Abolition of Man* (1944), by British novelist C. S. Lewis, rounded out the volume with a warning of the folly of humanity's perceived "conquest of Nature," setting a tone of humility in the face of uncertainty for early aspirations of an ecological economics.

The hand-picked essays framed "an emerging paradigm shift in political economy," as Daly asserted in the first sentence of his introductory essay. Referencing Thomas Kuhn's *The Structure of Scientific Revolutions* (1962), Daly contrasted the day-to-day, cumulative process of most science with the disruptive discoveries that occasionally arose to challenge conventional wisdom. In "normal science" the established paradigm is rarely questioned. Those who do are often labeled "fringe," including past "heretics" who insisted that the Earth was not the center of the universe, the vast diversity of life was not created in a cosmological instant, and human economies cannot grow forever on a finite planet.

In Daly's work, I had found a blueprint for learning (and now teaching) principles of ecological economics, one that I return to often for guidance on an unfinished journey. His career spans six decades, touching nearly every voice in the creation, naming, and evolution of ecological economics. Born in 1938 in Houston, Texas, at the tail end of the Great Depression, Daly witnessed firsthand the struggle of working-class America set against the backdrop of the Texas oil boom. The son of a hardware store owner, he knew the callused hands and furrowed brow of blue-collar work, but the deprivation of poverty was most glaring during a trip through Mexico after high school. He chose economics as his course of study at hometown Rice University, read Samuelson cover to cover, and, like other young men of his generation, concluded the solution to poverty and all social ills was economic growth.

We might have never heard of Herman Daly if his interest in economics began and ended with Samuelson, as it did for generations of students. However, Daly was a voracious reader, a side effect of having polio as a boy and missing the Texas football craze of his classmates. In college, he developed a particular taste for economic history, including *The Affluent Society* by Harvard economist John Kenneth Galbraith, a best-selling 1958 exposé of growing private consumerism and shrinking public investment. Galbraith was Harvard's post-Keynesian foil to Samuelson's neo-Keynesian synthesis. Galbraith asked whether economic production can be defended "as satisfying wants if that production creates the wants" to begin with. Through Galbraith, Daly learned about John Maynard Keynes, Thorstein Veblen, Henry George, and other heretics who questioned the ultimate purpose of economics in their own life and times.

During graduate school at Vanderbilt University in Nashville, Tennessee, Daly continued his search for broader conceptions of economic progress. After reading Rachel Carson's *Silent Spring* in 1962, Daly again had more questions than answers for mainstream economics. Galbraith was concerned that uncontrolled, growth-obsessed capitalism would perpetuate the divide between the rich and poor. Carson's critique cut much deeper. She questioned "an era dominated by industry, in which the right to make a dollar at whatever cost is seldom challenged." With the acumen of a scientist and the pen of a poet, Carson called on humanity to "come to terms with nature . . . to prove our maturity and our mastery, not of nature but of ourselves."

For Daly, a city boy from Houston, coming to terms with nature would become a life-long journey. At Vanderbilt, self-proclaimed "Harvard of the south," his exploration began in the most unlikely of places. Graduate economics programs, especially those competing for attention from the Ivy League, were not exactly a wellspring for interdisciplinary thought or challenges to the orthodoxy. Mimicry was rewarded. Dissent discouraged. Yet there was one heretic who had earned the respect of the mainstream early in his career but had increasingly strayed from the script. In Nicholas Georgescu-Roegen, Daly found a dissident like none other.

A world-class statistician from Romania, Georgescu had studied in Paris and London before a Rockefeller fellowship brought him to Harvard in 1934. There he was influenced by Joseph Schumpeter, the Austrian political economist who believed that capitalist economies were constantly evolving and innovating, and coined the term "creative destruction." He also became lifelong friends with future Nobel laureate Wassily Leontief, a fellow statistician driven to measure the vast interdependencies that make economic production possible, not simply assume untested conditions for fantastical market equilibrium.

Georgescu had an opportunity to join the faculty at Harvard at the end of his fellowship but returned instead to the University of Bucharest to serve a nation at the tenuous crossroads of East and West. When the postwar spread of communism put Western-leaning academics in the crosshairs of the Soviet Union, Georgescu and his wife escaped to the United States in 1948 as stowaways on a foreign freighter. The influence of Schumpeter and other heterodox economists had since waned, so Georgescu traded an uncertain future at Harvard for job security at Vanderbilt.[36]

Harvard's loss was Daly's gain. He found in Georgescu a mentor with one foot firmly planted in the status quo while the other tested the thin ice all around. None other than Paul Samuelson praised Georgescu as "a scholar's scholar, an economist's economist" in the foreword to *Analytical Economics*, a 1966 collection of papers from Georgescu's foundational work in mathematical economics.[37] These early contributions to economic theory put his name in the mix of annual Nobel speculation. But at sixty years old, his long simmering dissatisfaction with the orthodoxy came boiling over. In a new introduction to *Analytical Economics*, he argued that the metaphor of a pendulum, of market economies always returning to equilibrium, simply didn't hold up to scientific scrutiny. The better comparison was with an hourglass, a one-way process that converted limited resources capable of doing useful work into useless waste.

Georgescu saw the laws of thermodynamics as governing the economic process, not a dated Newtonian conception of a clockwork Universe. The first law states unequivocally that matter and energy cannot be created or destroyed. When you burn a lump of coal to heat water, make steam, spin turbines, and generate electricity, the energy and material building blocks of the lump don't magically disappear. The coal has been transformed into heat, ash, sulfur oxides, carbon dioxide, and other "waste," but this law of energy conservation says there is no "away."

In economics, as with the study of all biophysical systems, Georgescu understood that we're stuck with the ultimate initial condition—atoms of the Earth and photons from the Sun.

If thermodynamics ended with the first law, then perhaps the circular flow diagram of households and firms endlessly swapping inputs and outputs could be salvaged. Economies could be forever sustained by consuming their own waste, and prices could maintain market equilibrium. As long as the economy's tailpipe could feed back to its gas tank, the perpetual motion machine of the circular flow could spin indefinitely. But herein lies the rub of the second law. The entropy law, the centerpiece to Georgescu's "bioeconomics," states that all closed systems move from order (low entropy) to disorder (high entropy). The economy, like any heat engine, simply speeds up this natural process of decay from useful to useless.

In graduate economics seminars at Vanderbilt, Daly witnessed Georgescu apply the principles of physics to economics. In Georgescu's masterpiece on *The Entropy Law and the Economic Process*, he argued that since economies operate in a finite natural world, depletion and pollution are inevitable. No amount of market pricing, technological optimism, or wishful thinking could change the laws of thermodynamics, the only physical theory that Einstein was convinced "will never be overthrown."[38] Like any other living system, economies were limited by their supply of energy—ultimately, the Sun. Living off the stored sunshine of fossil fuels means we would eventually run out. Daly was convinced that economics should no longer focus on the efficiency of this one-way process but instead on the scale of an economy the Earth can sustain.

Just shy of his thirtieth birthday in 1968, while a visiting professor in the poverty-stricken region of Ceará in northeastern Brazil, Daly published his own game plan on "Economics as a Life Science" in the University of Chicago's top-tier *Journal of Political Economy*. Inspired by Georgescu, Boulding, and Leontief, he described an economic system interdependent with and limited by nature's sources and sinks. The seeds of a truly "ecological" economics were planted, followed by a decade of teaching, research, writing, and collaborations at Louisiana State University (LSU) that culminated in *Steady-State Economics* in 1977, Daly's own magnum opus.

Daly started with the idea that infinite economic growth on a finite planet was both physically impossible and morally wrong. He built on his mentor's work for the physical part, and for moral reasoning he reached back to the age of classical economics, when "the ethical content was at least as important as the analytic content."[39] At the height of the classical era in 1857, John Stuart Mill argued for the desirability of a "stationary state" in the second volume of his *Principles of Political Economy*,[40] writing,

> If the earth must lose that great portion of its pleasantness which it owes to things that the unlimited increase of wealth and population would extirpate from it, for the mere purpose of enabling it to support a larger, but not a happier or a better population, I sincerely hope, for the sake of posterity, that they will be content to be stationary, long before necessity compels them to it.

In the 1970s, Daly described Mill's stationary state as "even more relevant today than in his own time." He tweaked the term, borrowing from the language of ecology, to signal a move away from past interpretations of "stationary" as stagnant. Growth and exploitation are certainly prioritized in the competitive, pioneer stage of a young ecosystem, Daly argued. But with age comes a new focus on durability, supported by dynamism, cooperation, and lived experience. A steady-state model shifted the goal away from blind expansion of the economy and toward purposeful improvement of the human condition.

~

Moving beyond growth—the theme of our meeting in Chile—was core to the early vision of ecological economics imagined by the field's founders. In the 1970s and 1980s, those raised on Galbraith's affluent society, Boulding's spaceship Earth, Ehrlich's population bomb, Georgescu's entropy problem, Meadows' limits to growth, and Daly's steady-state economics were questioning the dogma of growthism. What was the purpose of growth? Who received the benefits, and who paid the costs? Does economic growth always and everywhere equate to human progress? If not growth, then what?

One response came from a mix of scholars who crossed paths with Daly throughout the 1970s and 1980s. These included Bob Costanza, who collaborated with Daly first as a postdoc and then as a junior faculty member at LSU between 1980 and 1988. Costanza had studied under Howard T. Odum, a pioneering systems ecologist at the University of Florida. Like Daly, Odum came to focus on the energy and material basis of the economy early in his career, influencing a long line of heretics from the ecology side, including AnnMari Jansson and Carl Folke at Stockholm University in Sweden and Charlie Hall at the State University of New York's College of Environmental Science and Forestry. Other contemporaries of Daly included disgruntled economists who questioned the wisdom of a Western-led growth agenda, such as Richard Norgaard at the University of California, Berkeley and Joan Martinez-Alier at the Autonomous University of Barcelona. These were among the leaders of the burgeoning field, which was formalized in the 1980s and 1990s through an international society, academic journal, and new research institutes devoted to ecological economics.[41]

These early efforts were influenced by a parallel response to the growth agenda within the United Nations bureaucracy. As early as the 1972 UN Conference on Human Development in Stockholm, the "beyond growth" narrative was vetted on the global diplomacy stage. The historic meeting introduced Maurice Strong to the world, presiding as secretary-general of the conference and welcoming representatives from 113 nations. The resulting "Stockholm Declaration" included twenty-six principles to "inspire and guide the peoples of the world in the preservation and enhancement of the human environment" and 109 recommendations under a framework for environmental action.

Questions over the benefits and burdens of economic growth featured prominently in the deliberations. Conference proceedings made clear that "the concept of 'no growth' could not be a viable policy for any society, but it was necessary to rethink the traditional concepts of the basic purposes of growth."[42] Debate summaries further noted, "Many speakers, from both developing and developed countries, agreed that the ruthless pursuit of gross national product, without consideration for other factors, produced conditions of life that were an affront to the dignity of man." Taking a human rights approach to environmental protection, these early UN efforts declared, "The requirements of clear air, water, shelter and health were undeniable needs and rights of man."

The Stockholm conference led most immediately to the creation of the United Nations Environment Programme, with Maurice Strong appointed its first director, and set into motion a prolonged reconciliation between the agendas of economic development and environmental protection. The development side certainly had a head start with the founding of the United Nations Development Programme seven years earlier. The UNDP administrator is the third highest-ranking official in the UN hierarchy, so development has always had a clear and obvious prioritization over environment. However, the Stockholm Declaration opened new questions over what kind of development and for whose benefit.

It took ten years, but the UN General Assembly eventually established the World Commission on Environment and Development to search for answers. Chaired by Norway's recent (and soon to be again) prime minister Gro Harlem Bruntland, the commission was immediately at odds with 1980s US and UK hegemony. Initially funded by the governments of Canada, Denmark, Finland, Japan, the Netherlands, Norway, Sweden, and Switzerland, their work was an international response to the dismantling of environmental policy under Reagan and Thatcher. During the nine hundred days from its first October 1984 gathering to the delivery of findings in April 1987, the commission set out on the most inclusive process to date, holding deliberative meetings and public hearings in all regions of the world with "senior government representatives, scientists and experts, research institutes, industrialists, representatives of non-governmental organizations, and the general public."[43]

As if the world needed a reminder of what was at stake, one month into the commission's work gas tank explosions in San Juanico, outside Mexico City, killed hundreds and severely burned thousands more. A month later, leaks at the Union Carbide pesticide plant in Bhopal, India, killed thousands and severely injured hundreds of thousands more in the largest industrial disaster in history. Over their nine-hundred-day fact-finding mission, a famine in Ethiopia killed over a million people and displaced millions more, an estimated 60 million people died throughout sub-Sahara Africa of diarrheal diseases related to unsafe drinking water and malnutrition, and the Chernobyl nuclear reactor explosion on April 26, 1986, blanketed Europe with radioactive fallout that increased the risk of cancer to many millions for many years to come.

Environmental disasters, endemic poverty, debt crises, and Cold War politics all pointed to a global development path that placed the future in peril. The Brundtland Commission's final report on *Our Common Future* stressed the interdependent fate of all humanity, as well as the inseparability of their dual mandate of economic development and environmental protection. They called for a vision of development "that meets the needs of the present without compromising the ability of future generations to meet their own needs," the often-cited and impossible to dismiss definition of "sustainable development." Limits to growth were acknowledged but not in absolute terms. Instead, environmental limits on the economy were viewed as a function of the "present state of technology and social organization," which "can be both managed and improved to make way for a new era of economic growth."

Was this a disruption of the status quo or just another step down the well-worn road of economism? Certainly, the 1987 report legitimized decades of work on shifting the development narrative, leveraged by the founding of the International Society for Ecological Economics at meetings in Barcelona, Spain, that same year. The commission's work was an evolution of Robert Kennedy's speech that asked what "makes life worthwhile" back in 1968. It resurfaced the admonition of Simon Kuznets, chief architect of macroeconomic accounting, who warned in 1934, "The welfare of a nation can scarcely be inferred from a measurement of national income." Although the Brundtland Commission couldn't break free from the spell of economic growth, its mandate for a "new era of economic growth" challenged the chorus of the Econocene emanating from the World Bank, IMF, and regional development banks ever since the collapse of Bretton Woods. In a call for "reorienting multilateral financial institutions," they noted the particular influence of the World Bank "both as the largest single source of development lending and for its policy leadership, which exerts a significant influence on both developing countries and donors."

After the Brundtland report, Daly saw a crack in the development policy window. He took the bait and in 1988 left LSU to join the World Bank's environment department as a senior economist at the invitation of Robert Goodland. Goodland was known as the "conscience" of the bank, appointed as its first ecologist ten years earlier to screen development projects for their environmental and human rights impacts.[44] Daly joined his "loyal opposition of environmentalists," including longtime World Bank economist Salah El Serafy, who led efforts to green the United Nations System of National Accounts in cooperation with UNEP.[45]

Leveraging three careers' worth of intellectual leadership and political capital, they got to work on operationalizing sustainable development. Daly focused on incorporating the principles of a steady-state economy. One of his most significant books, *For the Common Good*, with theologian John Cobb, was written while he was at LSU and published in his first full year at the World Bank. They didn't pull any punches in criticizing the state of economics as a discipline and profession. The first one hundred pages lambasted the dangerous abstractions of economic theory, including the circular flow model of the economy and selfish actor model of humanity. "New beginnings" for economics were then framed as re-embedding the economy within the ecosystem and the individual within community.

This "person-in-community" and "communities of communities" approach called for new energy, food, labor, and land systems and a revitalized progressive agenda to reform university education, empower community governance, right-size national economies, and restructure global trade. A suite of recommended policy reforms included shifting taxes onto depletion and pollution, broadening worker participation in management and ownership, building more self-sufficient national economies, and reducing military spending. *For the Common Good* was a blueprint for "redirecting the economy toward community, the environment, and a sustainable future."

The book received high marks from those already onboard the sustainable development train. Kenneth Boulding wrote, "Its critique of economic doctrine is shattering." Paul Ehrlich was equally laudatory, writing, "No one who is concerned with solving the human predicament can afford to be without this book." When the Brundtland Commission received the coveted Grawemeyer Award for Ideas Improving World Order in 1991, Daly and Cobb were recognized the following year. In the decades to come, Daly's work was acclaimed the world over, including by Sweden's Honorary Right Livelihood Award, The Netherlands' Heineken Prize for Environmental Science, Norway's Sophie Prize, Italy's Medal of the Presidency, and Japan's Blue Planet Prize.

However, then and now, public praise didn't translate into professional popularity, especially among World Bank economists. Although the idea of sustainable development was gaining traction, Daly's long-standing critique of boundless growth put him at odds with World Bank leadership. In one memorable exchange, the bank's chief economist, Lawrence Summers, was on a conference panel at the Smithsonian Institution discussing the twenty-year update to the Club of Rome's *Limits to Growth* report, now titled *Beyond the Limits*.[46] During Q&A, Daly rose to ask Summers whether the size of the economy relative to the ecosystem was important and worthy of economists' attention. In economics lingo, was the "optimal scale" of the economy of concern? Summers' reply was short and dismissive: "That's not the right way to look at it."[47]

To the bank's chief economist (and future secretary of treasury and president of Harvard), the "right way" to look at any and all decisions was through the lens of economic efficiency. To Summers and much of his economic brethren, global markets could and should be trusted to properly value and allocate environmental impact to nations with the lowest costs. Any limits would only be temporary as prices adjusted, innovation responded, and pollution and depletion were optimized. The "right way" to look at environmental costs is through the cold calculus of opportunity cost, where populations with the lowest wages and shortest lifetimes should welcome the chance to be the global economy's tailpipe. As Summers asked in an internal World Bank memo, leaked to *The Economist* magazine earlier that year, "Shouldn't the World Bank be encouraging *more* migration of the dirty industries to the LDCs [least developed countries]?"[48]

To Summers, "the economic logic behind dumping a load of toxic waste in the lowest-wage country is impeccable," and because the "initial increments of pollution probably have very low cost," it follows that "under-populated countries in Africa are vastly under-polluted." He further deduced, "The demand for a clean environment for aesthetic and health reasons is likely to have very high income-elasticity." Perhaps reflecting on his own income potential over a high life expectancy due to costly treatment of Hodgkin's lymphoma early in his career, he argued, "The concern over an agent that causes a one-in-a-million change in the odds of prostate cancer is obviously going to be much higher in a country where people survive to get prostate cancer than in a country where under-5 mortality is 200 per thousand."

In the Summers disciplinary bubble, it was ethical to increase the odds of mortality to a low-wage worker in order to decrease the odds to a high-salary earner. Unsustainable development was simply a temporary problem of relative limits imposed by the economic laws of supply and demand, not absolute limits imposed by the moral laws of humanity or the physical laws of the universe. Granted, the Brundtland Commission also dodged the question of absolute limits, as did the World Bank's 1992 *World Development Report* overseen by Summers, the first in its fifteen years of annual reporting to address links between development and environment. In Daly's review of early drafts in preparation for the Earth Summit in Rio de Janeiro, he had asked that a diagram of the economy be edited to include an enveloping environmental system. After two ignored requests to place a circle labeled "economy" inside a square labeled "environment," the figure was left out altogether.

In response, Goodland, Daly, and El Serafy assembled their own report for Rio, "Environmentally Sustainable Economic Development: Building on Brundtland."[49] The introduction made clear that "it is no longer tenable to make economic growth, as conventionally perceived and measured, the unquestioned objective of economic development policy." Chapter 1, Figure 1 had two versions of a "growing economic subsystem" inside a "finite global ecosystem": a nineteenth-century "empty world" with a small box in big circle and a late-twentieth-century "full world" with a big box in the *same* big circle. This was simple enough for a kindergartener to comprehend, let alone a PhD from Harvard. All the appeals to develop global technology, stabilize the population, and redistribute income were in the mix, but in the zero-sum game of box-in-circle they made clear that "more growth for the poor must be balanced by negative throughput growth for the rich."

The World Bank refused to publish the edited compilation despite a contributed chapter by econ rock star Jan Tinbergen, the very first Nobel laureate in economics. Tinbergen's diagnosis that "society is steering by the wrong compass" included an increasingly mainstream view to revise national income accounting to include environmental losses. His conclusions hit all the Bruntland highlights but added a priority for economic policies that "permit no further production growth in rich countries." The unavoidable conclusion implied by an embedded economy—that some must do without excess so that others can simply get by—has been dodged ever since.

From that year's UN Conference on Environment and Development in Rio, through the Rio+20 UN Conference on Sustainable Development in 2012, to the Sustainable Development Goals adopted by 193 nations in 2015, new goals and language for the next "new era of growth" have been put forth, but it's growth in a finite system all the same. The upturned blades of the "great acceleration" hockey sticks just keep accelerating. When the UN Framework Convention on Climate Change was opened for signature at the 1992 Earth Summit, carbon dioxide levels at the Mauna Loa observatory in Hawaii were at 356 parts per million, already above an accepted margin of safety for climate stability. In 2021, average annual atmospheric concentrations surpassed 416 with no signs of leveling off. In fact, more than half of carbon pollution from the start of the industrial era in 1751 through 2015 was emitted after 1987.[50] In other words, the tons of industrial carbon emitted in the twenty-seven years after Brundtland equaled the total from the 237 years before.

The impact of a growing human population with growing economic demands on the rest of life has been even more striking. The Convention on Biological Diversity also opened for signature at the 1992 Earth Summit, a multilateral treaty that all UN member states have since ratified with the exception of the United States. Despite the institution of National Biodiversity Strategies and Action Plans by 191 of 196 parties to the convention,[51] the lack of progress on conserving biodiversity is shocking. A 2019 global assessment by a UN panel combed over fifteen thousand scientific publications and a large body of indigenous and local knowledge, concluding that "around 1 million species already face extinction, many within decades." That's nearly one in nine species slated to vanish from the Earth in a blink of geologic time. Draw a growing square inside a fixed circle and the cause is obvious. As the global assessment found, two decades into the twenty-first century, "seventy-five percent of the land surface is significantly altered, 66 percent of the ocean area is experiencing increasing cumulative impacts, and over 85 percent of wetlands (area) has been lost."[52]

Gro Brundtland was certainly correct in her foreword to *Our Common Future*, that development and environment are "inseparable," but not in the direction she hoped for the future. The commission concluded that to achieve sustainable development, per capita incomes worldwide needed to grow at least 3 percent per year, and more like 5 percent in developing economies of Asia, 5 percent in Latin America, and 6 percent in Africa and West Asia, to have any impact on absolute poverty. They assumed that a "five- to tenfold increase in economic activity in less than half a century" could be made "sustainable" through technological advances to meet basic human needs while conserving natural resources. But again, the solution has been growth in a finite system all the same.

To be sure, progress on reducing the extremes of poverty has been significant. The World Bank proudly claims "marked progress on reducing poverty—the first of the world's Sustainable Development Goals—over the past decades."[53] In 2015, 10 percent of the world's population lived on less than a global poverty line of $1.90 a day, down from nearly 36 percent in 1990. However, the unavoidable conclusion is that higher incomes in both rich and poor nations have led to more depletion, pollution, and extinction. Also, more time devoted to generating market income can mean less time for the so-called informal care economy, unpaid family and community activities that are foundational to human well-being.

If we're aspiring to $1.90 per day per person in the full expression of a market society, then perhaps there's enough planet to go around with some leftovers for the rest of life. If success means more communities dependent on the vagaries of a globalized economy controlled by concentrated interests, then development is on the right track. Yet before Brundtland and ever since, the poverty math largely ignores the other end of the income spectrum, those with obscenely more than their fair share.

To keep the growth model in play, incomes grow just enough to make life tolerable for the lowest rungs of the economic ladder, but no one at the top is expected to give an inch to make any room. As with any feudal system, the poor must instead be convinced that their fate is tied to further accumulation of the rich, be they nobility, clergy, or capitalists. As Cambridge economist Ha-Joon Chang describes, "Once poor people are persuaded that their poverty is their own fault, that whoever has made a lot of money must deserve it and that they too could become rich if they tried hard enough, life becomes easier for the rich."[54]

The inconvenient truth of truly sustainable development is that it can't be achieved solely by ensuring necessities for the poor without reducing the luxuries of the rich. If we recognize the physical limits of the planet, infinite economic growth is off the table as the solution to poverty. More efficient growth also falls short in the long run as resources become cheaper, resulting in more depletion and pollution. In a zero-sum game, growth can alleviate the plight of the poor only by limiting the glut of the rich. Yet Brundtland, the World Bank, the United Nations, and every nation on the face of the Earth approach economic, social, and environmental crises with the same general solution: grow everything for everybody. As Donella Meadows put it, "The world's leaders are correctly fixated on economic growth as the answer to virtually all problems, but they're pushing it with all their might in the wrong direction."[55]

Daly spent a career charting a new direction, most notoriously during his six-year penance from working within the belly of the beast. In his 1994 farewell speech, on the occasion of the World Bank Group's fiftieth anniversary, Daly couldn't resist the opportunity "to pontificate and to prescribe a few remedies for the Bank's middle-aged infirmities." He prescribed first "a few antacids and laxatives to cure the combination of managerial flatulence and organizational constipation" of the bank's internal leadership. He followed with a prescription for external relations, to get "some new eyeglasses and a hearing aid" to overcome an "unrealistic vision of development as the generalization of Northern overconsumption to the rapidly multiplying masses of the South."

If we extend the metaphor nearly three decades later, the bank and the worldview it has come to represent are long past remedies. It's high time for retirement.

CHAPTER 5

A New Story

> If you wish to make an apple pie from scratch, you
> must first invent the universe.[1]
>
> —Carl Sagan

All cultures have an origin story. Mine starts in chapter 1, verse 1 of the Book of Genesis: "In the beginning God created the heaven and the earth."[2] Light followed darkness. Then water, then land. He filled the heavens with stars, and the Earth with grass, trees, and beasts. And on the sixth day, man was created in God's own image, "to rule over the fish of the sea and the birds of the air, over the livestock, and over all the earth itself and every creature that crawls upon it." From the pews of St. Mary's, I was taught that the universe was invented for us in a cosmological instant, with plenty of apples for pie.

The image of man atop a ladder of nature, one rung from the angels and two from an almighty God, is the foundation of Western philosophy. Man subservient to God, woman subordinate to man, together with our charge to "be fruitful, and multiply, and fill the earth and subdue it." But as the Old Testament story goes, the first two humans screwed things up by page 2. Adam and Eve disobeyed the word of God (her fault, of course) and were kicked out of the Garden of Eden, and humanity fell from an original state of innocence and a life of plenty to perpetual guilt and hardship.

As Francis Bacon wrote in *The Great Instauration*, "Man by the fall, fell at the same time from his state of innocence and from his dominion over creation." A seventeenth-century architect of the scientific method, Bacon framed modernity as a redemption project: "Both of these losses can in this life be in some part repaired; the former by religion and faith, the latter by arts and science." As historian Carolyn Merchant wrote, the central narrative of Western culture became to "reclaim the lost Eden by reinventing the entire earth as a garden." In the modern era, "Science, technology, and capitalism have provided the tools, male agency the power and impetus."[3]

Economics was born of this master narrative with humanity separate from heaven above and nature below. "Natural resources" were privately owned and progress was made through "improving" the land. The charge to "be fruitful, and multiply" justified endless growth, along with exploitation of people and the planet. As society grew increasingly secular, the economy itself became the focus of our idolatry, money the means to reclaim Eden, and economists the priests of progress.

I've spent a life of disquiet with this culture of dominance. As a child I knelt in prayer at the Roman Catholic church, made to feel small and submissive in the feigned presence of an ominous God. I was taught to fear power so that I could then yield it over others. In church and school alike, I memorized laws that separated me from other, present from past, and civilization from the wild.

Yet in the outdoors of my youth I rambled freely in the woods, breathed in air exchanged with white pine and red oak, and drank from cold lakes fed by mountain brooks. Beneath the night sky, with the sound of crickets and frogs in my ears, I felt part of something larger, on a timeless journey through a creative universe.

Later in life, I discovered other cosmologies that broke free from the strict anthropocentrism of Abrahamic religions. Eastern theologies and Indigenous narratives appealed to my sense of belonging to, not ruling over, the natural world. I learned to question Western constructs from other spiritual wanderers such as Daniel Quinn, Fritjof Capra, and Ursula Le Guin.

In *Ishmael*, Quinn reinterpreted the Book of Genesis as a struggle between "leaver" (hunter–gather) and "taker" (agricultural) cultures through an imagined conversation between man and gorilla. In the *Tao of Physics*, Capra illuminated the "basic oneness of the universe" by merging theoretical physics with Eastern mysticism. In *The Dispossessed*, Le Guin contrasted capitalism with anarchy in made-up worlds of science fiction that tested the principles of the society into which I was born.

Imagining a Socratic dialogue with a gorilla philosopher, exploring the quiet crossroads between science and spirituality, and puzzling through "ambiguous utopias" on make-believe planets are feats of creative thinking. They inspire a new cultural narrative that knocks man off the top of the ladder of nature. A new story that embeds humanity within the full community of life. A new definition of progress as shared, restorative, and balanced. And a new economics born from a new worldview.

In search of a new story, let's consider an astronomical perspective. If astronomer Carl Sagan had made an economy "from scratch" it certainly wouldn't have started with humans on Day 6, let alone a narrow conception of *Homo economicus*. Astronomy reveals an origin story through the images of powerful telescopes peering into the depths of the universe, charting a 13.8-billion-year history from the Big Bang to the present.

Traveling the furthest back in time so far, the Planck telescope in 2013 mapped the cosmic microwave background, the earliest fingerprint of the Big Bang, just 380,000 of our solar years after Year 0. Peering back 13 billion years ago, the Hubble Space Telescope revealed 10,000 galaxies in a dark spot in the night sky, the size of a straw hole for an earthly observer. Do the math and our Milky Way is one of perhaps two trillion galaxies in the *known* universe.

What, then, is the significance of a hairless ape that arose just 300,000 years ago on a grassy savanna on a planet formed from a cloud of dust 4.54 billion years ago? Our evolution on one of an estimated trillion trillion (1×10^{24}) planets circling around one of a billion trillion (1×10^{21}) stars is an extraordinary story but requires no external hand of a divine creator.

In this origin story, the universe created itself, evolving from atomic particles to hydrogen atoms, from gas clouds to star nurseries, from supernovas to chemical elements, and from planetary systems to an extraordinary diversity of life in at least one. A Big Bang cosmology links the physical evolution of the universe to the biological evolution of life. As "big" historian David Christian quotes an "anonymous wit" in his *Maps of Time*, "Hydrogen is a light, odorless gas which, given enough time, changes into people."[4]

Astronomy provides no support for human exceptionalism. Our lifetimes are counted as revolutions around one of sextillion stars, more stars in the universe than all the grains of sand on Earth.[5] There were 7.9 billion of us on the 2,021st lap around the sun since the turn of the Gregorian calendar from before Christ (BC) to *anno Domini* (AD). Those alive in 2021 totaled perhaps 7 percent of the 108 billion "modern" humans born in the last 50,000 years.[6] *Homo sapiens* is one among an estimated 8.7 million species in existence on Earth today,[7] just a twig on the family tree of life, alive for just 0.007 percent of our planet's history, less than an instant since the Big Bang.

By the numbers, the significance of my own fifty-two laps is underwhelming. Yet I feel smaller in a story of humanity created in God's image than in a cosmic voyage through an ever-evolving universe. I feel closer to the celestial heavens when I imagine the oxygen in my blood being forged in the belly of a star than when I read a book written by a chosen people to make the case for their chosen-ness.

What David Christian calls the "Goldilocks" conditions of life on Earth instills a deep sense of obligation to reverse our destruction of this infinitesimal corner of the universe.[8] Perhaps we are unexceptional in the grand scope of things, living out our lives in a cosmological instant. However, a humble perspective of our home reveals the undeniable interdependence we have on each other and on all life.

Sagan spoke often of this humility, most memorably when unveiling a final portrait of Earth taken by Voyager 1.[9] As the spacecraft finished its flybys of Jupiter and Saturn and began its exit from our solar system, Sagan suggested NASA turn the camera around for one last photo of home on Valentine's Day, 1990. Earth appeared as just a fraction of a pixel, "on a mote of dust suspended in a sunbeam," he would later write.[10]

To Sagan, the iconic photo in Voyager's Family Portrait series "underscores our responsibility to deal more kindly with one another, and to preserve and cherish the pale blue dot, the only home we've ever known." A perfect charge for forging a new economic story.

~

When I teach my large undergraduate course in ecological economics, I typically start with a "Where do you stand?" exercise. Across the blackboard I denote a spectrum of opinion, with "Strongly Agree" to "Agree" on one side of the classroom, "Disagree" to "Strongly Disagree" on the other. In the middle, "Neutral." Students are asked to stand up, consider a series of three statements, and "vote with their feet" across the rows of the lecture hall.

The first statement is, "Economic growth and environmental protection are fundamentally in conflict with one another." After round 1 of the shuffling settles, a predictable bell-shaped curve materializes. Now the fun begins, as I ask why they stand where they do, including an invitation to walk their opinion elsewhere if they're otherwise persuaded.

Students in the "disagree" tail of the distribution often concede that growth as currently measured has some degree of conflict with environmental protection but argue it's not "fundamental." They give examples of an economy growing in clean and green ways through renewable energy, ecotourism, or the service sector more generally. Someone usually claims that demand for environmental protection comes with higher incomes and that "poor" people, communities, or entire countries must first grow to deal with the very impacts of that growth. The conclusion from this side of the room is that economies can grow in more efficient ways to limit environmental impact. There is a "greener" way.

The big clump in the middle want more clarification, especially over the word *fundamentally*. They'd like to redefine growth as something else, perhaps citing an example of "beyond GDP" discussed in an environmental studies class. Someone might quote a vague recollection of the Brundtland Commission or mention the UN Sustainable Development Goals but admit they've never thought beyond the handwaving of the sustainability discourse. The middle doesn't like the either–or nature of the statement. They want the benefits of growth but not its costs, yet they struggle with whether growing the economy forever (however defined) is possible and even desirable. There must be a "middle" way.

Then there's the "agree" side. To them—especially the outlier or two hugging the classroom wall—growth is growth. They argue that if an economy is growing it must be further depleting and polluting a finite planet. Someone might counter the "green growth" argument with the "rebound effect," where efficiency makes resources cheaper per unit, which ultimately leads to more depletion and pollution. An efficient machine might use half as much energy and so run twice as much time. Also, higher incomes may demand cleaner local environments but continue to demand pollution-intensive goods from abroad. Green growth at a planetary scale is an illusion because there is no "away." We need a "new" way.

Round 1 of our classroom exercise opens up a series of questions to explore in the weeks ahead. There are empirical questions about both the possibility and desirability of green growth, the Shangri-La of sustainable development. There are scientific questions about the Earth's capacity to provide resources and absorb wastes at the current size of the global economy, let alone something bigger. There are ethical questions about who benefits from the growth model, who pays the costs, and whether our single species should make more room for the rest of life.

Discussions lead to the next statement to consider: "There should be a limit to the amount of money that an individual can earn in today's society." Reactions to round 2 are visibly more personal as students confidently reshuffle to their new stance. A bell-shaped curve materializes again but more skewed to the "agree" side (at least in Vermont).

The side that disagrees offers the usual cultural norms of a capitalist society. Limits on earnings subdue motivation, inhibit entrepreneurship, and stifle innovation. If you work hard, take risks, and play by the rules, then you deserve every penny you earn. It's the equality of opportunity that matters, not of outcome. Those who strongly disagree tend to be quite skeptical about who would set limits on income and how. And besides, don't millionaires and billionaires give away lots of *their* money to charitable causes?

The majority in the middle again want more clarity, especially on the word *limit*. If these are "soft" limits—such as progressive tax structures with higher incomes paying higher tax rates—some would drift over to the "agree" side. If "hard" limits included an imposed cap on income, many would join the "disagree" camp. Someone often argues that society's focus should instead be on lifting the unfortunate up from the bottom, not unfairly punishing the successful at the top. Could we better incentivize the wealthy to support just causes with their hard-won earnings?

The proportion of students who agree with limiting income usually dive into the 1 percent narrative. This side is troubled with growing inequality in the United States and around the world. They often want to unpack the word *earn*. Let the individual keep earned income from the sweat of their brow but not capture the unearned returns from the work of others, investments of society, and resources of the environment. Billionaires are possible only in an unjust society. Why should the tiniest fraction of the 1 percent decide whether and how to spend unearned income on tax-deductible causes?

This second round opens a discussion on what is fair and unfair in society. There are biological questions about the capacity of our social primate species to both compete and cooperate. There are institutional questions at the intersection of law, governance, and culture that determine which attributes of human behavior will be selected and reinforced. There are political questions over who exactly is served by an old economics of narrow self-interest and White privilege versus a new economics of community well-being and reciprocity.

The first two stances are about the sustainable size and fairness of the economic system. They are well outside the purview of most economics classes. However, the final statement is squarely within the realm of a self-proclaimed science of choice: "Free markets will ultimately solve our environmental problems."

The march to the "disagree" side of the room is determined, with a clear majority quick to dismiss free markets as the panacea to environmental problem solving. They voice concerns over alignment of short-term, for-profit motives with long-term, for-planet interests. Some want to believe that voting with their dollars can make a difference but are skeptical that consumer choice alone will solve the climate or extinction crises. If I replace "will ultimately" with "can help," the bell-shaped curve materializes again.

The folks in the middle want clarification over the word *free*. Does *free* imply absence of any and all government oversight? Let the market do its thing but within clear boundaries set by society. Voting by ballot must take precedence over voting by billfold. The center of the room wants to strike a balance between the invisible hand of the market with the invisible handshake of social norms and the invisible foot of government. If I strike *free* to further modify the statement to "Markets can help . . .," more heads bob in agreement.

Rarely does someone strongly advocate for a purely free market approach, although occasionally a student steps out from under the peer pressure and makes the case. The "agree" position usually stems more from distrust of government than from blind faith in markets. In a twenty-year old's voice I can hear a parent raised on Reaganisms and a culture that claims government rarely solves anything. If I replace "free markets" with "government," the "disagree" side of the room barely budges, and any proponents of market-based solutions eagerly join their colleagues.

This third and final statement leads to questions over the dichotomy of market and government. This opens up rich discussions over the right scale of governance, the design of checks and balances in both private and public spheres, and, a topic near and dear to my heart, the role of education in informing civic duty in a global society. As an economics education of "I" has crowded out a civics education of "we," there is no shortage of questioning and rethinking our culture's bedtime stories.

As novelist Ursula Le Guin wrote to her own students, "There are no right answers to wrong questions."[11] The hope is that these polarizing statements inspire questions worth asking in building a new economics. Asking what minimum size of an economic system is needed to support flourishing livelihoods and an interdependent web of life is the right question. Likewise, asking what's fair and unfair in our economic relationships should preclude any delusions that just outcomes will magically emerge from a narrow model of self-interest.

The answers won't be precise x–y coordinates on a blackboard, but surely the wrong question is how to make markets more efficient to merely slow planetary destruction. The answers won't conform to a single story told from a chosen people, but surely the wrong question is how to sustain an economy that serves the wants of the few by forsaking the needs of the many. The answers won't be "grow the economy" to nearly every question asked, but surely doing the same thing over and over again and expecting a different result is, as Alcoholics Anonymous is purported to have first said, a kind of insanity.

~

To design a new economy, let's first consider the carbon question. The planet is warming because of a growing human population and economy. Burning fossil fuels, catalyzing cement, raising livestock, and converting forests and soils from sinks to sources all add up to more carbon than can be absorbed by the ocean and through photosynthesis. Carbon dioxide concentrations exceeded an annual average of 416 parts per million (ppm) in 2021, a level not approached since the "mid-Piacenzian Warm Period" of the Pliocene epoch, about 3 million years ago. This is beyond a level when the global average temperature was 3°C to 4°C hotter (5.4–7.2°F) and sea levels 20 meters higher (over 65 feet).[12]

Within my own family, I need go back only six generations to reach "preindustrial" concentrations of 280 ppm. When my maternal grandmother was born in 1908, CO_2 levels were just under 300 ppm,[13] the outer bound of all eleven interglacial intervals over the last 800,000 years.[14] By the time my mom was born in 1943, the ppm ticker was at 311. Since 1950, over the course of just my parents' generation, CO_2 concentrations have grown more than 100 times faster than the interglacial warming of the entirety of the Holocene, the 11,700-year geological epoch of the current era.[15]

The 2014 Fifth Assessment Report (AR5) of the Intergovernmental Panel on Climate Change (IPCC) concluded that humanity has already warmed the planet by about 1°C since preindustrial times. The result has been "multiple observed changes in the climate system" including "more frequent heatwaves" and "an increase in the frequency, intensity and/or amount of heavy precipitation events at the global scale."[16] When the first installment of the Sixth Assessment Report dropped on August 9, 2021, the physical science conclusions were even more dire—what UN secretary general António Guterres called a "code red for humanity."[17]

When I first engaged in climate change research in 1991 in the initial months of graduate school, the alarm bells were sounding that the 1980s were the hottest decade on record. Then the 1990s broke the record. Then the 2000s. Then the 2010s included eight of the ten hottest years ever recorded, with the droughts, fires, floods, and extreme weather events to show for it.

Consider the year 2019, like something out of a science fiction movie. Fires in Australia consumed 25 million acres and killed over one billion animals.[18] Extreme droughts in Central America displaced hundreds of thousands of people.[19] The Southern Hemisphere suffered the third deadliest tropical cyclone on record in March, matched five months later by the second strongest Atlantic hurricane. Historic floods breached riverbanks throughout the United States during the wettest year in recorded history.[20] The Greenland ice sheet lost more ice mass than in any year on record, and the seas north of Alaska hit summertime temperatures a full 7°C (14°F) above long-term averages.[21]

Common weather vocabulary now includes terms like "bomb cyclone," "superstorms," "megadroughts," and "polar vortexes." Climate scientists note that global warming isn't the singular cause of any single extreme event but warn that it does dramatically change the odds. Record-breaking heat and drought that proceeded Australia's 2019 fires were four times more likely under human-induced climate change than without. December 17 was the hottest Australian day in recorded history, averaging 40.9°C (105.6°F) for the continent, with the south-central coast nearing 50°C (122°F).[22] Under a 2°C global warming scenario, these extreme temperatures are eight times more likely.[23]

Beyond 2°C, the odds of destabilizing Earth's climate increase further. Beyond 2°C, tipping points are possibly crossed where a range of carbon cycle feedbacks further accelerate global warming. Beyond 2°C, a "Hot-house Earth" pathway becomes more likely, a trajectory described in a 2018 review in the *Proceedings of the National Academy of Sciences* as triggering "abrupt, non-linear responses" with "serious disruptions to ecosystems, society, and economies."[24] Beyond 2°C, well past the upper bounds of past interglacial periods, is looking very likely.

In fact, despite thirty years of international agreements, treaties, and national emission targets, business as usual currently puts the planet on course for 3°C to 5°C warming by 2100. Despite all the sustainable development rhetoric and green growth strategies, the last five years of the 2010s were the hottest five years on record. Despite all the climate science, modeling, and reports since the UN Framework Convention on Climate Change was adopted on May 9, 1992, greenhouse gas emissions are still rising from a global economy still largely run on the combustion of carbon fuels.

While temperature records were broken year after year in the 2010s, so too were demands for oil, natural gas, and coal.[25] Global car sales hit all-time highs of over 97 million vehicles in 2017 and 2018.[26] Coal-fired electricity grew 54 percent in China, 121 percent in India, and 50 percent in the rest of Asia between 2010 and 2018.[27] Annual growth in natural gas consumption hit a new global high in 2018, with every region of the world consuming at record levels.[28]

Near the end of the decade, there were signs that global coal demand was leveling but only by swapping one fossil fuel for another. Growth in renewable energy also took a small bite out of growing electricity demand in the 2010s, but investment in new capacity was less than one quarter of the $1 trillion spent per year on new fossil fuel exploration, extraction, and transport.[29] The International Energy Agency estimates another $20 trillion of oil, gas, and coal development is (quite literally) in the pipeline through 2040.[30]

So the carbon question is, How far and how fast does the world economy need to cut carbon pollution to stay within a 1.5 to 2°C threshold? More specifically, what's left to burn and what needs to stay in the ground? The 2018 IPCC special report on "Global Warming of 1.5°C" estimated that humanity has 580 gigatons of CO_2 emissions remaining for a 50/50 chance of staying within 1.5 degrees.[31] With 2010 as a base year, net CO_2 emissions (the difference between new sources and new sinks) would need to be cut 45 percent by 2030 and reach "net zero" by 2050 for a possibility of "no or limited overshoot of 1.5°C." To stay within 2°C, the world has a little more wiggle room with 25 percent reductions by 2030 and net zero by 2070.

How do we pull this off? The near universal answer has been—drumroll please—to grow the economy more efficiently with new technologies. The overarching storyline is green growth, modeled by all 116 IPCC scenarios in the Fifth Assessment Report with a chance of staying below 2°C.[32] The Hail Mary of the most trusted scientific synthesis on climate science and modeling is to "decouple" a growing global economy from energy, materials, and resulting greenhouse gas emissions—the biblical emancipation project at unprecedented scale, scope, and pace.

It is certainly true that the ratio of economic output over input has improved for labor, energy, materials, land, and more. New technologies and know-how have helped the economy grow more efficiently in a virtuous cycle. With *more* growth there's *more* capital to invest in *more* research to create *more* technology for *more* growth. With laser focus on the margin, the story holds up. Resource and pollution limits aren't seen as ultimate constraints to growth but rather temporary obstacles to overcome through technical progress, one step at a time.

But therein lies the rub between emission limits and marginal gains in efficiency. The inconvenient truth is that increasing efficiency at the margin doesn't necessarily lead to decreasing environmental impact in the aggregate. If the *next* unit of labor or energy is more productive than the last, then each new unit of production is using less resources and spewing less pollution. However, zoom out to the global scale, or over longer time horizons, and total depletion and pollution *increase* with efficiency.

As ecological economist Herman Daly described, "'Efficiency first' sounds good, especially when referred to as 'win–win' strategies or more picturesquely as 'picking the low-hanging fruit.'"[33] But in fact, putting efficiency first makes "frugality less necessary."

Humanity has become more efficient at mining for minerals. So we mine more minerals. We're more efficient at burning fossil fuels, so we burn more fossil fuels. Generation after generation, we have become more efficient at farming the land, fishing the sea, and drilling for oil, so we farm more land, fish more sea, and drill baby drill. The hockey stick diagrams of global depletion and pollution have accelerated to meet the demands of more people and more economy because we're more efficient than ever at plundering the Earth. We slow down or reverse course only when a resource collapses or the economy contracts.

This rebound effect was long ago identified by William Stanley Jevons in *The Coal Question*. One of the architects of the marginalist revolution in economics, Jevons wrote in 1865 that whatever "conduces to increase the efficiency of coal, and to diminish the cost of its use, directly tends to augment the value of the steam-engine, and to enlarge the field of its operations." With greater efficiency of coal discovery, mining, processing, and burning came greater use of coal.

Jevon's paradox, as it came to be known, is as true for the world's twenty-first-century carbon question as it was for Britain's nineteenth-century coal question. In 1990, the ratio of global GDP output to global energy input, in dollars per kilogram of oil equivalent, was 3.5. By 2014, the ratio was at 8.2, a more than doubling of energy productivity in just fifteen years. But a more efficient global economy didn't consume less energy. Quite the opposite. Total energy consumption over the same time period grew 59 percent, and CO_2 emissions grew 63 percent.[34]

Global energy, in aggregate, also didn't become more renewable during this more than doubling of productivity. Since 1990, the share of renewable energy in the global mix has fluctuated between 17 and 18 percent,[35] the majority of which is large-scale hydropower constructed decades ago.[36] At the margin, the decoupling story celebrates growth in renewables, but at best new solar panels and wind turbines have only partially offset growing energy demand.

Greener megawatts added to the global mix also require new carbon burned for production, shipment, installation, and maintenance. The carbon payback period—the run time to offset the carbon pollution generated from manufacturing and installing new solar, wind, biomass, geothermal, and hydro power—can vary from a year to a decade or more.[37,38] The transition to greener energy demands will also have an upfront carbon cost. For example, the manufacture and assembly of an average 2-ton electric vehicle—the star of the decoupling story—produces over three tons of CO_2.[39]

Omissions in carbon accounting are rampant in most decoupling claims. Again, at a circumscribed view of the margin, a country like the United States seems to be making great strides in bending the CO_2 curve while growing the economy. Former US president Barack Obama boasted in a 2017 essay in *Science* that "CO_2 emissions from the energy sector fell by 9.5% from 2008 to 2015, while the economy grew by more than 10%."[40] By counting only pollution produced within US borders, Obama claimed that "GHG mitigation need not conflict with economic growth" and that the "latest science and economics provide a helpful guide for what the future may bring."

But even a cursory glance at carbon "embodied" in US trade throws more shade on the dream of decoupling. More than one fifth of CO_2 pollution produced in China was driven by exports to the United States.[41] In fact, China is far and away the largest net exporter of embodied CO_2, with most headed across the Pacific to the United States, far and away the world's largest net importer. When all the CO_2 burned to produce a product is assigned to the country that uses the product rather than the one that created it, the United States is responsible for the lion's share of *global* CO_2 emissions, the only carbon account that truly matters.

At best, between 1990 and 2015, the global economy achieved mild, "relative" decoupling of CO_2 emissions. Real GDP per capita grew on average 2.14 percent per year, while CO_2 emissions grew 1.89 percent per year.[42] However, given a hard constraint of a 1.5°C or 2°C carbon budget, the dream of decoupling matters only if it is "absolute." As the economy goes up, emissions must go down, and fast. Yet even the most optimistic scenarios of cutting emissions while growing the economy require heroic assumptions quite different from empirical evidence.

Consider again the 116 IPCC mitigation scenarios with a 50/50 chance of limiting warming to 2°C or less. Each scenario assumes the global economy will grow at 2 to 3 percent a year, with a pace and scale of decoupling well beyond recent history.[43] At 2 percent a year, the size of the global economy will double in thirty-six years. At 3 percent, a doubling takes just twenty-four years. Yet the dream of decoupling assumes away a carbon rebound from this growth. Decoupling also ignores the upfront carbon burned in an accelerated transition to renewables. And it pretends the global South will simply decarbonize like the global North by ignoring the pollution embodied in trade.

Even the most optimistic scenarios—with energy efficiency gains two to three times greater than recent trends *and* renewable energy development two to five times faster than recent years—can't meet the necessary carbon cuts without one more magic trick.[44] Nearly every mitigation roadmap in the climate policy literature, including 101 of the 116 IPCC "stay within 2°C" scenarios of the Fifth Assessment Report, can't achieve decoupling far enough and fast enough without relying "on the availability and widespread deployment of bioenergy with carbon capture and storage (BECCS)."[45]

BECCS is the metaphorical genie in the bottle. This last-ditch effort to grow the global economy while capping carbon would require planting, harvesting, and burning massive tree plantations for energy, then capturing and storing CO_2 emissions on site and underground for eternity. This highly speculative solution would require fifteen thousand negative-emission bioenergy plants worldwide,[46] fueled by tree plantations covering land more than two times the size of India.[47] As Jason Hickel and Giorgos Kallis conclude in their comprehensive review of the green growth storyline, "Relying on these 'negative emissions technologies' allows for a much larger carbon budget (about double the actual size)" and thus "allows politicians to postpone the need for rapid emissions reductions."[48]

Politicians love this climate action plan because it doesn't require much action. The narrative assumes that technological advance in wealthy importing countries will *eventually* take hold in poorer exporting countries. Higher incomes and changing preferences will *eventually* shift lifestyles to greener consumption. Profit motives and self-interest will *eventually* leave carbon in the ground. Business-as-usual will *eventually* get the job done.

In this fantasy, affluent countries most responsible for climate disruption get a pass. The United States has produced 25 percent of historical CO_2 emissions, much more if they are assigned to American consumption. The twenty-eight countries of the European Union account for another 22 percent of historical emissions.[49] Nearly half of all carbon pollution since the dawn of industrialization has benefited the development of just 10 percent of the current global population. Green growth ensures that these inequities will persist through "good" intentions imposed by the very colonial powers that most benefited from grimy growth.

To find a more honest assessment, you must look outside the established political consensus. For example, an analysis of IPCC scenarios published by the Institute for New Economic Thinking states that "the road to 'Hothouse Earth' is paved with good intentions."[50] The authors conclude that "marginal, incremental, improvements in energy and carbon efficiency cannot do the job and that what is needed is a structural transformation." Their unavoidable conclusion is that "establishment economics lacks the instruments and approaches to analyze exactly this."

A genuine response to the carbon question requires a hard break from the past, especially the core economic logic of perpetual growth, technology saviors, and colonial power. The good news is there are plenty of antiestablishment approaches to choose from where growth is no longer sacred, green or not.

~

Principal among the critics of green growth is my tribe of ecological economists. We have long asked whether growth eventually becomes "uneconomic," when diminishing benefits of a growing economy drop below its increasing costs.

The logic doesn't stray far from the mainstream. As GDP per capita rises, there is an undeniable upside to more private consumption, first to satisfy essential needs and then unessential wants. Higher-income nations also have more tax revenue for investment in health, education, environmental quality, and infrastructure. However, as is generally assumed in all flavors of economics, diminishing returns eventually kick in, with each new unit of private consumption and public investment contributing less and less to individual satisfaction and overall social welfare.

On the cost side, economists assume the opposite relationship with scale. Beyond initial efficiencies gained from economies of scale, the marginal costs of production eventually increase at an increasing rate. These include on-the-books land, labor, and capital costs, as well as uncounted pollution and depletion costs. There are also increasing opportunity costs of doing something else with the time and resources devoted to economic activities.

The calculus of marginal benefits and marginal costs is at the very center of the microeconomic mainstream but is somehow ignored by its macroeconomics counterpart. The opportunity costs of a growing economy are conspicuously absent in conventional textbooks. When GDP per capita is used as shorthand for human well-being, all spending is counted as a benefit, no matter the purpose (want or need) or person (rich or poor). However, the *net* contribution of GDP growth to human well-being clearly depends on tradeoffs, distribution, and externalities.

Consider the opportunity cost of paid work. Every hour of market compensation is an hour lost with family, community, or leisure. Paid time is counted in national income accounts and weighted by a market price. Unpaid time is ignored and thus undervalued in market societies with GDP as the lodestar. Yet caring for children, helping out a neighbor, or rejuvenating your mental and physical health *away* from work also contributes to the well-being of society.

Or consider the regrettable expenditures counted as benefits in the all-dollars-are-created-equal GDP accounts. Public spending on military, disasters, and crime all boost GDP. But is a nation better off in a perpetual state of war, in constant repair from hurricanes and wildfires, or in spending more on prisons than schools? Private spending on divorce lawyers, medical bills from preventable diseases, and cement walls around gated communities also contribute to GDP. By these measures, the United States is exceedingly well off. But are Americans any happier or healthier with the most military spending, most incarcerated citizens, and most single-parent homes in the world?

Then there are the full costs of production and consumption to consider. GDP counts the depletion of a nation's oil and mineral stocks, unsustainable harvest of forests and fisheries, and mining of soil nutrients by industrial agriculture as short-term current income instead of long-term asset depreciation. GDP records urban sprawl as houses built, roads paved, and commuters gassing up but ignores the loss of storm surge protection from wetlands, ecological resilience of unfragmented forests, and food security from prime farming acreage. And GDP privileges the private benefits of current consumption over the social costs of future global climate disruption.

When environmental externalities are counted and priced—again, within the wheelhouse of the orthodoxy—large swaths of the global economy would be uneconomical. A comprehensive study for The Economics of Ecosystems and Biodiversity initiative, led by the business consulting group Trucost, concluded that none of the world's top twenty polluting sectors by region would be profitable if forced to pay the full environmental and social costs of production.[51] Considering just one sector in one region, an International Monetary Fund study found that the United States alone spends ten times more on subsidizing the true costs of the oil industry than on all federal spending on education.[52]

These arguments aren't new, but they have been largely ignored at the altar of economic growth. Herman Daly and John Cobb considered the question of net returns to growth in *For the Common Good* in 1989. Together with Cobb's son Clifford and drawing on decades of literature from environmental and natural resource economics, they constructed an Index of Sustainable Economic Welfare (ISEW) for the US economy, the precursor to the Genuine Progress Indicator (GPI) now calculated for all fifty US states and at least seventeen countries.[53]

Straight out of the playbook of welfare economics, tallying the ISEW or GPI begins with a series of adjustments to personal expenditures, the largest portion of GDP. The first accounts for diminishing returns to income, the long-forgotten idea described by Arthur Pigou in *The Economics of Welfare*. Very simply, another dollar of income to a debt-strapped student generates more welfare than another dollar to Amazon founder Jeff Bezos, on track to be the world's first trillionaire by 2026.[54]

Other economic adjustments include accounting for the net benefits of major household expenses such as cars, washing machines, and computers that should last longer than three years. Calculating the difference between sale price and annual economic services penalizes a throwaway economy (at least for big purchases) rather than celebrating it as a sign of success, as the global North has typically done. Less money spent on consumer durables because of longer product lifetimes, frugal reuse and repurposing, and, when all else fails, recycling of component parts should be a sign of progress, not lamented as a drag on the economy.

Time use also factors into this conception of genuine economic progress. In any given year, for every American searching for work counted in the official unemployment rate, there's another who has given up or is working part-time while still looking for full-time employment. When, in April 2020, the US official unemployment rate peaked at a post–World War II high of 14.7 percent, the underemployment rate hit 22.8 percent,[55] a more accurate gauge of the plight of nearly one quarter of the labor force.

On the flipside, there are plenty of workers who would love to cut back a fifty- or sixty-hour work week, not work two or three jobs to make ends meet, or just afford to take a few days off. Among OECD countries in 2019, the United States ranked tenth of thirty-seven in total hours worked per worker, more than 25 percent higher than in countries such as Denmark, Norway, and Germany.[56] One reason for longer hours with similar standards of living is that the United States is also the only industrialized nation without a paid parental leave policy.[57] A 2015 Pew Research Center analysis found that both parents worked full-time in nearly half of two-parent households, compared to under one third in 1970.[58]

The United States also stands out among wealthy peers as the only nation without federally guaranteed paid vacation days. After a year on the job, workers in the European Union are guaranteed a minimum of twenty vacation days,[59] with no related tradeoff in labor productivity. Eight of the top ten OECD nations with the highest worker productivity are EU members, all at or under a thirty-hour average work week. The United States is the exception, ranked fifth in productivity but with the twentieth longest work week.[60] In return for longer, more productive hours for the average US worker, wages adjusted for inflation have been flat since the late 1970s.[61] That's not progress by any reasonable measure of fairness or balancing work, family, and personal time.

There are also hours and hours of work in the so-called informal economy that are uncounted in GDP. Unpaid care for children, older adults, or the disabled isn't counted. Household work like cooking, cleaning, laundry, and maintenance isn't counted. Work for a homeless shelter, fire department, blood drive, youth sports team, bird census, community garden, and other volunteer activities that make up the fabric of our communities isn't counted. According to the 2019 American Time Use Survey, the average American adult spent over twelve hours a week doing household chores, nearly five hours caring for others, and about two hours with organizational, civic, and religious activities.[62]

Much of this unpaid work is unevenly distributed between women and men, hidden by per capita statistics. On average, women are paid eighty cents to the dollar of men's pay in the formal US economy yet put in 62 percent more hours of unpaid work in the informal economy.[63] The comparison is even more inequitable for Black and Hispanic women. If unpaid household labor were compensated at average US wage rates, the average American woman would make an extra $40,000 a year.

Finally, the GPI calculation goes to great lengths to estimate costs imposed on the national and global commons from a growing economy. There are daily human health costs from air, water, and noise pollution. There are accumulating costs from paving, developing, and otherwise fragmenting our wetlands, farmlands, and forests. There are long-term costs from depleting the ozone layer, disrupting the global climate, and consuming nonrenewable resources faster than substitutes can be developed. Together the economic losses from these environmental costs accounted for more than a 40 percent reduction to the personal consumption starting point in recent US GPI estimates.[64]

Here's the punchline: By this estimate, the United States has been in a progress recession since the late 1970s. Past ISEW and current GPI studies incorporate about twenty-five adjustments to GDP, some positive and some negative. Although the details of both national and state-level estimates can vary, the general trends do not. As GDP per capita ticks up year after year, barring a few recessions along the way, GPI per capita has flatlined and, for some US states, is headed downwards. The same general conclusion has been reached in at least seventeen national GPI studies from around the world. Although some countries have stretched the net gains from growth a bit longer than the United States, all have entered recent decades of uneconomic growth.

The conclusion that bigger isn't always better has also been reached outside the narrow confines of monetary metrics. For example, the Gallup–Sharecare Well-Being Index has surveyed Americans' perceptions of their lives and daily experiences since 2008. In-depth interviews include questions on sense of purpose, social relationships, financial security, relationship to community, and physical health.[65] Hawaii has taken the top spot among US states a record seven times despite ranking thirty-ninth in total gross state product and twelfth in per capita terms.[66] Vermont has long been the smallest state economy (and thirty-fourth in per capita terms in 2019), yet it is consistently in the top ten for this broader measure of well-being.

Internationally, Gallup well-being research in 2014 included more than 146,000 surveys in 145 countries and areas.[67] The tiny economies of Panama, Costa Rica, and Puerto Rico ranked highest. The United States, with the largest economy in the world, came in twenty-third place, behind nine Latin American nations that have been advised for decades to follow the US economic model of "success." In the community well-being category—summarized as "liking where you live, feeling safe and having pride in your community"—the United States ranked forty-first.

Other life satisfaction surveys that go back many decades tell the same story: High national income doesn't directly translate into higher life satisfaction. Since 1972, the US General Social Survey has asked, "Taken all together, how would you say things are these days? Would you say that you are not too happy, pretty happy or very happy?"[68] The percentage of people responding "very happy" was never higher than 38 percent, reached in 1974. Average happiness for the sample has treaded water from 1972 to 2018, wiggling up and down within a narrow range. Over the same period, real US GDP per capita grew by nearly 130 percent,[69] average square footage of new homes grew by over 60 percent,[70] and the adult obesity rate grew by a staggering 163 percent.[71]

Americans are quite literally bigger than ever but not universally better off in the bargain. We shop more, drive more, and eat more than most. But look behind the curtain and the largest economy in the world is ranked thirty-seventh in life expectancy (and declining in recent years).[72] The United States has the second highest rate of poverty among wealthy nations (over 17 percent in a low-unemployment year).[73] Suicide rates increased by 33 percent between 1999 and 2017, the tenth leading cause of death overall and second for the population between ten and thirty-four years old, the highest by far among high-income nations.[74]

Dig deeper into the statistics and significant differences appear between geographies, gender, ethnicity, and race. Male life expectancy is eighty-two years in affluent Fairfax County, Virginia, yet a half day's drive away, in McDowell County, West Virginia, an average guy in the heart of coal country can expect to live only sixty-four years.[75] Whereas one in ten White Americans lived in poverty in 2018, that rate was one in four for Native Americans and one in five for African Americans.[76] US suicides reached a twenty-five-year high in 2017, and the rate for military veterans was 1.5 times the adult average.[77] Youth identifying as lesbian, gay, and bisexual were nearly five times more likely to attempt suicide than their peers.[78]

A society built on the illusion of infinite economic growth will eventually face the sobering reality of physics, but there's often a long delay between resource collapse and social decay. History is filled with the ashes of fallen empires, failed states, and the social limits to growth. Economic growth is worshiped as the universal approach to development despite growing income inequality within and between nations. The US economy is heralded as the strongest in the world despite spending more and more on healthcare with less and less healthy outcomes. The perennial rhetoric of an all-access-pass to the American dream is actually stamped with your race, gender, sexuality, birthplace, and centuries of divergent power and wealth between the haves and have-nots.

Efforts to measure genuine progress, well-being, and happiness are rooted in a new story. A story that breaks from the one-size-fits-all prescription of growth, green or otherwise. A new narrative that puts public health ahead of private gain. A new economy with benefits that are widely shared and costs evenly distributed. A global model that is a race to the middle, eradicating the desperation of poverty by vanquishing the obscenity of gluttony.

As economic anthropologist Jason Hickel wrote in the early days of the 2020 COVID crisis, "If your economy requires people to consume things they don't need or even want, and to do more of it each year than the year before, just in order to keep the whole edifice from collapsing, then you need a different economy."[79]

The question is: Will we make an inevitable transformation by design or by disaster?

~

In early 2020, the worldwide spread of a novel coronavirus brought the global health system and economy to its knees in just a few short months. The COVID-19 virus, the cause of the second severe acute respiratory syndrome (SARS) pandemic of the twenty-first century, spread faster and farther than any virus in human history. On New Year's Eve, Chinese authorities reported forty-one cases of a "mysterious pneumonia."

By the end of June there were over 10 million confirmed cases in 185 countries and over 500,000 human lives lost.[80] By the end of the year, the cumulative case count was over 90 million in all countries on Earth and approaching 2 million deaths.[81]

As the global public health system mobilized and traced disease origins and pathways, it became clear this was a particularly contagious respiratory pathogen. To limit the spread, the early medical consensus was to wash our hands, not touch our faces, and stay at least 6 feet apart. If keeping distant wasn't possible, wear a mask. When epidemiologists confirmed that the virus could be carried and spread by those without SARS symptoms, the need to impose strict social distancing for everyone, healthy or not, led to widespread stay-at-home orders.

China was hit hardest early on, followed by Italy and the United States. The US federal government was slow to respond, largely deferring to state and local officials to issue advisories and mandates. However, by April nonessential parts of the economy were shut down in forty-three of fifty states. We could go grocery shopping but not much else. Large crowds were discouraged or outright banned. Travel restrictions between states and with other nations became common. Mayors, governors, task forces, and public health officials made plea after plea to our better natures to help "flatten the curve."

I'll leave it to others to comment on the widespread political denial, misinformation, and lack of coordination that characterized the US response. What's indisputable is that the nation quickly became the global hotspot. Older adults and those with compromised immune systems suffered the highest death rates, particularly in dense living spaces such as nursing homes. Social determinants of health such as poverty, discrimination, and low education levels led to disease prevalence two to four times greater in Black and Hispanic communities.[82] Shortages of personal protective equipment, ventilators, and intensive care beds quickly stressed the national healthcare system, particularly in the outbreak of New York City that was killing over five hundred people a day by early April.[83]

By May the stay-at-home orders and other public health measures were reducing new infections. The five-day moving average of new confirmed cases in the United States peaked at over thirty-two thousand in early April and dropped below twenty thousand by early June.[84] The daily death toll peaked on April 17 at close to five thousand but by June fell below one thousand per day for most of the month, including eight days below five hundred.[85] Shortages of critical medical supplies started to subside. Testing and contact tracing were containing many new outbreaks. Most folks were doing their part in controlling the spread of the virus, and it was working.

It *was* working. Six months into the pandemic, a study titled "The Cure Is Not Worse than the Disease" by a group of health economists estimated that up to 2.7 million American lives could be saved if strict public health measures stayed in place through the end of the year, including restrictions on economic activity.[86] But by the 4th of July— US Independence Day—the world's largest economy had grown impatient with doctor's orders. A familiar debate over free choice and individual rights was shaping public policy, as well as questions over whether the economic losses due to limits on personal freedoms were worth the lives saved.

The economic impacts from the shut-down were in uncharted territory. First-time unemployment claims jumped to an all-time high of over 6.8 million in the last week of March, nearly nineteen times the fifty-three-year average, shattering the previous record of 695,000 set back in October 1982.[87] Over 52 million people filed jobless claims from mid-March through mid-July,[88] nearly one-third of US households were late or missed their mortgage or rental payments in July,[89] and 5.4 million laid-off workers lost their employer-sponsored health insurance between February and May in the middle of the worst pandemic since 1918.[90] During the second quarter of the year, April through June, the

US economy contracted at an annual rate of 32.9 percent, more than three times the size of any loss since the advent of GDP accounting.[91]

Larry Kudlow, assistant to the president for economic policy and director of the National Economic Council, had lamented since the outset that the economic cost of a shut-down would be "too great" and that the United States would need "to make some difficult trade-offs."[92] He wasn't alone. A sample of April headlines included "Restarting America Means People Will Die. So When Do We Do It?" in the *New York Times Magazine*, "Economics v. Epidemiology: Quantifying the Trade-off" in the *Wall Street Journal*, and "A Grim Calculus: COVID-19 Presents Stark Choices between Life, Death, and the Economy" in *The Economist*. One of the more infamous soundbites came from Dan Patrick, lieutenant governor of Texas, who offered up the lives of senior citizens to reopen the economy because "there are more important things than living and that's saving this country."[93] By country, he meant economy.

And so, after less than a month of widespread lockdown, the economy started to open back up. State by state, stay-at-home orders were lifted and restrictions on private enterprises and public spaces relaxed. Nonessential businesses like restaurants, bars, and hair salons were some of the first to open their doors with capacity limits. However, absent any national mandates, presidential leadership, or reliable social norms, public health policy devolved into inconsistent state and local government recommendations and pleas to social distance and to wear a mask.

By early June, the curve was flat no more. A rapid increase in new cases brought the five-day moving average above sixty-eight thousand by the end of July, more than twice the April peak.[94] The daily death toll climbed back above one thousand.[95] "Superspreading" events of large crowds of people in close contact with each other in confined spaces were traced to many outbreaks. One study warned that as few as 10 percent of infected people could drive 80 percent of cases through everything from birthday parties and crowded bars to summer camps and choir practice.[96]

On August 1, Dr. Deborah Birx, coordinator of the White House's coronavirus task force, warned that the United States had entered a "new phase" in which COVID-19 was "extraordinarily widespread."[97] By September 1, with just 4 percent of the world's population, the United States had nearly 24 percent of the world's COVID-19 cases. By the end of the year, daily new cases were above 225,000 and climbing, the daily death toll was approaching four thousand,[98] and an average of 79 percent of hospital intensive care units were occupied nationwide (with more than one fifth of hospitals with ICUs above 95 percent capacity).[99] Despite Donald Trump's no-fault claim of "it is what it is," dramatic differences with all but a few countries in the world suggested this was a disaster of our own making.

We were living, as *Atlantic* staff writer George Packer wrote early on, in a "failed state."[100] By his diagnosis, the "coronavirus didn't break America." Rather, "it revealed what was already broken." The virus exploited a set of "underlying conditions" that included "a corrupt political class, a sclerotic bureaucracy, a heartless economy, [and] a divided and distracted public." But these were just the symptoms of a failed system. The US experiment in both democracy and capitalism was in shambles, built on a foundation of fairytales spun by the superstitions of economics, the language of the ruling class.

The virus revealed the vulnerability of global supply chains built on cheap energy and exploited labor. It exposed the lack of resilience in our basic societal systems, most strikingly apparent in widespread failures of our medical and food systems. It highlighted the dependence on an undervalued and underpaid essential workforce in producing, stocking, and delivering necessities. It laid bare a legacy of structural racism that predetermined access to healthcare, job prospects, and public safety based on the color of your skin.

Although these interrelated crises were surprising to some, they were also the obvious result of intentional erosion of trust in government, faith in science, and duty to the common good. The decision to wear a face mask came to symbolize the dividing line between support of or resistance to government's role in upholding public health, acceptance or denial of science in informing public policy, and allegiance to self or society. At the height of the culture wars over whether face coverings infringe on "freedom of choice," US surgeon general Jerome Adams tweeted on June 14, "Ultimately it is a choice we make, and I hope it's made based on the best available/current science, and a desire to do all we can to help others and ourselves/our communities."[101]

As with decades of climate science denial and obfuscation, a science-informed democracy was butting heads with a preference-privileged economy. A US response based on individualism and nationalism crashed into the reality of an interdependent global society. But with crisis comes opportunity. The impetus to write this book was originally the crisis of the Great Recession and the opportunity for a new economics that was bubbling up from social movements such as Occupy Wall Street, Black Lives Matter, and a reborn progressive politics. However, the nation quickly got back to "normal," and a deeply unequal system of power, income, and opportunity persisted.

The recovery from COVID-19 presents yet another opportunity for a new economics to emerge. Some old blueprints for economic transformation have been dusted off and given new relevance. Others are being generated by new alliances, new conversations, and a more inclusive approach to our shared future. All will ultimately depend on reexamining our origin stories and master narratives to understand how we arrived at this moment so that we might chart a different path ahead.

CHAPTER 6

A New Economics

The universe is a communion of subjects, not a collection of objects.[1]

—Thomas Berry

Suppose you and a stranger are offered one hundred US dollars to share. You're handed a hundred bills and told to offer any amount to Jane or John Doe. If they accept, you dole out their share, keep your own, and then go about your merry way. But here's the catch. If they reject your offer, neither of you gets a cent. What would you do?

When this ultimatum game is played with real money, most people offer half, and the stranger accepts. Of course, there are always a few who offer a bit less than an even split and folks generally accept, but only to a point. When offers drop below 20 percent, the chance of the stranger saying "take a hike" becomes much higher.

These results seem perfectly reasonable from the point of view of *Homo sapiens*. Despite rumors to the contrary, people across countries and cultures have a general sense of fairness, worry about their social reputation (even among perfect strangers), and will reciprocate with either kindness or retaliation depending on whether feeling respected or slighted. As a social primate, it's rational to be fair and just to punish those who break from social norms, even by harming ourselves in the process.[2]

Yet for the caricature of *Homo economicus*, offering anything more than a dollar is deemed "irrational" and therefore not predicted. From the perspective of an isolated, self-maximizing individual, the optimal decision is to offer a dollar and keep ninety-nine. Even offering a penny and asking for change would be fine. If you're on the receiving end of a stingy offer, who cares; you're now a little bit richer at the margin.

The very idea of reciprocal behavior—you scratch my back, and I'll scratch yours—is inconsistent with a core economic assumption about how individuals make decisions. To put a fine point on it, without "independent utility functions" the entire edifice of neoclassical economics falls apart. My well-being does not depend on yours in the rational actor model. Ultimatum offers described as "fair" by most players are deemed "anomalies" in Econ 101. In fact, of the dozens of ultimatum games documented, only one group of humans behaves close to the model: brainwashed economics students.[3]

Evidence of interdependent—dare I say "cooperative"—decision making is even more striking in common-pool resource games. In these experiments, participants are presented with a choice between contributing to the betterment of the group or looking out for themselves. Participants tend to cooperate when everyone's decisions are disclosed, groups are communicating well, and there are transparent, enforceable sanctions for those who step outside social norms. In contrast, selfish strategies develop when decisions are kept secret, communication between participants is not possible or allowed, and rules are viewed as arbitrary or unenforceable.[4]

For example, I play a game in classes with a payout table based on individual choices of being a "1" or a "0." The first column in the table determines the payouts based on the number of people who choose to be a 1, from none to everyone. The second column shows the payout to the 1s, starting at nothing and increasing by increments of $4. The third column shows the payout to the 0s, who always get $50 more than the 1s. So, in a class of sixty students, if everyone chooses 1, everyone gets $240. If no one chooses 1, everyone gets $50. Then there's all the combinations in between.

After explaining the rules, I joke to "see the dean" after class for their cash payment, then start the game. Students are instructed to tear off a corner from their notes and anonymously write down whether they are a 1 or a 0. I then collect the scraps in a hat and tally up the totals. In a typical undergraduate class, less than half choose 1. So, in our hypothetical class of sixty, if twenty-five students choose 1, their payout is $100 each, and the thirty-five 0s each get $150.

After a mixture of grumbling and giggling, we play the game again. This time everyone is again instructed to choose 1 or 0 but also asked to write down their name so that I can announce the 0s. In this public round of decision making, we quite reliably get eighty percent or more of the class to choose 1. So, if forty-eight choose 1 and twelve choose 0, the payout to the 1s increases to $192, but the 0s still make $50 more at $242. When I call out the 0s and ask them to stand and be recognized, some blush a bit with embarrassment while a few beam with pride that their gamble paid off.

Of course, this is all pretend money, but in a third round I increase the stakes. I will again announce the 0s, each of whom will be docked a full letter grade off their midterm exam. With my threat of sanction in the air, I again tally their choices, and the number of 0s is usually just a few. Some always hold out, and one or two may even switch from 1 to 0 in protest. This occurs with fictional dollars weighed against real exam points, that is, if they believe I'll enforce the punishment.

My only success in reaching 100 percent cooperation is when we take the time for the 1s to talk with the few remaining 0s. Civil discourse toward common purpose wins out in the end. To be clear, this is only a game among peers in the safety of a classroom setting, but the discussion that ensues strikes at the heart of pursuing collective goals in the face of a cultural narrative of blind self-interest.

In an anonymous marketplace we are stripped away of our identities, social position, and obligations to all but ourselves. As isolated individuals at a single point in time we behave more like *Homo economicus*, an idealized model meant to equate the welfare of the group with the welfare of the individual. But it is the aggregation of these market choices that results in climate disruption, mass extinction, health pandemics, and a growing divide between the haves and have-nots. When market freedom and individual liberty take precedence over social harmony and broadly shared well-being, we impoverish the world one marginal choice at a time.

Cornell economist Alfred Kahn, an advisor to US president Jimmy Carter, called such outcomes the "tyranny of small decisions."[5] Each market choice can make sense in isolation as an individual weighs known, personal, immediate benefits and costs. At the margin, the isolated decision seems "rational." However, the sum of many small decisions over time can result in tyrannies that the original decision makers would have never voted for.

In Kahn's 1966 article, he was lamenting the closure of rail service between Ithaca and New York City. Citizens in a democracy, if given a vote, often choose to keep public services open and available by sharing the expense through paying taxes (whether you use the train or not). However, insufficient dollar votes from consumers in a market system ends up limiting public choice and creating unintended harm to all.

In my own work with citizen watershed groups, I've met with homeowners in typical American subdivisions on the outskirts of town who are seeking the quiet life, affordability, and a little extra space all to themselves. As these housing choices accumulate over time, so do the pressures on public resources. Although the isolated decision to buy a house in the suburbs makes sense, the original purchasers would never have voted for suburban sprawl and resulting "tyrannies" like traffic jams, failing public schools, or polluted waterways.[6]

Given an opportunity to discuss and plan for a common future, people make decisions that consider dependencies on one another. In fact, when my graduate students and I have facilitated discussions aided by computer models that show the cumulative impacts of small decisions on society and the environment, people vote for a different world. That's true not just with watershed councils but in public healthcare systems, employee-owned businesses, community land trusts, and other groups focused on a common purpose. We are willing to accept limits to individual choice for the greater good more often than is assumed.

In the *much* bigger picture, citizens don't consciously vote for climate breakdown, mass extinction, or widespread human misery. Yet as isolated consumers we are led to believe these are inevitable "externalities" of a species hardwired for self-interest. These crises of modernity are born of a very narrow part of the human persona drawn out and reinforced by a particular set of worldviews. When conditioned to think only about the here and now, we never ask where we are headed and why.

Tyrannies of small decisions emerge from a culture of individuality reinforced by an economics of isolated choices that denies the very interdependencies that make the world possible. They persist because those in power (the 0s) hold everyone else (the 1s) hostage in a winner-takes-all society. In a pandemic, the doctor or nurse operating within a for-profit, globally sourced, just-in-time, cost-cutting system didn't plan on equipment shortages and staffing bottlenecks during a public health crisis. Likewise, the Amazon shopper, Wall Street investor, and business entrepreneur make isolated decisions every day that make sense to household budgets, investment returns, and company profits but in aggregate do harm to themselves and each other along every link in the supply chain.

The looming question is, Can we break from a tyrannical world? What would it take to abandon an obsession with "me" and nurture instead a culture of reciprocity, restoration, and renewal? What would be required to suppress our competitive instincts and celebrate our cooperative natures? Could a new economics emerge as a study of the human household built on our evolutionary story as a social, interdependent species with a rich variety of experiences?

A new economics that is grounded in science, values cultural diversity, and embraces ethical deliberation not only is possible, its construction is well under way.

~

Edward O. Wilson, Pulitzer Prize–winning writer, biologist, and naturalist from Harvard University, set the goalposts for such a new economics in his 1998 masterpiece *Consilience*.[7] The culmination of a career of careful observation and scientific reason—ranging from the microscopic world of entomology to the macroscopic synthesis of sociobiology—*Consilience* challenged scholars to a "jumping together" of knowledge. To pass the consilience test for any particular field of study, one question must be answered: Does theory in your field hold up against theory in all others?

The natural sciences have provided one roadmap for bridging disciplinary divides. In one direction, consilience has occurred by reducing all physical phenomena to atoms, electrons, and ever smaller particles. What is known, taught, and studied in physics, chemistry, and biology has these basic building blocks in common. But knowledge of the inner workings of an atom cannot explain the dynamics of human society, let alone the complexities of life on Earth. The more challenging direction is consilience by synthesis, weaving together knowledge of the parts into a coherent story of the whole.

Evolutionary biology provides a foundation for this understanding. From the molecular time of DNA replication to geological time of plate tectonics, Darwin's theory of evolution by natural selection connects reproductive success with the evolution of all life, *Homo sapiens* included. The basic premise is that the attributes of a species will change over time through the interaction of genetic mutations and environmental conditions. Successful traits are then passed along through reproduction. These evolutionary processes, often punctuated by rapid environmental changes, then accumulate and differentiate population characteristics that explain the full diversity of life on Earth.

The theory of evolution—tested against an arsenal of evidence from paleontology and comparative morphology to gene sequencing and experimental evolution—is the glue that holds the sciences together. Science from the 1950s forward has upheld Darwin's main insights, with debate now limited to the fine points of evolutionary processes, such as how selective pressures work on the individual versus the group in social species such as our own. What is known and taught in a college biology class today is generally consilient with chemistry, physics, and all the various disciplines and subdisciplines of the natural sciences.

If we begin with a foothold in evolutionary biology, crossing the consilience bridge to the social sciences and humanities then requires one seemingly small step: expand the human environment to include culture. Our culture is a social environment that we co-create but not from scratch. It has a basis in biology and is shaped by our genetics. With some variation, we all see, hear, smell, taste, and touch our world in similar ways because we all belong to the same species. We therefore process and act on information in similar ways, even when our backgrounds and family histories are very different.

If we consider human biology and evolutionary history, the general sketch of consilience goes something like this. First, our genes determine how we sense and process information, which makes us more prone to developing certain cultural attributes than others. Next, attributes that translate into reproductive success over time become the dominant characteristics of our societies. Culture then either reinforces or suppresses our genetic inclinations in a grand dance called gene–culture co-evolution. We compete and we cooperate, we hate and we love, we make peace and we make war. The relative degrees depend on our cultural cues.

Making this connection between the natural sciences, social sciences, and humanities has been contentious, to put it mildly. In my world, where I'm a weathered bridge-builder between economics and ecology, the controversy boils down to this: Evolutionary explanations for behavior, culture, or more generally "human nature" run up against the master narrative of human exceptionalism. Evolutionary biology unseats the human from atop the ladder of nature, questions the superiority of Western culture, and unearths an entirely new direction for the social sciences and humanities that, to put it simply, would be more human.

Perhaps, as Wilson aptly describes, "The human mind evolved to believe in the gods" but "did not evolve to believe in biology."[8] Incorporating biology has been easier for academic fields that already examined the long span of history or adhered to the scientific method. For example, anthropology considers how human societies and cultures co-evolved with our environments. Historians have similarly taken tentative steps to considering human history in the context of a changing environment. Even psychology—once the poster child of mystical thinking about the "black box" of the human mind—has begun to incorporate the brain sciences and the material basis of thought, reason, and decision making.

For economics, I'll cut to the chase: The self-proclaimed decision science fails the consilience test miserably. Wilson accuses economics of being Newtonian, "because economic theorists aspire to find simple, general laws that cover all possible economic arrangements." Although this gives the illusion of consilience, it also ignores human nature, denies the physical basis of our economy, and circumscribes the entirety of humanity to the experience of largely White men of recent European descent. The isolated rational actor and disembodied economy at the center of mainstream theory persist in textbooks, classes, and models because modern economics has itself been isolated from other fields, people, and histories. As Wilson describes it, economics remains "hermetic" because its models have historically been "sealed off from the complexities of human behavior and the constraints imposed by the environment."

The consilience challenge for economists is to consider how the diversity of our cultures and environments co-evolved to affect economic behavior. To do so, Wilson recommends first searching the "borderland disciplines" that straddle economics and other fields. Away from the obsession with abstract mathematics, the narrowness of *Homo economicus*, and the fairytale of market equilibrium are interdisciplinary collaborations that embrace the complexity of the human animal and our interdependence on each other and our Earth-bound home.

∼

Collaborations between economists and neuroscientists in the nascent field of neuroeconomics represent one example of consilience taking shape. Through functional magnetic resonance imaging (fMRI), scientists can quite literally watch the human brain puzzle through decisions. One conclusion, perhaps obvious to everyone but economic theorists, is that emotions often trump rational thinking, particularly in a class of decisions that philosophers have long called moral dilemmas.

For example, a popular dilemma in philosophy classes is the trolley problem. Here's the scenario: A runaway train is about to kill five people stuck on the tracks. But with a flip of a switch from a distant control booth, you can divert the train to a spur where only one person will die. What would you do? Quick, what would you do?

For this and similar moral dilemmas, most people state they would divert the train. Saving five lives is clearly better than losing one. Using brain imaging, Princeton University researchers found a lack of "emotional interference" in "impersonal" decisions such as the trolley problem, meaning the parts of the brain associated with emotions didn't light up.[9] Study participants were also able to quickly access the working memory part of the brain, areas linked with ordinary processing of information.

Now let's make your decision more personal. With a few tweaks we have the footbridge problem. A runaway train is again going to kill five people, but this time you are on a bridge over the tracks with an innocent bystander. There is no switch to divert the train, but you can push the stranger off the bridge and onto the tracks, stopping the train with certainty. What would you do?

The math is the same, sacrifice one to save five, but most participants in this thought experiment won't shove the hapless stranger. In the fMRI imaging, Brodmann areas of the cerebral cortex light up and engage in emotional interference. The brain sees the act as more consequential than the outcome. Putting your hands directly on a person versus flipping a remote switch makes all the difference.

Experiments such as these move beyond the unproven, untethered calculus of utility maximization and open the door to tested, richer explanations of how people make economic decisions. Moral dilemmas that explore personal versus impersonal choices force us to consider our own culpability in the consequences of our decisions, not just the final (often faraway) outcome. An utterly unemotional quarterly retirement portfolio statement, the thoughtless ease of a point-and-click online purchase, or the mindless filling of a gas tank with the swipe of a credit card all make it easy to ignore cause and consequence. If we instead make economic decisions as engaged participants, bearing the responsibility of our actions, different choices result.

Beyond the neurobiology of decision making are much broader explorations of human perception, reason, and choice. In the borderland discipline of behavioral economics, collaborations between psychology and economics reveal hundreds of exceptions to the rational actor model. A Wikipedia tally of so-called cognitive biases is close to two hundred and counting.[10] A "cheat sheet" developed by author Buster Benson boils the list down to four key problem areas that our brains try to address, each suggesting a major overhaul of economics.[11]

First is information overload and the cognitive shortcuts we use to filter through all the noise to make a useful decision. For instance, we are biased by our personal expectations, beliefs, and a long list of decision tricks needed to get through the day. Then there's the challenge of making meaning out of the information we actually absorb. We weave together stories that connect past experiences, fill in the gaps, and reinforce stereotypes. Unsurprisingly to even the most casual observer of human nature, we are terrible at interpreting probability (normalcy bias), guessing what others are thinking (illusion of asymmetric insight), and predicting the future (hindsight bias).

Behavioral economists have explored many of these cognitive biases in the context of economic decision making. Findings from choice experiments such as the ultimatum game conclude that our preferences are highly contingent on social context, life histories, and conscious changes to our likes and dislikes with experience.[12]

We also have strict rules with regard to some choices. In certain circumstances, no substitute or payment to accept a loss will be accepted, what economists call "lexicographic" preferences.[13] What's your mom or kid worth in trade? What's the wholesale destruction of a species or environment worth? As contingent valuation research has demonstrated, leaving the answer blank to such questions does not mean $0. It means, "No deal!" And it turns out that how we value the future depends on how far out is considered.[14] Sure I'd prefer a reward now to later, but when time tradeoffs are considered in years instead of days or weeks, my impatience becomes less relevant.

These human responses directly undercut the core rational actor model, calling into question its usefulness for predicting economic behavior and designing economic policy.[15] Then there are Benson's third and fourth categories of cognitive biases, the proverbial nails in the coffin.

The third category summarizes mental shortcuts needed to act fast in the face of uncertainty, including overconfidence, egocentric, optimism, and novelty biases. These strategies help us act decisively in the moment but aren't exactly "rational" in hindsight. These biases cast much doubt on the certainty (or at least probabilities) baked into economic models. For instance, models that look at agriculture and climate change assume something akin to a clairvoyant farmer who seamlessly adjusts to a knowable, observable, predictable new climate by making super rational and intelligent decisions about new technologies, new cultivars, and new timing of when to till, sow, irrigate, fertilize, weed, harvest, store, and market a crop. When the models are adjusted to reflect how people actually respond to change, they show big delays with enormous economic costs. The policy advice quickly shifts from "everything will be alright, we'll figure it out as we go" to "it's time to overhaul the economy, and fast."[16]

Benson's final category includes our many memory biases. It should come as no surprise that we misattribute, make up, and in various ways "edit" our memories after the fact. We discard specifics and form generalities, resulting in stereotypes and prejudices. In the flood of daily information, we try to store away the useful and important bits, but our edits reinforce the many errors along the way. This category could judiciously be applied to economists themselves, who, just like other disciplinarians, have a gift for either ignoring history or changing it to fit their preconceived view of the world.

All summed and totaled, the myriad cognitive biases do not bode well for the bias-free rational actor model, either in predicting microeconomic behavior or making macroeconomic forecasts. As the age-old joke attributed to Paul Samuelson captures all too well, "Economists have successfully predicted nine of the last five recessions." In fact, a study by the International Monetary Fund looked at 153 recessions in sixty-three countries between 1992 and 2014, concluding that most were missed by economists.[17] One explanation is that economic forecasters themselves find it difficult to imagine low-probability, high-impact events. But beyond the cognitive limits or ego of any particular economist, it's also clear that the illusion of rationality looms large in forecasting models that assume economic agents seamlessly absorb new information, predictably respond to price signals, and quickly move to the fantastical unicorn of a full employment economy after any and all shocks to the system.

The hundreds of so-called anomalies to the rational actor model—what Keynes referred to in part as "animal spirits" in his 1936 treatise—are today an exploding area of research in the borderlands between economics and the behavioral sciences. Such collaborations are unpacking the "proximate" causes of choice, the *how* of decision making. However, the greater leap toward a consilient economics is investigating the "ultimate" cause, or *why* we make the decisions we do.

Here the research questions are much bigger in scope. In what environment are decisions being made? How do these environments (culture included) influence decision making? What's the typical range of behavioral responses, the so-called norm of reaction? Are there epigenetic rules—social and environmental cues that regulate gene expression—that bias human culture in one direction over another? Can deciphering our human natures explain today's dominant economic worldview? Can interdisciplinary research about decision making lead us toward a healthier relationship with each other and our home?

Such questions require us to push beyond the comfort zone of ahistorical, Western-centric disciplines such as economics and even beyond the anthropocentrism of the social sciences and humanities more generally.

Borderland disciplines such as institutional and evolutionary economics have long explored how culture, law, and governance affect economies. Hindsight suggests that institutions designed on principles of selfishness and greed will favor economies of vice and competition. However, we also have experience with institutions designed on principles of trust and transparency that enable economies of care and cooperation.

The modest proposition that economies shape, and are shaped by, culture has been explored by many outside the confines of the orthodoxy. For example, feminist scholars have researched the source and use of power to control and suppress in human societies. Neoclassical economics was born from a system that privileged White men and thus became defined by qualities traditionally associated with masculinity that prioritize monetary value, competition for resources, and the commodification of labor and the environment. In contrast, feminist economics emphasizes the necessity of reproduction in human society and investment in social assets such as public education, health systems, and dependent care. A focus on cooperative relationships and obligations to collective justice is a radical departure from the dominant narrative of justice as individual freedoms and rights.[18]

Other approaches to economics examine the long and full experience of humanity. For example, economic anthropology reaches much further back in time than the typical economic origin story of Adam Smith and *The Wealth of Nations*. In particular, the study of hunter-gather societies, who developed some of the most durable and resilient economies known to humankind, offers valuable insight into living with nature's cycles.[19] Exploration of the cultural values that underpin Indigenous economies has also found much agreement between ancient wisdoms and modern science.[20] Many ways of knowing find that it's our interdependencies that define us, not an illusion of liberty and property perpetuated in Western culture.

These broader perspectives start with an essential truth that all flavors of economics are normative, shaped by the goals, experiences, and blind spots of their practitioners. They also recognize that economies are a function of power and privilege, not a fairytale of frictionless economic equilibrium. And they consider the evolution of human nature, including how Western cultures perpetuate the myth that there are no limits to the fossil-fueled bonanza we call modernity.

When the full picture of evolution comes into focus, the bridges between the natural sciences, social sciences, and humanities become much more slippery, even treacherous to the untenured academic. For instance, even the most senior of scientists gets a little antsy (pun intended) when the "super-organism" of *Homo sapiens* is lumped into a limited club of ultrasocial species of bees and ants.[21] Yet the fact that our species appropriates one third or more of the Earth's terrestrial net primary productivity—the product of photosynthesis that's the foundation to all living systems—opens unavoidable questions about the state and fate of human society.[22]

For insight on what our nonhuman relatives can teach us about human economies, we return again to E. O. Wilson. In his 1975 tome *Sociobiology*, Wilson crafted a far-reaching analysis of how social behavior evolves.[23] The 5-pound, seven-hundred-page, meticulously sourced book wouldn't have caused much of a fuss beyond the halls of academia if the distinguished entomologist had stuck to the nonhuman world. But the final chapter applied insights from the study of beehives, ant colonies, lion prides, monkey troops, and many other-than-human social organizations to the only-humans-allowed domain of sociology and psychology. A rare front-page book review in the *New York Times* was a sure sign of the influence, as well as controversy, to follow.[24]

Arguing that the evolution of social behavior is a sort of dance between genes and culture, Wilson and colleagues foretold the explosion of research into the origins of altruism, cooperation, and ethics. The synthesis tentatively suggested that biology shapes nearly all aspects of human culture, from language and art to politics and religion. Anthropology has long held that human societies throughout history and across the world share key cultural attributes, at least in broad brush strokes of common rituals and practice of courtship, parenting, division of labor, governance, and trade. But biological explanations for culture have always been off limits. Sociobiology broke that taboo, lending insight into our species' distinct advantages, particularly the human ability to cooperate to survive resource bottlenecks.

The sweeping synthesis Wilson stitched together has benefited from many additions through the years, especially from primatology, anthropology, and evolutionary psychology. In his call for consilience over two decades later, Wilson described how various disciplines could build bridges with contemporary science, perhaps none more importantly than economics. Take, for instance, the fact that we are biologically primed to bond tightly with people inside our own group and less likely to cooperate with others outside that group. These tensions between our cooperative and competitive natures have long been used by advertisers, sports franchises, and political campaigns to frame and influence our economic decisions. Consumerism is fueled by designing "arms races" through defining in-groups and out-groups. Multi-million-dollar sports franchises prey on our instincts for territorial defense. Political elections are won by scapegoating and stoking fear of those who don't look, speak, or pray like you.

But none of these manipulations that pull on our competitive instincts are cast in stone. We are equally capable of building cooperative ties between groups, designing collective actions, and tapping into our deeply evolved capacity for empathy. For example, research on parenting, mating, family structure, gender roles, and sexuality can help explain the persistent power hierarchies throughout our economy. However, this knowledge need not be an excuse for misogyny but rather suggests ways to break down systems of oppression and rebuild explicitly antisexist institutions. Similarly, examining the science of status seeking and territorial defense can help us turn away from conspicuous consumption and larceny of the commons in a winner-takes-all society. We can elevate instead new reference groups that celebrate respect, collaboration, and love.

Research into human nature also teaches us about how we make agreements, including forming trust, sniffing out cheaters, and developing social norms. Here there are many interactions between sociobiology and game theory in economics. Both show that our willingness to cooperate often comes down to the strengths of our social contracts. Simply put, no economic decisions are neutral. They all depend on the "what" and "why" of the rules of the game and especially on the "who" wrote them.

Making a decision as a member of a citizen jury, a town council, or a public governing board has a completely different social context than doing so as an anonymous consumer in a global marketplace. When we design fair, accountable, transparent decision-making processes we can make fair, accountable, transparent decisions! It turns out that in safe, respectful social settings we care about each other, we care about the future, and we care about life on Earth. When we understand humans as an evolving species within the full community of life, our interdependence becomes undeniable.

As I remind my students often, "We are related to our ancestors," human and nonhuman alike. Our species diverged from a common ancestor with other apes an estimated six to seven million years ago.[25] We survived the past not as isolated individuals but with intricate and delicate bonds to each other and the full diversity of life. Human history is littered with sagas of the rise and fall of complex societies, with much ecological devastation and blood spilt along the way, but as a global civilization we now have limited chances left to survive on a full planet.[26] Might we learn from our mistakes, lean in to our cooperative instincts, and build what Jeremy Rifkin has called an "empathetic civilization" to survive the future?[27]

As we choose a way forward for economics, there is much to learn from the borderland disciplines. Yes, humans are competitive and self-interested, but also highly cooperative, with evolved social norms of reciprocal fairness. Yes, we are short-sighted and willfully ignorant, but with dogged instincts to care for our young and safeguard their future. Yes, politics and economics can prey on our selfish instincts, but the drive to form bonds can help us realize our need for each other and the Earth we share with all life.

Most importantly, we are learning that contemporary economics has no place as a master narrative for humanity. But perhaps a new economics in service of a new economy might just save us from ourselves.

CHAPTER 7

A New Economy

> Not everything that is faced can be changed, but nothing
> can be changed until it is faced.[1]
>
> —James Baldwin

When you set out to recreate the world with revolutionary aims and spirit, expect to be accused of being too "radical." But if your theory of change is more incremental, working within the current system one small step at a time, you'll be called too "pragmatic." As an ecological economist, I've bounced between these poles, feeling like a chameleon when teaching and advising pragmatic steps in one breath while calling for radical political and economic reform in another. In my classes, by midsemester my students are usually confused and disoriented at best. At worst, they are overwhelmed and paralyzed. But with seven weeks to go in a fifteen-week term, I try my best to weave together these philosophical poles into something akin to "radical pragmatism."

At the height of the COVID-19 pandemic, Geoffrey Gertz and Homi Kharas of the Brookings Institution described radical pragmatism as "a willingness to try whatever works, guided by an experimental mindset and commitment to empiricism and measuring results."[2] In this sense, "pragmatism" is about "defining concrete problems, then asks what needs to be done, by whom and by when, to make progress." "Radical" implies that an honest assessment of problems will "often demand quite radical shifts from the status quo." Although people often "try whatever works" during a crisis, this approach can also be used to change systems proactively.

To reform the economy, radical pragmatism would draw on the lived experience of many people in many places at many times in history. What seems radical to some may be quite pragmatic to others. As an all-hands-on-deck approach, Gertz and Kharas recommend combining "the allocative efficiency of markets, the regulatory powers of governments, the innovation of science and technology, and the legitimacy and accountability of civil society." It brings to mind a line from a 2006 op-ed on climate action by Bill McKibben, "There are no silver bullets, only silver buckshot."[3]

For example, I've spent a career arguing for energy tax reform as one small step to address the climate emergency, particularly in the United States. Most nations have taxed fossil fuels to encourage energy efficiency, invest in public transport, and pivot toward renewables, with measurable results. However, the United States and a handful of oil-exporting countries are well outside the norm. Bringing our taxes in line with those of other countries is an obvious entry point for pressuring the status quo.

Consider a study by the Organization for Economic Development and Cooperation (OECD) that found the United States' "effective" carbon tax—converting current taxes on fossil fuels to a carbon equivalent—is one tenth the OECD country average and less than one twentieth the highest in Switzerland.[4] With the US federal gas tax stuck at 18.4 cents per gallon for nearly three decades, is it any wonder that the average American consumes nearly three times the fossil fuel energy of the average European and closer to four times the average human?[5]

To level the global marketplace and correct this ultimate market failure, economists of all stripes have argued for carbon taxes as a centerpiece to US climate action. The signatories to the "Economists' Statement on Carbon Dividends" in 2019 included twenty-eight Nobel laureate economists, four former chairs of the US Federal Reserve, and fifteen former chairs of the US Council of Economic Advisors.[6] This is not exactly a "radical" bunch calling for both a national carbon tax and international carbon tariffs to level the playing field.

Through energy tax reform, the US economy could reduce carbon emissions, decrease oil and gas dependence, increase economic competitiveness, and even offset regressive taxes elsewhere in the economy (the "double dividend" of pollution taxes). If the United States cannot muster the political will, then its trading partners could raise tariffs to harmonize energy taxes under the banner of free and fair trade. Imagine a World Trade Organization that enforced "standards raising competition" to bring nations *up to* the highest environmental standards, safest labor practices, and fairest employment compensation. Now that's radical pragmatism!

Harnessing market forces with progressive tax policy can also help close income and wealth gaps by shifting government finances off the backs of labor and onto the owners of capital. Again, the United States stands out as doing exactly the opposite. The wealth gap between the richest and poorest American families more than doubled between 1989 and 2016. By 2016, the top 5 percent of families held 248 times as much wealth as the bottom 40 percent.[7] In fact, the median annual wealth of the bottom 20 percent was at zero or in negative territory over the last thirty years. After decades of shifting taxes onto payrolls and off capital gains, wealth inheritance, and unearned income, 2018 was the first year in recent history when the 400 wealthiest Americans paid a lower tax rate than any other income group.[8] With this regressive tax structure, is it any wonder that the United States has one of the highest levels of income inequality in the global North?[9]

This growing economic inequality has dire consequences for health and well-being. In a landmark study titled *The Spirit Level*, social epidemiologists Richard Wilkinson and Kate Pickett found that nearly every social problem was worse in countries with high levels of income inequality.[10] Again, the United States is an anomaly as one of the most lopsidedly rich countries on Earth but with some of the worst social outcomes, including low levels of trust, social mobility, and life expectancy and high levels of mental illness, drug use, obesity, teenage births, infant mortality, imprisonment, and homicides. When blind economic growth doesn't produce broadly shared well-being, is it any wonder that so-called "radical" proposals from the political left—$15 minimum wage, universal healthcare, free college education, and wealth taxes—have become more mainstream?

Beyond tax reform, pragmatic strategies include breaking up monopolies, investing in public goods, and increasing transparency for consumers. These all fit the economist's pursuit of "perfect competition" while increasing efficiency, fairness, and equal opportunity. What's so radical about restoring checks and balances that promote open democracy over crony capitalism? What's so radical about upholding the very principles of competition that were designed to break up the monopolies of the robber barons and family dynasties? What's so radical about rating consumer products by their social and environmental impact? These textbook economic reforms in the name of maximizing economic welfare are "pragmatic" by any definition, and "radical" only when seen as opposing an affluent status quo.

However, these economic approaches to political and social reform can only go so far. Reversing course on the climate emergency, mass extinction, and the growing gap between the privileged and oppressed will require more than just steering market forces to achieve progressive social aims. Although it's true that higher taxes on fossil fuels around the world have incentivized energy efficiency and fuel switching, even energy taxes ten to twenty times higher in Europe than the United States have failed to break the "carbon lock-in" of high-income nations and their enabling carbon capitalists.[11]

Lock-in is a kind of dance between technology and institutions that creates feedback loops to reinforce the status quo. The more you use something, the cheaper it is to continuing using due to scale, learning, and network economies.[12] Monopolies and regulatory capture also lock us into bad policy and poor technology. The old guard of an industry stays ahead of competitors by spending profits on lobbying the powers-that-be for political advantages, including limiting regulations and securing subsidies. This perverse brand of co-evolution prevents better alternatives from ever gaining ground.

Consider a 2019 study from the International Monetary Fund. Staff from the not-so-radical IMF Fiscal Affairs Department estimated the global citizenry subsidized the fossil fuel industry to the tune of US$5.2 trillion, including direct payments to energy companies from taxpayers, health impacts from air pollution, and expenditures on climate adaptation.[13] That was equivalent to more than 6.5 percent of global GDP given away to one of the most established and profitable industries in the world. The United States alone spent ten times more on subsidizing fossil fuels than on federal support for education. Energy price reform can't do much to break carbon lock-in if one hand collects from coal, oil, and gas while the other writes them a check.

The consequences and challenges of carbon lock-in are very clear. The Carbon Tracker Initiative estimates 60 to 80 percent of listed reserves of coal, oil, and gas are "unburnable" if we are to reach 2°C targets of international climate accords.[14] This is known carbon that must be left in the ground, not burned more efficiently. Yet reliable technologies such as coal-fired electricity are costly to build but inexpensive to operate, locking in entire economies to carbon intensive investments.[15] Technologies such as internal combustion engines have entire support structures in place—from roads and gas stations to dealerships and mechanics—that lock in automobile purchases for decades.[16]

A radical break from this path will require serious restrictions, including banning new fossil fuel infrastructure, canceling mining and drilling leases on public lands and seas, and divesting from the fossil fuel industry.[17] Breaking the chain of carbon dependence at the very first link avoids lock-in and disrupts what OECD secretary general Ángel Gurría deemed "carbon entanglement" between government finances and taxing fossil fuels.[18] The alternative of politicians signing climate treaties while authorizing new oil and gas pipelines, exploration, and drilling is not just hypocritical, it's downright suicidal.

Incentivizing labor and capital by cutting taxes can make carbon lock-in even worse. More work and investment lead to more income and consumption, which create more carbon pollution, a rebound effect. Revenues from shifting taxes off workers and onto polluters could instead be used to free up time and lead to shorter work weeks, extended vacation and health days, and investments in job training for a post-carbon economy. There is widespread agreement among economists on the goal of full employment, where everyone who wants a job can find a job. But full employment doesn't require ever-expanding work, especially meaningless work just to keep the hamster wheel of economic growth spinning. In contrast, policies that shift time away from work and toward leisure, family, and community could help keep carbon in the ground while increasing quality of life.

Consider the example of Scandinavian countries where guaranteed parental leave, college education, healthcare, and paid vacations—no matter your job, income, or station in life—have enabled a high quality of life, fairer income distribution, and lower per capita energy consumption. These social investments haven't crippled Nordic economies or stifled individual freedom. Rather, they have enabled resilient communities and broadly shared well-being. In *The Nordic Theory of Everything*,

Finnish journalist Anu Partanen argues that the "overarching ambition of Nordic societies during the course of the twentieth century, and into the twenty-first, has not been to socialize the economy." Instead, contrary to American perceptions of a nanny state, the "goal has been to free the individual from all forms of dependency within the family and in civil society."[19] With universal access to healthcare, education, leisure, and childcare, human relationships are "unencumbered by ulterior motives and needs, and thus to be entirely free, completely authentic, and driven purely by love."

It's hard for me to wrap my American mind around a world where healthcare isn't tied to allegiance to your employer. Or where a college education is possible without a lifetime of student loan payments. Or where fathers share in paternity leave with mothers (up to 480 days in Sweden!). I was raised under a myth of individualism as separate from outside help. However, as Swedish historian Henrik Berggren explains, the Scandinavian experience has enabled "radical individualism in the land of social solidarity." He describes a "Swedish theory of love" where "authentic love and friendship are possible only between individuals who are independent and equal."[20]

An economy built on care, respect, and love need not be a radical dream, but the unresolved question is whether this is possible *without* more and more growth and higher and higher incomes. A country like Norway has received accolades for its social investments but has paid the bill partly through state-owned oil concessions in the North Sea. Although Scandinavian countries have provided for broad economic "needs," they still have high concentrations of perverse wealth.[21] Is full employment possible while breaking free from carbon lock-in and corrupt politics? Can we stop perpetual growth while reducing income, wealth, gender, and racial inequality? Could time be rebalanced between work, play, family, and community so that people are happier and healthier?

One answer comes from traditional Keynesian macroeconomic growth models that have been repurposed to reallocate time from the over-worked to the underemployed. The simulated results include less income inequality, higher quality of life, smaller economies, *and* lower carbon emissions. For example, system models designed by ecological econo-mist Peter Victor have demonstrated that downsizing the Canadian economy could significantly reduce greenhouse gas pollution through a renewable energy transition and shorter work weeks, all while maintain-ing full employment.[22]

There are also alternative storylines in climate models that achieve 1.5°C targets without a technological Hail Mary. For example, the International Institute for Applied Systems Analysis explored how "low energy demand" could lower emissions to Paris Agreement levels with-out fantastical assumptions about bioenergy with carbon capture and storage.[23] Their model includes reductions to production and consump-tion by simulating a sharing economy, for instance by moving away from private ownership of cars and other durable goods. As economic anthro-pologist Jason Hickel and colleagues argue, we urgently need more of these "post-growth climate mitigation scenarios."[24]

But plotting just transitions to low-carbon economies is not only a modeling exercise. The challenge is to design and implement strategies that "rightsize" our economies, what Oxford economist Kate Raworth describes in *Doughnut Economics* as "the space in which we can meet the needs of all within the means of the planet."[25] The inner ring of the doughnut defines the social foundation of a just space for society, including access to sufficient food, clean water and sanitation, energy, education, healthcare, and decent housing. It also includes minimum income, decent work, and access to networks of information and social support. Achieving these bare necessities requires gender equality, social equity, political voice, and peace and justice. The outer ring then defines the ecological ceiling of a safe space, including impacts from climate change, ocean acidification, chemical pollution, nitrogen and phosphorus loading, freshwater withdrawals, land conversion, biodiversity loss, air pollution, and ozone layer depletion.

Strategies that move the human community inside the doughnut would redefine the very purpose of and participation in economic development, starting with the ownership characteristics of capitalism. For example, in the realm of private enterprise, employee-owned companies are breaking away from the distant shareholder model and becoming more transparent and inclusive about management decisions. In the United States alone there were over 14 million participants in employee stock ownership plans in 2018, with assets over $1.4 trillion.[26] Expanding employee ownership has led to lower income inequality in the workplace, broader inclusion in management decisions, lower environmental impact, and greater productivity.[27]

Even more democratic "stakeholder" approaches to business enterprise and wealth management include community voices and interests beyond the workplace.[28] Gar Alperovitz, political economist and co-chair of The Next System Project, argues that a "quiet democratization" of wealth is happening "everywhere."[29] As a foundation to the "next American revolution," he notes that more than 40 percent of the US population are members of all sorts of cooperatives, including agricultural, electricity, banking, insurance, food, retail, healthcare, and artist co-ops.

For example, there were over five thousand credit unions in the United States in 2021, with a median asset size of $35 million.[30] From the largest (Navy Federal Credit Union, with nearly $112 billion in assets) to the smallest (Holy Trinity Baptist Credit Union, with $21,000), these member-owned cooperatives give every depositor a vote on business matters. The over 110 million credit union members in the United States tend to have nonprofit motivations closer to home, such as lending significantly more than for-profit commercial banks during the Great Recession and well into the recovery.[31] Credit unions are also a part of an array of community development financial institutions that serve low-income communities, areas that commercial banks have generally abandoned.[32]

The potential for prosocial behavior of nonprofit firms is also under-appreciated (and understudied). The nonprofit sector is the third larg-est employer in the United States, accounting for over 10 percent of the workforce.[33] Motivations beyond accumulating riches keep nurses tend-ing to the sick during a pandemic, convention centers sheltering the dis-placed during a hurricane, and firefighters working twenty-hour shifts to protect public and private property alike. Health, wealth, and well-being are always and everywhere a product of social cooperation and commu-nity investment. Conversely, billionaires and millionaires are possible only by exploiting unpaid and underpaid work, public investment, and our commonwealth of the Earth.

Engaged citizens are also designing new economies by restoring and protecting the watersheds of our streams, rivers, ponds, and lakes. They are organizing local food hubs through farmers markets and farm-to-plate initiatives that reduce food miles, support local agriculture, tran-sition to organics, and build food security. Through energy coopera-tives and municipally owned electric utilities, communities are knitting together resilient, renewable, locally organized energysheds that are shift-ing mindsets from not-in-my-backyard antagonism to yes-in-my-back-yard inclusion.[34]

It is through these forms of collective ownership and action that the elements of a new economy are emerging. In community after commu-nity, groups of people throughout the world are testing, bending, and changing the rules of the privatized economy. And yet many (myself included) are frustrated by the rate and scale of change. While we take our pragmatic steps, we long for more sweeping—yes, more radical—reform of the global economy.

And so we turn toward collective action, starting in our communi-ties and fanning outward. Community organizing has always been a wellspring of cultural evolution, albeit in fits and starts at one school, one neighborhood, and one watershed at a time. We know from experience that when mothers and fathers come together to advocate for safe and clean neighborhoods, change can happen. When marginalized groups and their allies lock arms and stand against discrimination, change can happen. When students organize and take to the streets for climate justice, change can happen.

But we also know that isolated protests on separate issues aren't enough. The secret sauce is when community organizing escalates into full-on social movement building. When moments become movements, watch out, change *will* happen, even in economics.

〜

Paul Samuelson famously said, "Science makes progress funeral by funeral: the old are never converted by the new doctrines, they simply are replaced by a new generation."[35] He was admittedly channeling the theoretical physicist Max Planck but certainly had economics in mind.

As a dominant social science tightly controlled by a small group of predominantly White men from a small club of elite institutions, the mainstream of economics has been slow to change. In much of recent history, an economist's identity flowed from the high priest they followed or school they studied. Did you pay homage to Keynes or Hayek? To Samuelson or Friedman? Where did you study, what textbook did you teach, and in which journal did you publish? Economics started as a moral philosophy and portended to be a social science, but today it seems more like a series of cults, albeit with highly influential memberships.

Granted, the mainstream has meandered between opposite poles. Debates over individualism versus social planning, private markets versus public governance, and decentralized versus centralized power have intersected with the movements of the day. The laissez-faire pole aligned with the conservative movement of the 1920s, and then again with the neoliberal turn of the 1970s and 1980s. More interventionist approaches found an audience with the progressive movements of the 1890s, 1930s, and 1960s. The social movements of past decades were influenced by and influential to the course of economics, regardless of any funerals.

This was certainly true of the 2010s, a turbulent decade at the crossroads of multiple movements. My own impulse to write this book came early in the shadow of the Great Recession and the groundswell of economic populism arising from Occupy Wall Street. In the Zuccotti Park encampment, I found kinship with those protesting a wide array of injustices. Their causes and convictions were on display in a variety of cardboard placards and sidewalk debates, but each shared a belief that too much power was in the hands of too few people.

The 2010s was also a decade when deep inequalities were swept out from under the rug of censored histories and willful ignorance. The Movement for Black Lives arose in defiance of state-sanctioned subjugation, persecution, and murder of Black men, women, and children across America. High-profile cases of sexual abuse, harassment, and discrimination went viral, igniting a #MeToo movement that indicted all corners of a patriarchal society. The climate movement was seized by our youth in an ultimate plea to safeguard their future. And all came to a head with the US presidential election of Donald Trump as wave upon wave of movements, countermovements, and a new age of discontent took hold around the world.

I remember waking to a stream of text messages early on the morning of November 9, 2016, the day after US elections. One from my fellow film producers, Jacob Smith and Kathryn Goldman, simply stated, "We're going to need a different ending!" We were on the home stretch of wrapping up a two-year journey documenting the resurgence of a progressive political movement in the United States. It began with a fateful trip to follow senator Bernie Sanders through the State of Iowa in his early exploration of a presidential run. In January 2015, the US senator was relatively unknown outside Vermont, but the resonance of his message from bookstores and classrooms to labor unions and community centers made us wonder whether the nation might embrace his call for a "political revolution."

Sanders was tapping into the growing sentiment that a perverse model of crony capitalism was failing the average American worker. His message was framed in the classic struggle of labor. As he described to a small gathering of union members in Cedar Rapids, Iowa, "Every worker in this room is producing more than he or she did twenty or thirty years ago. Are your wages going up and hours going down? Quite the contrary. People are working longer hours, in many cases for lower wages." His campaign centered on taking back power from the millionaire and billionaire class, the "other reality" in America where "the wealthiest people and the large corporations are doing phenomenally well."

As we watched the Sanders campaign heat up, our documentary film took shape. Audiences in the dozens swelled to auditoriums in the thousands. Our interviews with the movers and shakers in progressive politics confirmed what we were witnessing firsthand. Amy Goodman, long-time host of progressive radio show *Democracy Now!*, described the inspiration of "people banding together by the movements that are fighting for change, for justice, for sustainability, for the fate of the planet, for equality for all." Van Jones, CNN commentator and founder of Dream Corps, contrasted the race for the Democratic Party nomination as Hillary Clinton's "machine" versus the Sanders "movement." Robert Reich, former US secretary of labor and UC Berkeley economist, pontificated that the 2016 race was "no longer the old right versus left—do you want more government or less government—it's really anti-establishment versus establishment."

An early interview with Zephyr Teachout, a Fordham University professor and legal scholar who had run in the New York governor primaries, gave us the title we were looking for. As she described, "There is a sleeping giant of political anger and love that is in some ways waking up right now." While the resulting documentary, *Waking the Sleeping Giant*, followed the arc of the Sanders campaign—from political rallies and door-to-door canvassing to state primaries and the Democratic National Convention in Philadelphia—it was personal stories from the front lines of social change that ultimately shaped our film.[36]

The story of Sabrina Shrader, a West Virginia coal miner's daughter born into generational poverty, peeled back the illusion that hard work alone could get you ahead in a rigged economy. Inspired by Senator Sanders's grassroots campaign for president, Sabrina was rising from the failing economy of coal country to run for a seat in the West Virginia House of Delegates.

The story of Jan Williams, a school bus driver and local organizer for Black Lives Matter, bore witness to one of hundreds of protests across the country against police killings of Black men and women. Outside Los Angeles Police Department headquarters Jan called out "Say her name!" and allies replied "Wakiesha Wilson!" in protest of yet another Black woman who had mysteriously died in police custody.

The story of Kai Newkirk and Elise Whitaker, millennial organizers of Democracy Spring, showed the coalitions building around protecting voting rights and dismantling the influence of big money on US politics. At a mass sit-in on the US Capitol steps, activists from all walks of life and across many allied calls for justice were handcuffed and hauled away in police buses to a chorus of "Money ain't speech, corporations aren't people!"

While these stories shed light on long-standing struggles of class, race, and power that framed the 2016 elections, a decade of protest also gave voice to the future. In Vermont we organized youth climate action summits, a Vermont Youth Lobby, and a Vermont Youth Climate Congress to help embolden our leaders to turn vague climate goals into concrete climate action. As Friday sit-ins outside the Swedish Parliament by a single ninth grader evolved into one of the largest global protests in history, we were ready to join worldwide strikes of over four million students and workers on September 20 and 27, 2019. When Greta Thunberg addressed the United Nations that week in New York City, her eternal condemnation of those in power echoed across more than forty-five hundred protests in over 150 countries.

> You have stolen my dreams and my childhood with your empty words. And yet I'm one of the lucky ones. People are suffering. People are dying. Entire ecosystems are collapsing. We are in the beginning of a mass extinction, and all you can talk about is money and fairy tales of eternal economic growth. How dare you!

And as if the 2010s were not disruptive enough, a decade of intersecting economic, social, and environmental movements culminated with the onset of the deadliest pandemic in over a century. COVID-19 brought the world to its knees in 2020, claiming nearly 2 million lives in its first year of exponential spread, debilitating economies worldwide, and hitting the exploited, marginalized, powerless, and otherwise oppressed the hardest. As politicians made promises and plans to "get back to normal," an unsilenced majority screamed "no." Normal was already in crisis.

Normal was a White minority that clung to power by perpetuating a lie that all things are possible through hard work, fair play, and a little risk taking. Normal was a global climate unraveling as we tried to grow our way out of the latest economic recession. Normal was subverting democratic governance to a plutocracy controlled by the 0.001 percent.

But the lived experience of the global majority outside the purview of White privilege was one that demeaned, degraded, and demoralized fellow humans based on skin color, gender, ethnicity, sexual orientation, religion, and more. Communities around the world were already under siege from the worst-case scenarios of global climate change. In this world, historical precedent and the language of economics were shaping the rules of the so-called free market to favor obscene accumulation of wealth and political power.

Dominant economic ideology assumes away discrimination, wealth inheritance, money in politics, and the different starting lines of a winner-takes-all society. An organizing principle of economic efficiency doesn't make space for reparations to offset the momentum of injustice or the irreversible loss of entire ecosystems. The golden rule of economics, Pareto optimality, dictates that no one can be made worse off to make someone else better off, even by limiting the glut of the obscenely rich to meet the bare necessities of the historically exploited, human and other-than-human alike.

An economics born of and simultaneously ignorant of power and privilege reinforces that oppression, perpetuating psychological and physical violence on the most vulnerable members of society. A story of market freedom as equal opportunity to exchange labor, land, and capital ignores the backstory of a society built on theft and genocide, slavery and misogyny, plunder and mass extinction. The fiction of "free" markets as the organizing principle of democratic societies is the ultimate hypocrisy of Econ 101.

The intersecting social movements of the 2010s call for a new economics in support of a new economy. They have influenced and have been influenced by flavors of economics outside the mainstream. An economics that remembers history—including well-worn critiques of capitalism gone awry—and rejects the hegemony of one-size-fits-all neoliberalism. A new economics grounded in real lives of real people that breaks free from the chalkboard fable of "self-correction" and instead enables just and restorative systems by design.

In the pile-on of twenty-first-century crises, modest change following the next economist's funeral, metaphorical or otherwise, is a losing proposition. Instead, we need to look beyond the architects and high priests of mainstream economics to dramatically change the very soul of the discipline. Academia can play an important role in redesigning curricula, disciplines, and the very purpose of education. But new systems of knowing must be fed by systems of doing. The task at hand is nothing short of a revolution in classrooms, communities, and statehouses across the world, enabled by and connected to the social movements already under way.

~

For my small part as a privileged, White, cisgender, male professor at a US land-grant university built on the proceeds of stolen land, I'll conclude with new beginnings in education. Around the time I started thinking "yes, the world needs yet another book about economics," together with Peter Brown of McGill University, Ellie Perkins and Peter Victor of York University, and over eighty collaborators in academia and civil society, we launched an international initiative called Economics for the Anthropocene (E4A for short). The project started with an idea long held by ecological economists, that the teaching and practice of economics needed to reconcile with the biophysical realities of the Earth. Our work was born out of a rejection of what our colleague Eric Zencey called "infinite planet thinking," and E4A sought to animate and empower ecological economics as an alternative.[37]

In the 2010s, scientists were once again wrestling with inherent conflicts between a growing global economy and a finite planet. The Stockholm Resilience Centre assembled the latest evidence of the environmental damage inflicted by our species' seemingly insatiable appetite for more. By pressing against or across at least nine planetary thresholds, a bloated economy was eroding the very foundations of life on Earth.[38] This new project was meant to train graduate students to break free from disciplinary silos, shed the illusion of a values-free economics, and tackle problems by partnering with progressive think tanks, advocacy organizations, and community organizers.

We took inspiration from the latest bandwagon in academia, the naming of a geological epoch to recognize humanity's global impact. Geologists were debating whether and when we left the Holocene (the interglacial epoch that began nearly 12,000 years ago) and entered the Anthropocene, the age of humans. Some argued that the switch flipped with the dawn of modern agriculture and the accelerated, worldwide loss of soil that ensued. Others pegged it to the industrial use of coal that blanketed the globe with a layer of mercury deposition. My own view is that the Anthropocene commenced at the very moment of the Trinity Test, the first detonation of a nuclear bomb at 5:29 a.m. on July 16, 1945, near Jornada del Muerto, a New Mexican desert named by sixteenth-century Spanish conquistadors as "Dead Man's Route."

However, the debate was about more than getting the date right for the "age of humans"; it signaled a crossroads for humanity. One road declared victory, where naming a geological epoch in our honor completes a centuries-old emancipation project. In this story our species has escaped the toils of the Holocene. Technology and human ingenuity have liberated us from dependence on the land and each other. For at least the so-called developed nations, dominion is complete and the future is ours to do with what we please. Other countries need only catch up.

In contrast, our group of heretics imagined a different, much less worn path: a reconciliation project. On this road, the person, community, and society are embedded in a material universe, interdependent on each other and all life. Everything is relational, with no separation between human and other. For this journey, an entirely new social contract is needed, one that can halt the wholesale destruction of the Earth and build an age of restoration and renewal.

Clearly these interpretations of the Anthropocene are fundamentally at odds. Our intellectual leader and resident philosopher Peter Brown reminded us that this tension was nothing new, often referencing C. P. Snow's infamous 1959 "Two Cultures" lecture.[39] Snow, a British novelist and physical chemist, was the living embodiment of a "heretic" in postwar England. He argued that conflict between the sciences and humanities, pervasive at universities, was hindering solutions to the world's major problems. To Snow, the academy housed two "polar groups" with a "gulf of mutual incomprehension" in between.

Nowhere is this gulf more glaringly obvious than between science and economics, the principal target of our project. As I've tried to hammer home throughout these pages, separating the economy from energy and material flows fails any scientific scrutiny yet dominates the pedagogy and practice of economics. This isolated discipline confuses paper money and digital transfers with wealth, whereas most of Earth's true wealth is derived from photosynthesis. Economics clings to growth as the solution to the very problems created by growth. And the model of rational "man," central to economic models and policy advice, outright ignores modern behavioral sciences and common sense alike.

Economics had become what Peter Brown called an orphan discipline. Its intellectual parents died long ago, yet the untethered child roamed the halls of academia doing great harm. So we set out to find the orphan a home, starting with the natural sciences.

An economics at home with the sciences would study production as a physical transformation of Earth's materials and energy from the Sun, consistent with the laws of thermodynamics. It would recognize that the pace, distribution, and scale of this transformation affect the well-being of all life. In a more consilient economics, growth is understood as the initial stage of a maturing economy—a temporary means toward longer-term ends of stability, resilience, and longevity—not a futile pursuit of more for more's sake. People are seen as part of families, communities, and societies, as well as watersheds, foodsheds, energysheds, bioregions, and the entire Earth ecosystem. The infamous rational actor becomes a *human* actor whose economic decisions are based on emotions, personal values, and cultural influences rather than a Vulcan-like analysis of marginal utility.

What began as an effort to reform economics developed into an ambitious agenda to rethink education more broadly. If economics could be reimagined as a way to manage our relationships with each other and the Earth more ecologically, other disciplines could be similarly repurposed. Students of finance would think systematically about how the monetary system can support a healthy environment. Other academic orphans such as political science and law would rewrite our legal codes to stay well within Earth's safe operating limits. And philosophy and ethics—the hallmarks of academic anthropocentrism—would be reoriented around respect for all life with which we share the planet.

Our graduate students and faculty got to work building bridges between disciplines and also beyond the halls of academia. Collaborations with local climate activists, Indigenous leaders, and diaspora networks connected the theory of social change with the dynamism of collective action.[40] Workshops with new economy foundations and think tanks supported alliances to rethink finance, reform monetary systems, and build new metrics of shared prosperity.[41] Student internships and leadership positions—ranging from old-school advocates such as the David Suzuki Foundation to new-school collectives such as DegrowUS—helped orient graduate research around both established and emerging agendas for social change.

As E4A took shape, Peter Brown and I took inspiration from C. P. Snow and collaborated on a series of lectures of our own, tag teaming at international conferences in ecological economics, big history, complexity science, and political economy. These talks evolved into an article on "How Higher Education Imperils the Future" for *Balance*, a new publication of the Club of Rome, the patrons of the 1972 *Limits to Growth* report.[42] What came into focus was an unspoken truth that while the sciences were meticulously documenting environmental destruction, the social sciences and humanities were propping up the very systems of economics, law, governance, and philosophy that promote a planetary suicide pact.

These so-called normative disciplines consider "what ought to be" while often ignoring scientific realities. Yet the science side of the academy is not without blame as many scientists naively believe that knowledge of "what is" speaks for itself and will magically lead to action. To close this "gulf of mutual incomprehension" it became clear that our project needed to move beyond merely coming to terms with the Anthropocene of the present. We needed to envision and enable a new epoch for the future.

So our partnership took inspiration from the work of Thomas Berry, an ordained priest, cultural historian, and self-described "geologian" who spent his life bridging the divide between science, culture, and religion. Berry argued that the "Great Work" ahead of the new millennium is "to carry out the transition from a period of human devastation of the Earth to a period when humans would be present to the planet in a mutually beneficial manner."[43] For universities such as our own, Berry asked us to "decide whether [we] will continue training persons for temporary survival in the declining Cenozoic Era or whether [we] will begin educating students for the emerging Ecozoic."

In response to Berry's challenge, we envisioned a time when humanity would reject Western narratives of dominion and instead recognize humans as part of an ever-evolving universe. This conception of the future led us to Indigenous philosophies born of ancient bonds to land and sea. Narratives such as "buen vivir" from the Quechua peoples of the Andes declared that "good living" is possible only as part of community. The Zapatistas' call for "a world where many worlds fit" organized against the neoliberal homogenization of all cultures and communities. We found kinship with these voices and others that sought to dismantle exploitive, oppressive, overconsuming economies.

Economics was still a central focus of our partnership, but finding the orphan a home moved beyond merely reconciling with the realities of the Anthropocene and toward enabling an entirely new purpose. An economics working toward an Ecozoic era would view material growth as an early stage of development, not a permanent organizing concept of society. Characteristics such as resilience, cooperation, and frugality would take precedence over consumption, competition, and efficiency. An economy in service of flourishing human–Earth relations would reject extremes in waste and want, embrace cooperative arrangements in a sharing economy, and negotiate a political economy where well-regulated markets are our servants, not our masters.

While colonialism, industrialization, and globalism have distorted our sense of place, our souls still long for a connection to the land, waters, and life forces called home. Rediscovering that sense of belonging will help us turn away from consumerism, break the cycles of greed and oppression that have homogenized daily existence, and unlock the full expression of our humanity. As the final chapter of the fairytale of economics comes to its end, a new story is unfolding in its place. The work ahead will heal our bonds with the Earth, rekindle our love for one another, and reclaim our interdependent future. This is the unfinished journey of generations before to be good ancestors to the generations to come.

Acknowledgments

Mark Twain wrote in his autobiography, "There is no such thing as a new idea. It is impossible. We simply take a lot of old ideas and put them into a sort of mental kaleidoscope. We give them a turn and they make new and curious combinations." In reflecting on the years of "curious combinations" that resulted in this book, I certainly agree. These ideas evolved from conversations, collaborations, and care from family, colleagues, and students throughout my career. From ideas to writing to review, I owe many thanks to many people.

First to my wife, Pat. There would be no family, no home, and no career from which to write without her love and belief in unproven potential. To our sons, Louis and Jon, from whom we learned the meaning of true love. To my mother and father, thank you for your unending encouragement and undeserving praise. And to my brothers, Matt and David, whose shared life journey and love of the outdoors are reflected throughout these pages.

To my colleagues who have pushed, pulled, and stretched this book from pitches and proposals to outlines and drafts, thank you for your counsel and wisdom. For timely and insightful reviews, thanks in particular to Terry Bensel, David Christian, Herman Daly, Bob Devine, John Gowdy, David Korten, Richard Norgaard, Joe Roman, Juliet Schor, Amy Seidl, Jacob Smith, Gus Speth, and Stewart Wallace. Thanks especially to Herman for your leadership in ecological economics and to John for your mentorship and unwavering support throughout my career.

I've also had the good fortune to be a part of two boundary-pushing projects over the last decade, the source of some of my most current thinking. For the vision and courage to launch and sustain our Economics for the Anthropocene (E4A) and Leadership for the Ecozoic (L4E) partnerships, thanks to Peter Brown, Geoff Garver, Ursula Georgeoglou, Kate Greswold, Deissy Perilla, Ellie Perkins, Dina Spigelski, and Peter Victor. Thanks especially to Peter Brown for the passion and drive to refuse taking "no" for an answer again and again (and again).

The many students who have helped me harvest, test, and shape ideas worth writing about are too numerous to list. However, the recent doctoral students who have read, edited, and suffered the most throughout my writing ups and downs include John Adams, Sam Bliss, Matthew Burke, Christopher Clements, Meg Egler, Mairi-Jane Fox, Nate Hagens, Kelly Hamshaw, Katie Horner, Jolyon Larson, Rigo Melgar-Melgar, Maya Moore, Bonnie Pratt, Eduardo Rodriguez, Nina Smolyar, Phoebe Spencer, and Michael Wironen. Thank you for your leadership, inspiration, and advice throughout this project.

Beyond the intellectual and emotional support, I owe many thanks for financial support for graduate students and summer writing time from the Social Sciences and Humanities Research Council of Canada, Lintilhac Foundation, Peter Rose, Leadership for the Ecozoic Partnership, and David Blittersdorf Professorship of Sustainability Science and Policy. And for the patience, push, and privilege to finish a book that should have been done years ago, thank you to dean Nancy Mathews and associate deans Allan Strong, Jen Pontius, and Breck Bowden.

Finally, a special thanks to Dale Willman, my unofficial agent, for shopping around my proposal until we found the perfect publisher. This book might have never seen the light of day without Dale connecting me to Emily Turner, my editor at Island Press. The faith, support, and talent of Emily and her entire team make me want to get started on the next book right away, but alas my wife has me serving a writer's parole until we finish building the farm!

Notes

Preface. Promises of an Ecological Economics

1. "The worth of a songbird" is a reference to an influential article in the field of ecological economics on postnormal science by Funtowicz and Ravetz (1994).

Chapter 1. The Education of an Economist

1. Adelman (2004).
2. In a survey of economics graduate students in elite programs, 77 percent agreed with the statement that "economics is the most scientific of the social sciences." See Colander (2005).
3. There are a few noneconomists who have received a Memorial Nobel Prize, such as mathematician John Nash, for his contributions to game theory, and psychologist Daniel Kahneman, who was honored in 2002 for "having integrated insights from psychological research into economic science." Also, the first woman to be honored was Elinor Ostrom, in 2009, for her "analysis of economic governance, especially the commons."
4. Lazear (2000).
5. Fourcade et al. (2015).

6. Weyl (2017), cited in Fourcade et al. (2015).
7. Fourcade and colleagues point to a long line of research on prestige rankings of economics departments, composition of journal editorial boards and professional society officers, and hiring practices within the field. For example, see Han (2003).
8. Gross and Simmons (2007).
9. Fourcade et al. (2015).
10. Costanza et al. (1997).
11. From Nobel prize archives at https://www.nobelprize.org/prizes/economic-sciences/1992/summary/.
12. Frank (2008).
13. Levitt and Dubner (2005).
14. Ackerman and Heinzerling (2002).
15. Carlin and Sandy (1991).
16. Fourcade et al. (2015) report on trend data from the US Center for Education Statistics indicating that only economics and the physical sciences remain below a 30 percent threshold of doctorates awarded to women. Psychology, sociology, and the life sciences have all risen above 50 percent in recent years, and political science and public administration have reached 40 percent. Economics reached only a 20 percent level in the mid-1990s.
17. These examples were collated in Daly (2000).
18. Erickson (1993).
19. Konczal (2014).
20. Rampell (2011).
21. National Center for Education Statistics (2015).
22. Byrne (2014).

Chapter 2. Ascension of the Queen

1. Keynes (1936).
2. Wikipedia maintains an extensive and well-cited list of US city occupations. See https://en.wikipedia.org/wiki/List_of_Occupy_movement_protest_locations_in_the_United_States.

3. For a list of California Occupy protests and encampments, see https://en.wikipedia.org/wiki/List_of_Occupy_movement_protest_locations_in_California.

4. Agence France-Presse (2011).

5. Bell and Blanchflower (2011).

6. Data from the Federal Reserve Bank of St. Louis on "Real Median Household Income in the United States." See https://research.stlou isfed.org/fred2/series/MEHOINUSA672N.

7. Bivens et al. (2014).

8. Smith (2015).

9. Ibid.

10. Reich (2011).

11. Rampell (2011).

12. Roose (2011).

13. Ibid.

14. Harvard Political Review (2011).

15. DelReal (2011).

16. Read (2015).

17. Mankiw (2013).

18. Inman (2013).

19. Inman (2014).

20. From the open letter on "An International Student Call for Pluralism in Economics" by the International Student Initiative for Pluralism in Economics. See http://www.isipe.net/open-letter/.

21. From a letter to *The Guardian* by the Post Keynesian Economics Study Group. See http://www.theguardian.com/education/2013/nov /18/post-keynesians-comeback.

22. Although William Stanley Jevons (1835–1882) in England and Carl Menger (1840–1921) in Austria get credit for their own independent contributions to neoclassical theory, it was Walras who put a full model together, built on the calculus of maximizing producer profit and consumer utility.

23. Schumpeter (1954).

24. The metaphysics of Walras have been researched by many, including Koppl's (1992) work on "Price Theory as Physics." Walras's intention to develop a truly scientific social science is quoted by Koppl from an 1859 letter to Adolph Gueroult, editor of *La Presse*.

25. From the "George, Henry" entry in the American National Biography Online. See http://www.anb.org/articles/15/15-00261.html.

26. George (1868).

27. Writing from New York on January 25, 1905, Henry George Jr. wrote a reflection on his father's life in an introduction to the twenty-fifth anniversary edition of *Progress and Poverty*.

28. George (1871).

29. George (1879).

30. From Henry George Jr.'s introduction to George (1905).

31. From John Dewey's forward to *The Philosophy of Henry George* by Geiger (1933).

32. The Robert Schalkenbach Foundation is a good source of information on the influence of Henry George's work. The foundation was "organized in 1925 as an operating foundation to promote public awareness of the social philosophy and economic reforms advocated by Henry George." See http://schalkenbach.org/.

33. Sheppard (2014).

34. Kennedy (1886).

35. Marshall's lectures on Henry George were not available for many decades. They were reprinted in 1969 in *The Journal of Law and Economics*.

36. An account and analysis of the "debate" is found in Herbert (1979).

37. Kennedy (1886).

38. Gaffney and Harrison (1994).

39. Guo (2015).

40. From the *New York Times* archive, October 9, 1917. See https://www.nytimes.com/1917/10/09/archives/quits-columbia-assails-trustees-professor-charles-a-beard-says.html.
41. Sinclair (1923).
42. Hodgson (2002).
43. McKenna (2013).
44. Scottish Government (2015).
45. Cotula (2012).

Chapter 3. Growing a Market Society

1. See the "Charles E. Wilson" entry at the Automotive Hall of Fame, available at https://www.automotivehalloffame.org/honoree/charles-e-wilson/.
2. "Wilson Gets New Hearing" was the front-page headline to the *Chicago Tribune* on January 18, 1953. See http://archives.chicagotribune.com/1953/01/18/page/1/article/wilson-gets-new-hearing/index.html.
3. I attribute this distinction between invisible hand, handshake, and foot to David Collander, an institutional economist at Middlebury College, Middlebury, Vermont.
4. Presidential historians have not been kind to Warren Harding, routinely ranking him as one of the worst US presidents in history and one of the most corrupt. See the *US News and World Report* ranking of "The 10 Worst US Presidents" at https://www.usnews.com/news/special-reports/the-worst-presidents/slideshows/the-10-worst-presidents.
5. Tucker (2012).
6. Pigou (1920).
7. Keynes (1919).
8. An essay based on his November 1924 Sidney Ball lecture was published as a pamphlet by the Hogarth Press in July 1926 and later reprinted in Keynes (1932).

9. Say (1803).
10. Mellon (1924).
11. Estimates of the size of the economy before 1929 predated GDP accounting. The World War I estimate is based on Census data, cobbled together in various places, including a September 10, 2015, report from the Joint Economic Committee of the US Congress, available at https://www.jec.senate.gov/public/_cache/files/aeeff50d-dc8e-4e0b-ab9f-def32f184179/20150910-jec-spendingstudy.pdf.
12. Based on economic research from the Federal Reserve Bank of St. Louis, available at https://fred.stlouisfed.org/series/FYONGDA 188S.
13. From table 47 of chapter 6 from the third volume of the report written and edited by Simon Kuznets with the National Bureau of Research. Available at http://www.nber.org/chapters/c3060.pdf.
14. Cohan (2009).
15. A full list of executive orders is found at the FDR Library at Marist College. See http://www.fdrlibrary.marist.edu/archives/collections/franklin/.
16. From the *New York Times* archive, November 17, 1985. See http://www.nytimes.com/1985/11/17/nyregion/stuart-chase-97-coined-phrase-a-new-dea.html.
17. Downey (2009).
18. Keynes (1933).
19. Keynes (1936).
20. Noted in a quote from economist Richard T. Froyen from the University of North Carolina in Bureau of Economic Analysis (2000).
21. Report on "National Income, 1929–32" was issued from the acting secretary of commerce on January 4, 1934, in response to Senate Resolution 220 of the 72nd US Congress. Available at https://fraser.stlouisfed.org/files/docs/publications/natincome_1934/19340104_nationalinc.pdf.

22. Bureau of Economic Analysis (2000).
23. Zelizer (2001).
24. See "The New Spirit" from Walt Disney (1942), available on You-Tube at https://youtu.be/eMU-KGKK6q8.
25. Goodwin (2001).
26. For an abbreviated "History of the Gold Standard," see Kimberly Amadeo's entry in *The Balance*, available at https://www.thebalance.com/what-is-the-history-of-the-gold-standard-3306136.
27. See the "World Bank Group Timeline," available at https://timeline.worldbank.org.
28. LaFeber (2002).
29. From the online *Encyclopedia Britannica* entry by Michael Ray on "Why Did the Soviet Union Collapse?," available at https://www.britannica.com/story/why-did-the-soviet-union-collapse.
30. Huffington (2010).
31. Moggridge (1992).
32. Reprinted in volume 27 of "The Collected Writings of John Maynard Keynes," edited by Johnson and Moggridge (1978).
33. See https://www.whitehouse.gov/cea/.
34. From the August 11, 1963, *New York Times* obituary by Karen W. Arenson, available at https://www.nytimes.com/1983/08/11/obituaries/prof-joan-robinson-dies-at-79-cambrdige-university-economist.html.
35. Skousen (1997).
36. Thompson (2009).
37. Gunnar (1977).
38. Wikipedia provides a "List of Nobel Laureates by University Affiliation," available at https://en.wikipedia.org/wiki/List_of_Nobel_laureates_by_university_affiliation.
39. For a synopsis of "Stagflation and Its Causes," see Kimberly Amadeo's entry in *The Balance*, available at https://www.thebalance.com/what-is-stagflation-3305964.

40. Daggett (2010).

41. Locke (2009 [1689]).

42. Unger (1996).

43. The full speech is available to view on YouTube at https://youtu.be/qXBswFfh6AY.

44. Latson (2014).

Chapter 4. Coming of Age in the Econocene

1. From a May 3, 1981, interview by Ronald Butt published in the *Sunday Times*. See https://www.margaretthatcher.org/document/104475.

2. Bottomore (1991).

3. Norgaard (2015).

4. See the entry on the "Great Acceleration" from the International Geosphere-Biosphere Programme at http://www.igbp.net/global change/greatacceleration.4.1b8ae20512db692f2a680001630.html.

5. Mbaye and Moreno Badia (2019).

6. Unger (1996).

7. Archived at the John F. Kennedy Presidential Library and Museum at https://www.jfklibrary.org/learn/about-jfk/the-kennedy-family /robert-f-kennedy/robert-f-kennedy-speeches/remarks-at-the-univer sity-of-kansas-march-18-1968.

8. See the 2010 Mont Pelerin Society Directory, available at https:// www.desmogblog.com/sites/beta.desmogblog.com/files/Mont%20 Pelerin%20Society%20Directory%202010.pdf.

9. Plehwe (2009).

10. McPherson (1980).

11. Monbiot (2016).

12. Based on lobbying database from the Center for Responsive Politics, available at https://www.opensecrets.org/federal-lobbying/top -spenders.

13. Katz (2015).

14. A copy of the original August 23, 1971, confidential memo titled "Attack on American Free Enterprise System" is available at https://d1uu3oy1fdfoio.cloudfront.net/wp-content/uploads/2012/09/Lewis-Powell-Memo.pdf.
15. Hacker and Pierson (2010).
16. Blasko (2004).
17. Dowie (2002).
18. Edwards (1997).
19. Covington (1997).
20. Quoted in the report from National Committee for Responsive Philanthropy by Covington (1997).
21. From the "About Us" page of the Intercollegiate Studies Institute. See https://isi.org/about-us/.
22. Shiller (2012).
23. Cropper and Oates (1992).
24. Morgenstern (1997).
25. Schultze (1997).
26. Kramer (1978).
27. Stromberg (1978).
28. des Rosiers (2014).
29. Shabecoff (1981).
30. Rothman (2017).
31. Spash (2009).
32. Reel and Smith (2006).
33. Fischer (2009).
34. Letter from Milton Friedman to Augusto Pinochet, available at https://genius.com/Milton-friedman-letter-to-president-augusto-pinochet-annotated.
35. Fischer (2009).
36. Daly (1995).
37. Georgescu-Roegen (1966).

38. Holton and Elkana (1997).

39. Daly (1977).

40. Mill (1857).

41. Røpke (2004) provides an excellent early history of ecological economics.

42. United Nations (1973).

43. World Commission on Environment and Development (1987).

44. Blackwelder and Daly (2014).

45. From the acknowledgments of Daly (1996).

46. Meadows et al. (1992).

47. Recounted in Daly (1996).

48. Reprinted in the February 8, 1992, edition of *The Economist.*

49. Goodland et al. (1991).

50. Frumhoff (2014).

51. National biodiversity strategies and action plans are available at https://www.cbd.int/nbsap/.

52. Intergovernmental Science-Policy Platform on Biodiversity and Ecosystem Services (2019).

53. From the World Bank's "Poverty" page at https://www.worldbank.org/en/topic/poverty/overview.

54. Chang (2014).

55. Meadows (2000).

Chapter 5. A New Story

1. Sagan (1980).

2. Book of Genesis, New International Version, available at https://biblehub.com/genesis/.

3. Merchant (2013).

4. Christian (2004).

5. Blatner (2012).

6. Kaneda and Haub (2020).

7. Camilo et al. (2011).

8. See David Christian's TED talk "The History of Our World in 18 Minutes," available at https://www.ted.com/talks/david_christian_the_history_of_our_world_in_18_minutes.

9. See clips from the 1990 press conference in which Carl Sagan unveils the "Pale Blue Dot" image, available at https://youtu.be/7KBy_QsQDpE.

10. Sagan (1997).

11. Le Guin (1979).

12. de la Vega (2020).

13. Interactive graphic with supporting references available at https://www.sealevel.info/co2_and_ch4.html.

14. Historical CO_2 levels summarized in the National Oceanic and Atmospheric Administration's "Understanding Climate" series, available at https://www.climate.gov/news-features/understanding-climate/climate-change-atmospheric-carbon-dioxide.

15. World Meteorological Organization (2017).

16. Intergovernmental Panel on Climate Change (2014).

17. McGrath (2021).

18. Rice (2020).

19. Moloney (2019).

20. Masters (2020).

21. Lindsey (2019).

22. Australian Government (2020).

23. Readfearn (2020).

24. Steffen et al. (2018).

25. International Energy Agency data for oil at https://www.iea.org/reports/oil-information-2019, natural gas at https://www.iea.org/reports/natural-gas-information-2019, and coal at https://www.iea.org/reports/coal-2019.

26. Data on "Estimated Worldwide Automobile Production from 2000 to 2019" compiled by Statista, available at https://www.statista.com/statistics/262747/worldwide-automobile-production-since-2000/.

27. Data on "Every Coal Power Plant in the World (1927–2019)" compiled by Visual Capitalist, available at https://www.visualcapitalist.com/every-coal-power-plant-1927-2019/.
28. Data on "Natural Gas Domestic Consumption" compiled by the Global Energy Statistical Yearbook, available at https://yearbook.enerdata.net/natural-gas/gas-consumption-data.html.
29. Data on renewable energy investment from Frankfurt School, UNEP Collaborating Centre for Climate and Sustainable Energy Finance (2019). Data on fossil fuel investment from International Energy Agency (2016).
30. International Energy Agency (2017).
31. Intergovernmental Panel on Climate Change (2018).
32. Hickel and Kallis (2020).
33. Daly (2008).
34. World Bank data page for "GDP per unit of energy use," available at https://data.worldbank.org/indicator/EG.GDP.PUSE.KO.PP.
35. World Bank data page for "Renewable energy consumption," available at https://data.worldbank.org/indicator/EG.FEC.RNEW.ZS.
36. British Petroleum (2019).
37. Kenny et al. (2010).
38. Weisser (2007).
39. Sullivan et al. (2010).
40. Obama (2017).
41. Fan et al. (2017).
42. Schröder and Storm (2018).
43. Intergovernmental Panel on Climate Change (2000).
44. In a full review of mitigation scenarios, Hickel and Kallis (2020) cite the International Renewable Energy Agency (2018) roadmap as one of the more aggressive decarbonization strategies.
45. Intergovernmental Panel on Climate Change (2014).
46. Peters (2017).
47. Heck et al. (2018).

48. Hickel and Kallis (2020).
49. Ritchie (2019).
50. Schröder and Storm (2018).
51. Trucost (2013).
52. Coady et al. (2019).
53. Fox and Erickson (2018), Kubiszewski et al. (2013).
54. Sonnemaker (2020).
55. Data accessed on August 11, 2020, from the US Bureau of Labor Statistics. See https://www.bls.gov/news.release/empsit.t15.htm.
56. Data accessed on August 11, 2020, from the Organisation for Economic Co-operation and Development. See https://data.oecd.org/emp/hours-worked.htm.
57. Livingston and Thomas (2019).
58. Pew Research Center (2015).
59. McCarthy (2017).
60. Johnson (2017).
61. Desilver (2018).
62. Data accessed on August 17, 2020, from the US Bureau of Labor Statistics. See https://www.bls.gov/charts/american-time-use/activity -by-sex.htm.
63. Hess (2018).
64. Fox and Erickson (2018).
65. See "How Does the Gallup-Sharecare Well-Being Index Work?," available at https://www.gallup.com/175196/gallup-healthways-index-methodology.aspx.
66. Witters (2019).
67. Gallup-Healthways (2014).
68. Data accessed on August 18, 2020, from the General Social Survey. See https://gss.norc.org/.
69. Data accessed August 18, 2020, from the Federal Reserve Bank of St. Louis. See https://fred.stlouisfed.org/series/A939RX0Q048SBEA.

70. Perry (2016).

71. Fryar et al. (2016).

72. Data accessed January 11, 2020, from the United Nations Development Programme: See http://hdr.undp.org/en/content/latest -human-development-index-ranking.

73. Merelli (2017).

74. Hedegaard et al. (2018), Tikkanen and Abrams (2020).

75. Lowrey (2014).

76. Data accessed August 19, 2020, from Poverty USA, an initiative of the Catholic Campaign for Human Development. See https://www. povertyusa.org/facts.

77. US Department of Veterans Affairs (2019).

78. Centers for Disease Control and Prevention (2016).

79. Twitter @jasonhickel, posted May 1, 2020.

80. Neilson and Woodward (2020).

81. Data accessed on January 10, 2021, from the Johns Hopkins Coronavirus Resource Center. See https://coronavirus.jhu.edu/.

82. Godoy and Wood (2020).

83. Data accessed on July 31, 2020, from City of New York. See https:// www1.nyc.gov/site/doh/covid/covid-19-data.page.

84. Data accessed on July 30, 2020, from the Johns Hopkins Coronavirus Resource Center. See https://coronavirus.jhu.edu/data/new-cases.

85. Data accessed on July 30, 2020, from the European Centre for Disease Prevention and Control. See https://github.com/owid/covid -19-data/blob/master/public/data/ecdc/new_deaths.csv.

86. Yakusheva et al. (2020).

87. Data accessed on July 30, 2020, from the Federal Reserve Bank of St. Louis. See https://fred.stlouisfed.org/series/ICSA.

88. Data for the March 21 through July 18 reports accessed on July 30, 2020, from the Federal Reserve Bank of St. Louis. See https://fred. stlouisfed.org/series/ICSA.

89. Adamczyk (2020).
90. Dorn (2020).
91. Data accessed on July 30, 2020, from the US Bureau of Economic Analysis. See https://www.bea.gov/news/2020/gross-domestic-product-2nd-quarter-2020-advance-estimate-and-annual-update.
92. Wise (2020).
93. Samuels (2020).
94. Data accessed on July 30, 2020, from the Johns Hopkins Coronavirus Resource Center. See https://coronavirus.jhu.edu/data/new-cases.
95. Data accessed on July 30, 2020, from the European Centre for Disease Prevention and Control. See https://github.com/owid/covid-19-data/blob/master/public/data/ecdc/new_deaths.csv.
96. Aschwanden (2020).
97. Stracqualursi (2020).
98. Data accessed from the COVID-19 Dashboard by the Center for Systems Science and Engineering at Johns Hopkins University. See https://www.arcgis.com/apps/opsdashboard/index.html#/bda7594740fd40299423467b48e9ecf6.
99. Conlen et al. (2021).
100. Packer (2020).
101. Buchwald (2020).

Chapter 6. A New Economics

1. Berry (1999).
2. Bowles and Gintis (2002).
3. Carter and Irons (1991), Oosterbeek et al. (2004).
4. Ostrom et al. (1992).
5. Kahn (1966).
6. Erickson et al. (2004).
7. Wilson (1998).

8. Ibid.

9. Greene et al. (2001).

10. Wikipedia "List of Cognitive Biases," accessed February 3, 2021, at https://en.wikipedia.org/wiki/List_of_cognitive_biases.

11. Buster Benson's "Cognitive Bias Cheat Sheet," accessed February 3, 2021, at https://medium.com/better-humans/cognitive-bias-cheat-sheet-55a472476b18.

12. Albert and Hahnel (1990), Bowles (1998).

13. Spash (2000).

14. Laibson (1997).

15. Gowdy and Erickson (2005).

16. Wright and Erickson (2003).

17. An et al. (2018).

18. Spencer et al. (2018).

19. Gowdy (1998).

20. Groenfeldt (2003).

21. Gowdy (2021).

22. Imhoff et al. (2004).

23. Wilson (1975).

24. Rensberger (1975).

25. Choi (2017).

26. See Tainter (1988) and Diamond (2005).

27. Rifkin (2010).

Chapter 7. A New Economy

1. This quote is from a manuscript titled "Remember This House," about Medgar Evers, Dr. Martin Luther King, Jr., and Malcolm X that Baldwin began but never completed before his death in 1987. Thanks to Carolyn Finney, author of *Black Faces, White Spaces* (2014), for highlighting Baldwin's timeless words in an April 16, 2021, Gund Institute webinar.

2. Thanks to Jolyon Larson for introducing me to this concept and article during an online spring 2021 "COVID class" we taught together on energy system transitions. See Gertz and Kharas (2020).
3. McKibben (2006).
4. OECD (2013).
5. Data accessed on July 27, 2021, from Our World in Data, fossil fuel consumption per capita, 2019. See https://ourworldindata.org/grapher/fossil-fuels-per-capita.
6. See the statement published as a commentary in the *Wall Street Journal* on January 16, 2021, at https://www.wsj.com/articles/economists-statement-on-carbon-dividends-11547682910.
7. Schaeffer (2020).
8. Saez and Zucman (2019).
9. In the latest Gini index data assembled by the World Bank, the United States has the highest level of income inequality among all high-income nations. See https://data.worldbank.org/indicator/SI.POV.GINI.
10. Wilkinson and Pickett (2009).
11. Research on the carbon lock-in phenomenon has been led by Peter Erickson of the Stockholm Environment Institute. See Erickson et al. (2015).
12. Arthur (1989).
13. Coady et al. (2019).
14. Carbon Tracker (2013).
15. Hood (2014).
16. Geels (2005).
17. Lazarus and van Asselt (2018).
18. Gurría (2013).
19. Partanen (2016).
20. From an English synopsis of the book Är *Svensken Människa?* (*Is the Swede Human?*), by Lars Trägårdh and Henrik Berggren. See https://darkwing.uoregon.edu/~scan/berggren.pdf.

21. Bird (2014).
22. Victor (2019).
23. Grubler et al. (2018) (cited in the Hickel and Kallis 2020 review).
24. Hickel et al. (2021).
25. Raworth (2017).
26. Latest data from the National Center for Employee Ownership, accessed August 10, 2021, at https://www.nceo.org/articles/employee-ownership-by-the-numbers.
27. Dudley and Rouen (2021).
28. Venkatesan et al. (2020).
29. Alperovitz (2013).
30. Data accessed November 18, 2021, from MX Technologies. See https://www.mx.com/moneysummit/biggest-us-credit-unions-by-asset-size/.
31. Cororaton (2018).
32. Rubin (2007).
33. McClimon (2019).
34. Thomas and Erickson (2021).
35. Backhouse (2017).
36. See https://wakingthesleepinggiant.com/.
37. Zencey (2012).
38. Rockström et al. (2009).
39. Snow's talk was delivered on May 7, 1959, at the University of Cambridge as part of the influential Rede Lecture series and published as a book later that year. See Snow (1959).
40. Perkins (2019).
41. Svartzman et al. (2020).
42. Brown and Erickson (2016).
43. Berry (1999).

Bibliography

Ackerman, Frank, and Lisa Heinzerling. 2002. "Pricing the Priceless: Cost–Benefit Analysis of Environmental Protection." *University of Pennsylvania Law Review* 150, no. 5: 1553–84.

Adamczyk, Alicia. 2020. "32% of U.S. Households Missed Their July Housing Payments." CNBC, July 8. https://www.cnbc.com/2020/07/08/32-percent-of-us-households-missed-their-july-housing-payments.html.

Adelman, Clifford. 2004. *The Empirical Curriculum: Changes in Postsecondary Course-Taking, 1972–2000.* Washington, DC: US Department of Education.

Agence France-Presse. 2011. "'Indignant' Protests to Go Global on Saturday." *Philippine Daily Inquirer*, October 15. http://newsinfo.inquirer.net/76663/indignant-protests-to-go-global-on-saturday.

Albert, Michael, and Robin Hahnel. 1990. *A Quiet Revolution in Welfare Economics.* Princeton, NJ: Princeton University Press.

Alperovitz, Gar. 2013. *What Then Must We Do? Straight Talk about the Next American Revolution.* White River Junction, VT: Chelsea Green Publishing.

An, Zidong, João Tovar Jalles, and Prakash Loungani. 2018. "How Well Do Economists Forecast Recessions." Working Paper no. 18/39, International Monetary Fund, Washington, DC. https://www.imf.org/en/Publications/WP/Issues/2018/03/05/How-Well-Do-Economists-Forecast-Recessions-45672.

Arthur, W. Brian. 1989. "Competing Technologies, Increasing Returns, and Lock-In by Historical Events." *The Economic Journal* 99, no. 394: 116–31.

Aschwanden, Christie. 2020. "How 'Superspreading' Events Drive Most COVID-19 Spread." *Scientific American*, July 23. https://www.scientificamerican.com/article/how-superspreading-events-drive-most-covid-19-spread1/.

Aspromourgos, Tony. 1986. "On the Origins of the Term 'Neoclassical.'" *Cambridge Journal of Economics* 10, no. 3: 265–70.

Australian Government. 2020. *Annual Climate Statement 2019*. Melbourne: Australia Bureau of Meteorology. http://www.bom.gov.au/climate/current/annual/aus/2019/.

Backhouse, Roger E. 2017. *Founder of Modern Economics: Paul A. Samuelson. Volume 1: Becoming Samuelson, 1915–1948*. Oxford, UK: Oxford University Press.

Bell, David N. F., and David G. Blanchflower. 2011. "Young People and the Great Recession." Discussion Paper no. 5674, Institute for the Study of Labor, Bonn, Germany. http://ftp.iza.org/dp5674.pdf.

Berry, Thomas. 1999. *The Great Work: Our Way into the Future*. New York: Bell Tower.

Bird, Mike. 2014. "Why Socialist Scandinavia Has Some of the Highest Inequality in Europe." *Business Insider*, October 14. https://www.businessinsider.com/why-socialist-scandinavia-has-some-of-the-highest-inequality-in-europe-2014-10.

Bivens, Josh, Elise Gould, Lawrence Mishel, and Heidi Shierholtz. 2014. "Raising America's Pay: Why It's Our Central Economic Policy Challenge." Briefing Paper #378, Economic Policy Institute, Washington, DC. http://www.epi.org/publication/raising-americas-pay.

Blackwelder, Brent, and Herman Daly. 2014. "Remembering Robert Goodland." *The Daly News*, January 22. https://steadystate.org/remembering-robert-goodland/.

Blasko, Andrew. 2004. *Reagan and Heritage: A Unique Partnership*. Washington, DC: The Heritage Foundation. https://www.heritage.org/conservatism/commentary/reagan-and-heritage-unique-partnership.

Blatner, David. 2012. *Spectrums: Our Mind-Boggling Universe from Infinitesimal to Infinity*. New York: Bloomsbury.

Bottomore, Tom. 1991. "Economism." In Tom Bottomore, Lawrence Harris, V. G. Kiernan, and Ralph Miliband, eds. *A Dictionary of Marxist Thought*, 2nd ed. Oxford, UK: Blackwell.

Bowles, Samuel. 1998. "Endogenous Preferences: The Cultural Consequences of Markets and Other Economic Institutions." *Journal of Economic Literature* 36: 75–111.

Bowles, Samuel, and Herbert Gintis. 2002. "Homo reciprocans." *Nature* 415: 125–27.

British Petroleum. 2019. *BP Statistical Review of World Energy 2019*, 68th ed. London: BP. https://www.bp.com/content/dam/bp/business-sites/en/global/corporate/pdfs/energy-economics/statistical-review/bp-stats-review-2019-full-report.pdf.

Brown, Peter G., and Jon D. Erickson. 2016. "How Higher Education Imperils the Future: An Urgent Call for Action." *Balance* 2: 42–48.

Buchwald, Elisabeth. 2020. "Why Do So Many Americans Refuse to Wear Face Masks? Politics Is Part of It—But Only Part." *MarketWatch*, June 28. https://www.marketwatch.com/story/why-do-so-many-americans-refuse-to-wear-face-masks-it-may-have-nothing-to-do-with-politics-2020-06-16.

Bureau of Economic Analysis. 2000. "GDP: One of the Great Inventions of the 20th Century." *Survey of Current Business* 80: 6–9. https://www.bea.gov/scb/account_articles/general/0100od/maintext.htm.

Byrne, John A. 2014. "Why the MBA Has Become the Most Popular Master's Degree in the US." *Fortune*, May 13. http://fortune.com/2014/05/31/mba-popular-masters-degree/.

Camilo, Mora, Derek P. Tittensor, Sina Adl, Alastair G. B. Simpson, and Boris Worm. 2011. "How Many Species Are There on Earth and in the Ocean?" *PLoS Biology* 9, no. 8: e1001127.

Carbon Tracker. 2013. *Unburnable Carbon 2013: Wasted Capital and Stranded Assets.* London: Carbon Tracker.

Carlin, Paul S., and Robert Sandy. 1991. "Estimating the Implicit Value of a Young Child's Life." *Southern Economic Journal* 58, no. 1: 186–202.

Carter, John R., and Michael D. Irons. 1991. "Are Economists Different, and If So, Why?" *Journal of Economic Perspectives* 5, no. 2: 171–77.

Centers for Disease Control and Prevention. 2016. "Sexual Identity, Sex of Sexual Contacts, and Health-Related Behaviors among Students in Grades 9–12: United States and Selected Sites, 2015." *Morbidity and Mortality Weekly Report* 65, no. 9: 1–202. https://www.cdc.gov/mmwr/volumes/65/ss/pdfs/ss6509.pdf.

Chang, Ha-Joon. 2014. *Economics: The User's Guide.* New York: Bloomsbury Press.

Choi, Charles Q. 2017. "Fossil Reveals What Last Common Ancestor of Humans and Apes Looked Liked." [sic] *Scientific American,* August 10. https://www.scientificamerican.com/article/fossil-reveals-what-last-common-ancestor-of-humans-and-apes-looked-liked/.

Christian, David. 2004. *Maps of Time: An Introduction to Big History.* Berkeley: University of California Press.

Coady, David, Ian Parry, Nghia-Piotr Le, and Baoping Shang. 2019. "Global Fossil Fuel Subsidies Remain Large: An Update Based on Country-Level Estimates." Working Paper no. 19/89, International Monetary Fund, Washington, DC. https://www.imf.org/en/Publications/WP/Issues/2019/05/02/Global-Fossil-Fuel-Subsidies-Remain-Large-An-Update-Based-on-Country-Level-Estimates-46509.

Cohan, Adam. 2009. "The First 100 Days." *Time,* June 24. http://content.time.com/time/specials/packages/article/0,28804,1906802_1906838_1906979-1,00.html.

Colander, David. 2005. "The Making of an Economist Redux." *The Journal of Economic Perspectives* 19, no. 1: 175–98.

Conlen, Matthew, John Keefe, Lauren Leatherby, and Charlie Smart. 2021. "How Full Are Hospital I.C.U.s Near You?" *The New York Times*, January 11. https://www.nytimes.com/interactive/2020/us/covid-hospitals-near-you.html.

Cororaton, Anna. 2018. "The Impact of Objectives on Firm Decisions: Bank and Credit Union Lending in the Great Recession." SMU Cox School of Business Research Paper no. 18-36. https://papers.ssrn.com/sol3/papers.cfm?abstract_id=3281376#.

Costanza, Robert, Ralph d'Arge, Rudolf de Groot, Stephen Farber, Monica Grasso, Bruce Hannon, Karin Limburg, Shahid Naeem, Robert V. O'Neill, Jose Paruelo, Robert G. Raskin, and Marjan van den Belt. 1997. "The Value of the World's Ecosystem Services and Natural Capital." *Nature* 387, no. 6630: 253–60.

Cotula, Lorenzo. 2012. "The International Political Economy of the Global Land Rush: A Critical Appraisal of Trends, Scale, Geography and Drivers." *Journal of Peasant Studies* 39, no. 3–4: 649–80.

Covington, Sally. 1997. *Moving a Public Policy Agenda: The Strategic Philanthropy of Conservative Foundations*. Washington, DC: National Committee for Responsive Philanthropy.

Cropper, Maureen L., and Wallace E. Oates. 1992. "Environmental Economics: A Survey." *Journal of Economic Literature* 30, no. 2: 675–740.

Daggett, Stephen. 2010. *Cost of Major U.S. Wars*. Washington, DC: Congressional Research Service. https://fas.org/sgp/crs/natsec/RS22926.pdf.

Daly, Herman E. 1977. *Steady-State Economics*. San Francisco: W.H. Freeman.

Daly, Herman E. 1995. "On Nicholas Georgescu-Roegen's Contributions to Economics: An Obituary Essay." *Ecological Economics* 13, no. 3: 149–54.

Daly, Herman E. 1996. *Beyond Growth: The Economics of Sustainable Development*. Boston: Beacon Press.

Daly, Herman E. 2000. "Why Smart People Make Dumb Mistakes." *Ecological Economics* 34, no. 1: 1–2.

Daly, Herman E. 2008. "Frugality First." In Luk Bouckaert, Hendrik Opdebeeck, and László Zsolnai, eds. *Frugality: Rebalancing Material and Spiritual Values in Economic Life*. Oxford, UK: Peter Lang Academic Publishers.

de la Vega, Elwyn, Thomas B. Chalk, Paul A. Wilson, Ratna Priya Bysani, and Gavin L. Foster. 2020. "Atmospheric CO_2 during the Mid-Piacenzian Warm Period and the M2 Glaciation." *Scientific Reports* 10: 11002.

DelReal, Jose A. 2011. "Students Walk Out of Ec 10 in Solidarity with 'Occupy.'" *The Harvard Crimson*, November 2. http://www.the-crimson.com/article/2011/11/2/mankiw-walkout-economics-10/.

Desilver, Drew. 2018. "For Most U.S. Workers, Real Wages Have Barely Budged in Decades." Fact Tank, Pew Research Center, August 7. https://www.pewresearch.org/fact-tank/2018/08/07/for-most-us-workers-real-wages-have-barely-budged-for-decades/.

des Rosiers, Jared. 2014. "Exemption Process under the Endangered Species Act: How the God Squad Works and Why." *Notre Dame Law Review* 66: 825–62.

Diamond, Jared. 2005. *Collapse: How Societies Choose to Fail or Succeed*. New York: Viking Penguin.

Dorn, Stan. 2020. "The COVID-19 Pandemic and Resulting Economic Crash Have Caused the Greatest Health Insurance Losses in American History." Families USA, July 13. https://www.familiesusa.org/resources/the-covid-19-pandemic-and-resulting-economic-crash-have-caused-the-greatest-health-insurance-losses-in-american-history/.

Dowie, Mark. 2002. "Learning from the Right." *The New York Times*, July 6. https://www.nytimes.com/2002/07/06/opinion/learning-from-the-right-wing.html.

Downey, Kristin. 2009. *The Woman behind the New Deal: The Life and Legacy of Frances Perkins*. New York: Anchor Books.

Dudley, Thomas, and Ethan Rouen. 2021. "The Big Benefits of Employee Ownership." *Harvard Business Review*, May 13.

Edwards, Lee. 1997. *The Power of Ideas: The Heritage Foundation at 25 Years.* Ottawa, IL: Jameson Books.

Erickson, Jon D. 1993. "From Ecology to Economics: The Case against CO_2 Fertilization." *Ecological Economics* 8: 157–75.

Erickson, Jon D., Karin Limburg, John Gowdy, Karen Stainbrook, Audra Nowosielski, Caroline Hermans, and John Polimeni. 2004. "An Ecological Economic Model for Integrated Scenario Analysis: Anticipating Change in the Hudson River Watershed." In Randall J. F. Bruins and Matthew T. Heberling, eds. *Economics and Ecological Risk Assessment: Applications to Watershed Management.* Boca Raton, FL: CRC Press.

Erickson, Peter, Sivan Kartha, Michael Lazarus, and Kevin Tempest. 2015. "Assessing Carbon Lock-in." *Environmental Research Letters* 10, no. 8: 084023.

Fan, Jing-Li, Xin Pan, and Jia-Quan Li. 2017. "Production-Based and Consumption-Based CO_2 Transfers among Major Economies: A Flow Chart Analysis." *Energy Procedia* 105: 3499–506.

Finney, Carolyn. 2014. *Black Faces, White Spaces: Reimagining the Relationship of African Americans to the Great Outdoors.* Chapel Hill: UNC Press.

Fischer, Karin. 2009. "The Influence of Neoliberals in Chile before, during, and after Pinochet." In Philip Mirowski and Dieter Plehwe, eds. *The Road from Mont Pèlerin: The Making of the Neoliberal Thought Collective.* Cambridge, MA: Harvard University Press.

Fourcade, Marion, et al. 2015. "The Superiority of Economists." *The Journal of Economic Perspectives* 29, no. 1: 89–113.

Fox, Mairi-Jane V., and Jon D. Erickson. 2018. "Genuine Economic Progress in the United States: A Fifty State Study and Comparative Assessment." *Ecological Economics* 147: 29–35.

Frank, Robert H. 2008. *The Economic Naturalist: Why Economics Explains Almost Everything.* London: Virgin.

Frankfurt School, UNEP Collaborating Centre for Climate and Sustainable Energy Finance. 2019. *Global Trends in Renewable Energy*

Investment 2019. Frankfurt, Germany: Frankfurt School of Finance and Management. https://www.unenvironment.org/resources/report /global-trends-renewable-energy-investment-2019.

Frumhoff, Peter. 2014. "Global Warming Fact: More than Half of All Industrial CO_2 Pollution Has Been Emitted Since 1988." Union of Concerned Scientists Blog, December 15. https://blog.ucsusa.org/ peter-frumhoff/global-warming-fact-co2-emissions-since-1988-764.

Fryar, Cheryl D., Margaret D. Carroll, and Cynthia L. Ogden. 2016. "Prevalence of Overweight, Obesity, and Extreme Obesity among Adults Aged 20 and Over: United States, 1960–1962 through 2013–2014." Health E-Stats, National Center for Health Statistics, July. https://www.cdc.gov/nchs/data/hestat/obesity_adult_13_14/ obesity_adult_13_14.htm.

Funtowicz, Silvio, and Jerome R. Ravetz. 1994. "The Worth of a Songbird: Ecological Economics as a Post-Normal Science." *Ecological Economics* 10, no. 3: 197–207.

Gaffney, Mason, and Fred Harrison. 1994. *The Corruption of Economics*. London: Shepheard-Walwyn Publishers.

Gallup-Healthways. 2014. *State of Global Well-Being: 2014 Country Well-Being Rankings*. Washington, DC: Gallup. https://wellbeingin-dex.sharecare.com/wp-content/uploads/2017/12/Country-Well-Be ing-Rankings-2015.pdf.

Geels, Frank W. 2005. "The Dynamics of Transitions in Socio-Technical Systems: A Multi-Level Analysis of the Transition Pathway from Horse-Drawn Carriages to Automobiles (1860–1930)." *Technology Analysis and Strategic Management* 17, no. 4: 445–76.

Geiger, George Raymond. 1933. *The Philosophy of Henry George*. New York: Macmillan. http://lvtfan.typepad.com/lvtfans_blog/2015/07/ john-deweys-foreword-to-geigers-the-philosophy-of-henry-george. html.

George, Henry. 1868. "What the Railroad Will Bring Us." *The Overland Monthly* 1, no. 4: 297–306. https://quod.lib.umich.edu/m/moajrnl/ ahj1472.1-01.004/293:1.

George, Henry. 1871. *Our Land and Land Policy, National and State.* San Francisco, CA: White and Bauer. https://hollis.harvard.edu/ primo-explore/fulldisplay/01HVD_ALMA211860278670003941/ HVD.

George, Henry. 1879. *Progress and Poverty: An Inquiry into the Cause of Industrial Depressions and of Increase of Want with Increase of Wealth, the Remedy.* London: K. Paul, Trench and Company.

George, Henry. 1905. *Progress and Poverty: An Inquiry into the Cause of Industrial Depressions and of Increase of Want with Increase of Wealth, the Remedy* (25th anniversary edition). Garden City, NY: Doubleday.

Georgescu-Roegen, Nicholas. 1966. *Analytical Economics: Issues and Problems.* Cambridge, MA: Harvard University Press.

Gertz, Geoffrey, and Homi Kharas. 2020. "Radical Pragmatism: Policy-Making after COVID." *Democracy*, October 16.

Godoy, Maria, and Daniel Wood. 2020. "What Do Coronavirus Racial Disparities Look Like State by State?" National Public Radio, May 30. https://www.npr.org/sections/health-shots/2020/05/30/86541 3079/what-do-coronavirus-racial-disparities-look-like-state-by-state.

Goodland, Robert, Herman Daly, and Salah El Serafy, eds. 1991. "Environmentally Sustainable Economic Development Building on Brundtland." Environment Working Paper 46, World Bank, Washington, DC. http://documents1.worldbank.org/curated/en /332821467989482335/pdf/multi-page.pdf.

Goodwin, Doris. 2001. "The Way We Won: America's Economic Break-through during World War II." *The American Prospect*, December 19. http://prospect.org/article/way-we-won-americas-economic-break through-during-world-war-ii.

Gowdy, John M., ed. 1998. *Limited Wants, Unlimited Means: A Reader on Hunter–Gatherer Economics and the Environment.* Washington, DC: Island Press.

Gowdy, John M. 2021. *Ultrasocial: The Evolution of Human Nature and the Quest for a Sustainable Future.* Cambridge, UK: Cambridge University Press.

Gowdy, John M., and Jon D. Erickson. 2005. "The Approach of Ecological Economics." *Cambridge Journal of Economics* 29, no. 2: 207–22.

Greene, Joshua D., R. Brian Sommerville, Leigh E. Nystrom, John M. Darley, and Jonathan D. Cohen. 2001. "An fMRI Investigation of Emotional Engagement in Moral Judgment." *Science* 293, no. 5537: 2105–8.

Groenfeldt, David. 2003. "The Future of Indigenous Values: Cultural Relativism in the Face of Economic Development." *Futures* 35, no. 9: 917–29.

Gross, Neil, and Solon Simmons. 2007. "The Social and Political Views of American Professors." Working Paper, Harvard University Symposium on Professors and Their Politics.

Grubler, Arnulf, Charlie Wilson, Nuno Bento, Benigna Boza Kiss, Volker Krey, David McCollum, Narasimha D. Rao, Keywan Riahi, Joeri Rogelj, Simon De Stercke, Jonathan Cullen, Stefan Frank, Oliver Fricko, Fei Guo, Mat Gidden, Petr Havlík, Daniel Huppmann, Gregor Kiesewetter, Peter Rafaj, Wolfgang Schoepp, and Hugo Valin. 2018. "A Low Energy Demand Scenario for Meeting the 1.5°C Target and Sustainable Development Goals without Negative Emissions Technologies." *Nature Energy* 3: 515–27.

Gunnar, Myrdal. 1977. "The Nobel Prize in Economic Science." *Challenge* 20, no. 1: 50–52.

Guo, Jeff. 2015. "The Protestors Who Are Trying to Upend the Fantasy World of Economics." *The Washington Post*, January 5. https://www.washingtonpost.com/news/storyline/wp/2015/01/05/the-protesters-who-are-trying-to-upend-the-fantasy-world-of-economics/.

Gurría, Ángel. 2013. "The Climate Challenge: Achieving Zero Emissions." Lecture by the OECD Secretary-General, London, UK, October 9. http://www.oecd.org/about/secretary-general/the-climate-challenge-achievingzero-emissions.htm.

Hacker, Jacob S., and Paul Pierson. 2010. *Winner-Take-All Politics*. New York: Simon and Schuster.

Han, Shin-Kap. 2003. "Tribal Regimes in Academia: A Comparative Analysis of Market Structure across Disciplines." *Social Networks* 25, no. 3: 251–80.

Harvard Political Review. 2011. "An Open Letter to Greg Mankiw." *Harvard Political Review*, November 2. http://harvardpolitics.com/harvard/an-open-letter-to-greg-mankiw/.

Heck, Vera, Dieter Gerten, Wolfgang Lucht, and Alexander Popp. 2018. "Biomass-Based Negative Emissions Difficult to Reconcile with Planetary Boundaries." *Nature Climate Change* 8: 151–55.

Hedegaard, Holly, Sally C. Curtin, and Margaret Warner. 2018. "Suicide Mortality in the United States, 1999–2017." Data Brief no. 330, National Center for Health Statistics, November. https://www.cdc.gov/nchs/products/databriefs/db330.htm.

Herbert, Robert F. 1979. "Marshall: A Professional Economist Guards the Purity of His Discipline." In Robert V. Andelson, ed. *Critics of Henry George: A Centenary Appraisal of Their Strictures on "Progress and Poverty."* Plainsboro, NJ: Associated University Press (reprinted in the *American Journal of Economics and Sociology* 63, no. 2, 2004).

Hess, Abigail. 2018. "Here's How Much More Women Could Earn if Household Chores Were Compensated." CNBC, April 10. https://www.cnbc.com/2018/04/10/heres-what-women-could-earn-if-household-chores-were-compensated.html.

Hickel, Jason, Paul Brockway, Giorgos Kallis, Lorenz Keyßer, Manfred Lenzen, Aljoša Slameršak, Julia Steinberger, and Diana Ürge-Vorsatz. 2021. "Urgent Need for Post-Growth Climate Mitigation Scenarios." *Nature Energy*, August 4.

Hickel, Jason, and Giorgos Kallis. 2020. "Is Green Growth Possible?" *New Political Economy* 25, no. 4: 469–86.

Hodgson, Geoffrey M. 2002. *How Economics Forgot History: The Problem of Historical Specificity in Social Science*. Abingdon, UK: Routledge.

Holton, Gerald, and Yehuda Elkana. 1997. *Albert Einstein, Historical and Cultural Perspectives: The Centennial Symposium in Jerusalem*. Princeton, NJ: Princeton University Press.

Hood, Christina. 2014. "Policies and Actions to 'Unlock' High-Emissions Assets: The Example of Coal-Fired Power Generation." In International Energy Agency, *Energy, Climate Change and Environment: 2014 Insights*. Paris: International Energy Agency.

Huffington, Ariana. 2010. "Guns vs. Butter 2010." *The Huffington Post*, May 25. http://www.huffingtonpost.com/arianna-huffington/guns-vs-butter-2010_b_548620.html.

Imhoff, Marc L., Lahouari Bounoua, Taylor Ricketts, Colby Loucks, Robert Harriss, and William T. Lawrence. 2004. "Global Patterns in Human Consumption of Net Primary Production." *Nature* 429, no. 6994: 870–73.

Inman, Phillip. 2013. "Economics Students Aim to Tear Up Free-Market Syllabus." *The Guardian*, October 24. https://www.theguardian.com/business/2013/oct/24/students-post-crash-economics.

Inman, Phillip. 2014. "Economics Students Call for Shakeup of the Way Their Subject Is Taught." *The Guardian*, May 4. https://www.theguardian.com/education/2014/may/04/economics-students-overhaul-subject-teaching.

Intergovernmental Panel on Climate Change. 2000. *Emissions Scenarios: A Special Report of Working Group III of the Intergovernmental Panel on Climate Change*. Cambridge, UK: Cambridge University Press.

Intergovernmental Panel on Climate Change. 2014. *Climate Change 2014: Synthesis Report. Contribution of Working Groups I, II and III to the Fifth Assessment Report of the Intergovernmental Panel on Climate Change*. Geneva, Switzerland: IPCC.

Intergovernmental Panel on Climate Change. 2018. *Global Warming of 1.5°C: An IPCC Special Report*. Geneva, Switzerland: IPCC.

Intergovernmental Science-Policy Platform on Biodiversity and Ecosystem Services. 2019. *Global Assessment Report on Biodiversity and Ecosystem Services of the Intergovernmental Science-Policy Platform on Biodiversity and Ecosystem Services*. Bonn, Germany: IPBES Secretariat. https://ipbes.net/global-assessment.

International Energy Agency. 2016. *World Energy Investment 2016*. Paris, France: IEA. https://www.iea.org/reports/world-energy-invest ment-2016.

International Energy Agency. 2017. *World Energy Outlook 2017*. Paris, France: IEA. https://www.iea.org/reports/world-energy-out look-2017.

International Renewable Energy Agency. 2018. *Global Energy Transformation: A Roadmap to 2050*. Abu Dhabi, UAE: IREA.

Johnson, David. 2017. "These Are the Most Productive Countries in the World." *Time*, January 4. https://time.com/4621185/worker -productivity-countries/.

Johnson, Elizabeth, and Donald Moggridge, eds. 1978. *The Collected Writings of John Maynard Keynes*. London: Royal Economic Society.

Kahn, Alfred E. 1966. "The Tyranny of Small Decisions: Market Failures, Imperfections, and the Limits of Economics." *Kyklos* 19, no. 1: 23–47.

Kaneda, Toshiko, and Carl Haub. 2020. "How Many People Ever Lived on Earth." Population Reference Bureau, Washington, DC, January 20. https://www.prb.org/howmanypeoplehaveeverlivedonearth/.

Katz, Alyssa. 2015. *The Influence Machine: The US Chamber of Commerce and the Corporate Capture of American Life*. New York: Spiegel and Grau.

Kennedy, Robert C. 1886. "Reform—By George." *Harp Week*, Cartoon of the Day. https://www.harpweek.com/09cartoon/BrowseByDate-Cartoon.asp?Month=October&Date=23.

Kenny, R., Colin Law, and Joshua M. Pearce. 2010. "Towards Real Energy Economics: Energy Policy Driven by Life-Cycle Carbon Emission." *Energy Policy* 38, no. 4: 1969–78.

Keynes, John Maynard. 1919. *The Economic Consequences of the Peace*. London: Macmillan.

Keynes, John Maynard. 1932. *Essays in Persuasion*. London: MacMillan.

Keynes, John Maynard. 1933. "An Open Letter to President Roosevelt." *The New York Times*, December 31. http://www.la.utexas.edu/users/ hcleaver/368/368KeynesOpenLetFDRtable.pdf.

Keynes, John Maynard. 1936. *The General Theory of Employment, Interest and Money*. London: Macmillan.

Konczal, Michael. 2014. "Frenzied Financialization." *Washington Monthly*, November/December. http://www.washingtonmonthly.com/magazine/novemberdecember_2014/features/frenzied_financialization052714.php.

Koppl, Roger. 1992. "Price Theory as Physics: The Cartesian Influence in Walras." *Methodus*, December (now the *Journal of Economic Methodology*).

Kramer, Bruce M. 1978. "The 1977 Clean Air Act Amendments: A Tactical Retreat from the Technology-Forcing Strategy?" *Urban Law Annual* 15: 103–57.

Kubiszewski, Ida, Robert Costanza, Carol Franco, Philip Lawn, John Talberth, Tim Jackson, and Camille Aylmer. 2013. "Beyond GDP: Measuring and Achieving Global Genuine Progress." *Ecological Economics* 93: 57–68.

LaFeber, Walter. 2002. *America, Russia, and the Cold War, 1945–2002*. Ithaca, NY: Cornell University Press.

Laibson, David. 1997. "Golden Eggs and Hyperbolic Discounting." *Quarterly Journal of Economics* 112: 443–77.

Latson, Jennifer. 2014. "Walt Disney, Ronald Reagan and the Fear of Hollywood Communism." *Time*, October 20. https://time.com/3513597/huac-hollywood-hearings/.

Lazarus, Michael, and Harro van Asselt. "Fossil Fuel Supply and Climate Policy: Exploring the Road Less Taken." *Climatic Change* 150: 1–13.

Lazear, Edward P. 2000. "Economic Imperialism." *The Quarterly Journal of Economics* 115, no. 1: 99–146.

Le Guin, Ursula K. 1979. *The Language of the Night: Essays on Fantasy and Science Fiction*. New York: Ultramarine Publishing.

Levitt, Steven D., and Stephen J. Dubner. 2005. *Freakonomics: A Rogue Economist Explores the Hidden Side of Everything*. New York: William Morrow.

Lindsey, Rebecca. 2019. "2019 Arctic Report Card: Melt Season on Greenland Ice Sheet Rivals Record for Area and Duration." *Climate-Watch Magazine*, December 10. https://www.climate.gov/news-features/featured-images/2019-arctic-report-card-melt-season-greenland-ice-sheet-rivals-record.

Livingston, Gretchen, and Deja Thomas. 2019. "Among 41 Countries, Only U.S. Lacks Paid Parental Leave." Fact Tank, Pew Research Center, December 16. https://www.pewresearch.org/fact-tank/2019/12/16/u-s-lacks-mandated-paid-parental-leave/.

Locke, John. 2009. *Two Treatises of Government: A Translation into Modern English*. Manchester, UK: Industrial Systems Research (originally published in 1689).

Lowrey, Annie. 2014. "Income Gap, Meet the Longevity Gap." *The New York Times*, March 15.

Mankiw, N. Gregory. 2013. "Defending the One Percent." *Journal of Economic Perspectives* 27, no. 3: 21–34.

Marshall, Alfred. 1969. "Three Lectures on Progress and Poverty by Alfred Marshall." *The Journal of Law and Economics* 12, no. 1: 184–226.

Masters, Jeff. 2020. "The Top 10 Weather and Climate Stories of 2019." *Scientific American*, January 3. https://blogs.scientificamerican.com/eye-of-the-storm/the-top-10-weather-and-climate-stories-of-2019/.

Mbaye, Samba, and Marialuz Moreno Badia. 2019. "New Data on Global Debt." *IMF Blog*, January 2. https://blogs.imf.org/2019/01/02/new-data-on-global-debt/.

McCarthy, Niall. 2017. "American Workers Get the Short End on Vacation Days." *Forbes*, January 26. https://www.forbes.com/sites/niallmccarthy/2017/06/26/american-workers-have-a-miserable-vacation-allowance-infographic/?sh=31ffd965126d.

McClimon, Timothy J. 2019. "The Nonprofit 10 Percent." *Forbes*, May 14. https://www.forbes.com/sites/timothyjmcclimon/2019/03/14/the-nonprofit-10-percent/?sh=5543d9625f29.

McGrath, Matt. 2021. "Climate Change: IPCC Report Is 'Code Red for Humanity'." *BBC News*, August 9.

McKenna, Kevin. 2013. "Scotland Has the Most Inequitable Land Ownership in the West. Why?" *The Guardian*, August 10. https://www.theguardian.com/uk-news/2013/aug/10/scotland-land-rights.

McKibben, Bill. 2006. "Welcome to the Climate Crisis: How to Tell Whether a Candidate Is Serious about Combating Global Warming." *The Washington Post*, May 27.

McPherson, Harry C., Jr. 2000. "Walter Lippmann and the American Century." *Foreign Affairs*, Fall.

Meadows, Donella. 2000. "Leverage Points: Places to Intervene in a System." *Solutions* 1, no. 1: 41–49.

Meadows, Donella H., Dennis L. Meadows, and Jørgen Randers. 1992. *Beyond the Limits*. Post Mills, VT: Chelsea Green Publishing.

Mellon, Andrew W. 1924. *Taxation: The People's Business*. New York: Macmillan.

Merchant, Carolyn. 2013. *Reinventing Eden: The Fate of Nature in Western Culture*. New York: Routledge.

Merelli, Annalisa. 2017. "The US Has a Lot of Money, but It Does Not Look Like a Developed Country." *Quartz*, March 10. https://qz.com/879092/the-us-doesnt-look-like-a-developed-country/.

Mill, John Stuart. 1857. *Principles of Political Economy*, Volume 2. London: John W. Parker.

Moggridge, Donald E. 1992. *Maynard Keynes: An Economist's Biography*. Abingdon, UK: Routledge.

Moloney, Anastasia. 2019. "Hunger Driving Migration in Drought-Hit Central America: U.N." *Reuters*, August 14. https://www.reuters.com/article/us-central-america-drought-migration/hunger-driving-migration-in-drought-hit-central-america-un-idUSKCN1V423J.

Monbiot, George. 2016. "Neoliberalism: The Ideology at the Root of All Our Problems." *The Guardian*, April 15. https://www.theguardian.com/books/2016/apr/15/neoliberalism-ideology-problem-george-monbiot.

Morgenstern, Richard D. 1997. "The Legal and Institutional Setting for Economic Analysis at EPA." In Richard D. Morgenstern, ed.

Economic Analyses at EPA: Assessing Regulatory Impact. Abingdon, UK: Routledge.

National Center for Education Statistics. 2015. *Digest of Education Statistics, 2013*. NCES 2015-011. Washington, DC: US Department of Education.

Neilson, Susie, and Aylin Woodward. 2020. "A Comprehensive Timeline of the Coronavirus Pandemic at 1 Year, from China's First Case to the Present." *Business Insider*, December 24. https://www.businessinsider.com/coronavirus-pandemic-timeline-history-major-events-2020-3.

Norgaard, Richard. 2015. "The Church of Economism and Its Discontents." Great Transition Initiative, December. https://greattransition.org/publication/the-church-of-economism-and-its-discontents.

Obama, Barack. 2017. "The Irreversible Momentum of Clean Energy." *Science* 355, no. 6321: 126–29.

Oosterbeek, Hessel, Randolph Sloof, and Gijs Van De Kuilen. 2004. "Cultural Differences in Ultimatum Game Experiments: Evidence from a Meta-Analysis." *Experimental Economics* 7, no. 2: 171–88.

Organisation for Economic Co-operation and Development (OECD). 2013. *Taxing Energy Use: A Graphical Analysis*. Paris: OECD Publishing. https://www.oecd.org/tax/tax-policy/taxingenergyuse.htm.

Ostrom, Elinor, James Walker, and Roy Gardner. 1992. "Covenants with and without a Sword: Self-governance Is Possible." *American Political Science Review* 86, no. 2: 404–17.

Packer, George. 2020. "We Are Living in a Failed State." *The Atlantic*, June. https://www.theatlantic.com/magazine/archive/2020/06/underlying-conditions/610261/.

Partanen, Anu. 2016. *The Nordic Theory of Everything: In Search of a Better Life*. New York: HarperCollins.

Perkins, Patricia E., ed. 2019. *Local Activism for Global Climate Justice: The Great Lakes Watershed*. London: Routledge.

Perry, Mark J. 2016. "New US Homes Today Are 1,000 Square Feet Larger than in 1973 and Living Space per Person Has Nearly Doubled." American Enterprise Institute, June 5. https://www.aei.org/

carpe-diem/new-us-homes-today-are-1000-square-feet-larger-than-in-1973-and-living-space-per-person-has-nearly-doubled/.

Peters, Glen. 2017. "Does the Carbon Budget Mean the End of Fossil Fuels?" Climate News, Center for International Climate Research, Oslo, June 4. https://www.cicero.oslo.no/en/posts/klima/does-the-carbon-budget-mean-the-end-of-fossil-fuels.

Peterson-Withorn, Chase. 2021. "How Much Money America's Billionaires Have Made during the Covid-19 Pandemic." *Forbes*, April 30.

Pew Research Center. 2015. *Raising Kids and Running a Household: How Working Parents Share the Load*. Washington, DC: Pew Research Center. https://www.pewsocialtrends.org/2015/11/04/raising-kids-and-running-a-household-how-working-parents-share-the-load/.

Pigou, Arthur C. 1920. *The Economics of Welfare*. London: Macmillan.

Plehwe, Dieter. 2009. "Introduction." In Philip Mirowski and Dieter Plehwe, eds. *The Road from Mont Pèlerin: The Making of the Neoliberal Thought Collective*. Cambridge, MA: Harvard University Press.

Rampell, Catherine. 2011. "Out of Harvard, and into Finance." *The New York Times*, December 21. https://economix.blogs.nytimes.com/2011/12/21/out-of-harvard-and-into-finance/.

Raworth, Kate. 2017. *Doughnut Economics: Seven Ways to Think Like a 21st Century Economist*. White River Junction, VT: Chelsea Green Publishing.

Read, Richard. 2015. "A $280 College Textbook Busts Budgets, but Harvard Author Gregory Mankiw Defends Royalties." *The Oregonian*, February 12. http://www.oregonlive.com/education/index.ssf/2015/02/a_280_college_textbook_busts_b.html.

Readfearn, Graham. 2020. "Bushfire Crisis Conditions Eight Times More Likely under 2C Warming, Analysis Shows." *The Guardian*, March 4. https://www.theguardian.com/australia-news/2020/mar/05/bushfire-crisis-conditions-eight-times-more-likely-under-2c-warming-analysis-shows.

Reel, Monte and J. Y. Smith. 2006. "A Chilean Dictator's Dark Legacy." *The Washington Post*, December 11. https://www.washingtonpost.com/wp-dyn/content/article/2006/12/10/AR2006121000302.html.

Reich, Robert B. 2011. "The Limping Middle Class." *The New York Times*, September 3. http://www.nytimes.com/2011/09/04/opinion /sunday/jobs-will-follow-a-strengthening-of-the-middle-class.html.

Rensberger, Boyce. 1975. "Sociobiology: Updating Darwin on Behavior." *The New York Times*, May 28. https://www.nytimes.com /1975/05/28/archives/sociobiology-updating-darwin-on-behavior -sociobiology-integration.html.

Rice, Doyle. 2020. "Over 1 Billion Animals Feared Dead in Australian Wildfires, Experts Say." *USA Today*, January 8. https://www.usato day.com/story/news/world/2020/01/08/australian-fires-over-1- billion-animals-feared-dead-experts-say/2845084001/.

Rifkin, Jeremy. 2010. *The Empathic Civilization: The Race to Global Consciousness in a World in Crisis*. New York: Jeremy P. Tarcher, Inc.

Ritchie, Hannah. 2019. "Who Has Contributed Most to Global CO_2 Emissions?" Our World in Data, October 1. https://ourworldin data.org/contributed-most-global-co2.

Rockström, Johan, Will Steffen, Kevin Noone, Åsa Persson, F. Stuart Chapin III, Eric F. Lambin, Timothy M. Lenton, Marten Scheffer, Carl Folke, Hans Joachim Schellnhuber, Björn Nykvist, Cynthia A. de Wit, Terry Hughes, Sander van der Leeuw, Henning Rodhe, Sverker Sörlin, Peter K. Snyder, Robert Costanza, Uno Svedin, Malin Falkenmark, Louise Karlberg, Robert W. Corell, Victoria J. Fabry, James Hansen, Brian Walker, Diana Liverman, Katherine Richardson, Paul Crutzen, and Jonathan A. Foley 2009. "A Safe Operating Space for Humanity." *Nature* 461, no. 7263: 472–75.

Roose, Kevin. 2011. "At Top Colleges, Anti-Wall St. Fervor Complicates Recruiting." *The New York Times*, November 28. https:// dealbook.nytimes.com/2011/11/28/at-top-colleges-anti-wall-st-fer vor-complicates-recruiting/.

Røpke, Inge. 2004. "The Early History of Modern Ecological Economics." *Ecological Economics* 50, no. 3–4: 293–314.

Rothman, Lily. 2017. "9 Executive Orders That Changed American History." *Time*, February 6. https://time.com/4655131/executive -orders-history/.

Rubin, Julia Sass, ed. 2007. *Financing Low-Income Communities: Models, Obstacles, and Future Directions.* New York: Russell Sage Foundation.

Saez, Emmanuel, and Gabriel Zucman. 2019. *The Triumph of Injustice: How the Rich Dodge Taxes and How to Make Them Pay.* New York: W.W. Norton.

Sagan, Carl. 1980. *Cosmos.* New York: Random House.

Sagan, Carl. 1997. *Pale Blue Dot: A Vision of the Human Future in Space.* New York: Ballantine Books.

Samuels, Alex. 2020. "Dan Patrick Says 'There Are More Important Things than Living and That's Saving This Country.'" *The Texas Tribune,* April 21. https://www.texastribune.org/2020/04/21/texas-dan-patrick-economy-coronavirus/.

Say, Jean-Baptiste. 1803. *A Treatise on Political Economy; or The Production, Distribution, and Consumption of Wealth* (trans. C. R. Prinsep from the 4th edition of the French, Philadelphia: Lippincott, Grambo & Co., 1855. 4th–5th ed.).

Schaeffer, Katherine. 2020. "6 Facts about Economic Inequality in the U.S." Pew Research Center, February 7. https://www.pewresearch.org/fact-tank/2020/02/07/6-facts-about-economic-inequality-in-the-u-s/.

Schröder, Enno, and Servaas Storm. 2018. "Economic Growth and Carbon Emissions: The Road to 'Hothouse Earth' Is Paved with Good Intentions." Working Paper no. 84. New York: Institute for New Economic Thinking. https://www.ineteconomics.org/uploads/papers/WP_84.pdf.

Schultze, Charles L. 1997. *The Public Use of Private Interest.* Washington, DC: The Brookings Institution. https://www.brookings.edu/book/the-public-use-of-private-interest/.

Schumpeter, Joseph. 1954. *History of Economic Analysis.* London: Psychology Press.

Scottish Government. 2015. *Severe Poverty in Scotland.* Edinburgh: Scottish Government. https://www.gov.scot/publications/severe-poverty-scotland/.

Shabecoff, Philip. 1981. "Reagan Order on Cost-Benefit Analysis Stirs Economics and Political Debate." *The New York Times*, November 7. https://www.nytimes.com/1981/11/07/us/reagan-order-on -cost-benefit-analysis-stirs-economic-and-political-debate.html.

Sheppard, Barry. 2014. "Progress and Poverty: Henry George and Land Reform in Modern Ireland." *The Irish Story*, August 24. http://www .theirishstory.com/2014/08/24/progress-and-poverty-henry-george- and-land-reform-in-modern-ireland/#.WCjadNybH5A.

Shiller, Robert J. 2012. "Spend, Spend, Spend. It's the American Way." *The New York Times*, January 14. https://www.nytimes.com/2012/01/15/ business/consumer-spending-as-an-american-virtue.html.

Sinclair, Upton. 1923. *The Goose-Step: A Study of American Education.* Pasadena, CA: Author.

Skousen, Mark. 1997. "The Perseverance of Paul Samuelson's Economics." *Journal of Economic Perspectives* 11, no. 2): 137–52.

Smith, Charles H. 2015. "Here's Why Labor's Share of GDP Has Been Declining for 40 Years." *Business Insider*, September 22. http://www. businessinsider.com/why-labors-gdp-share-is-on-decline-2015-9.

Snow, Charles Percy. 1959. *The Two Cultures and the Scientific Revolution.* London: Cambridge University Press.

Sonnemaker, Tyler. 2020. "Jeff Bezos Is on Track to Become a Trillionaire by 2026." *Business Insider*, May 14. https://www.businessinsider. com/jeff-bezos-on-track-to-become-trillionaire-by-2026-2020-5.

Spash, Clive L. 2000. "Ecosystems, Contingent Valuation and Ethics: The Case of Wetland Re-creation." *Ecological Economics* 34: 195–215.

Spash, Clive L. 2009. "The New Environmental Pragmatists, Pluralism and Sustainability." *Environmental Values* 18, no. 3: 253–56.

Spencer, Phoebe, Patricia E. Perkins, and Jon D. Erickson. 2018. "Reestablishing Justice as a Pillar of Ecological Economics through Feminist Perspectives." *Ecological Economics* 152: 191–98.

Steffen, Will, Johan Rockström, Katherine Richardson, Timothy M. Lenton, Carl Folke, Diana Liverman, Colin P. Summerhayes, Anthony D. Barnosky, Sarah E. Cornell, Michel Crucifix, Jonathan

F. Donges, Ingo Fetzer, Steven J. Lade, Marten Scheffer, Ricarda Winkelmann, and Hans Joachim Schellnhuber. 2018. "Trajectories of the Earth System in the Anthropocene." *Proceedings of the National Academy of the Sciences* 115, no. 33: 8252–9.

Stracqualursi, Veronica. 2020. "Birx Warns US Is 'in a New Phase' of Coronavirus Pandemic with More Widespread Cases." CNN, August 2. https://www.cnn.com/2020/08/02/politics/birx-corona virus-new-phase-cnntv/index.html.

Stromberg, David B. 1978. "The Endangered Species Act Amendments of 1978: A Step Backwards?" *Boston College Environmental Affairs Law Review* 7, no. 1: 33–42.

Sullivan, J. L., A. Burnham, and M. Wang. 2010. *Energy-Consumption and Carbon-Emission Analysis of Vehicle and Component Manufacturing.* Argonne, IL: Argonne National Laboratory.

Svartzman, Romain, Joseph Ament, David Barmes, Jon D. Erickson, Joshua Farley, Charles Guay-Boutet, and Nicolas Kosoy. 2020. "Money, Interest Rates and Accumulation on a Finite Planet: Revisiting the 'Monetary Growth Imperative' through Institutionalist Approaches." In Robert Costanza, Jon D. Erickson, Joshua Farley, and Ida Kubiszewski, eds. *Sustainable Wellbeing Futures: A Research and Action Agenda for Ecological Economics.* Cheltenham, UK: Edward Elgar.

Tainter, Joseph A. 1988. *The Collapse of Complex Societies.* Cambridge, UK: Cambridge University Press.

Thomas, Austin, and Jon D. Erickson. 2021. "Rethinking the Geography of Energy Transitions: Low Carbon Energy Pathways through Energyshed Design." *Energy Research and Social Science* 74: 101941.

Thompson, Derrick. 2009. "An Interview with Paul Samuelson, Part One." *The Atlantic*, June 17. https://www.theatlantic.com /business/archive/2009/06/an-interview-with-paul-samuelson-part -one/19586/.

Tikkanen, Roosa, and Melinda K. Abrams. 2020. "U.S. Health Care from a Global Perspective, 2019: Higher Spending, Worse Outcomes?" The Commonwealth Fund, January 30. https://www.common

wealthfund.org/publications/issue-briefs/2020/jan/us-health
-care-global-perspective-2019.

Trucost. 2013. *Natural Capital at Risk: The Top 100 Externalities of Business*. London: Trucost. https://www.trucost.com/wp-content/ uploads/2016/04/TEEB-Final-Report-web-SPv2.pdf.

Tucker, Garland. 2012. *High Tide of American Conservatism: Davis, Coolidge, and the 1924 Election*. Austin, TX: Greenleaf Book Group.

Unger, Irwin. 1996. *The Best of Intentions: The Triumphs and Failures of the Great Society Under Kennedy, Johnson, and Nixon*. New York: Doubleday.

United Nations. 1973. *Report of the United Nations Conference on the Human Environment*. New York: United Nations. https://www. un.org/ga/search/view_doc.asp?symbol=A/CONF.48/14/REV.1.

US Department of Veterans Affairs. 2019. *2019 National Veteran Suicide Prevention Annual Report*. Washington, DC: US Department of Veterans Affairs. https://www.mentalhealth.va.gov/docs/data-sheets/2019/2019_National_Veteran_Suicide_Prevention_Annual_Report_508.pdf.

Venkatesan, Madhavi, Jon D. Erickson, and Christine Carmichael. 2020. "Principles of Stakeholder Engagement for Ecological Economics." In Robert Costanza et al., eds. *Sustainable Wellbeing Futures: A Research and Action Agenda for Ecological Economics*, Cheltenham, UK: Edward Elgar.

Victor, Peter. 2019. *Managing without Growth: Slower by Design, Not Disaster*. 2nd ed. Cheltenham, UK: Edward Elgar.

Weisser, Daniel. 2007. "A Guide to Life-Cycle Greenhouse Gas (GHG) Emissions from Electric Supply Technologies." *Energy* 32, no. 9: 1543–59.

Weyl, E. Glen. 2017. "Finance and the Public Good." In Edward L. Glaeser et al., eds. *After the Flood: How the Great Recession Changed Economic Thought*, Chicago: University of Chicago Press, 243–76.

Wilkinson, Richard, and Kate Pickett. 2009. *The Spirit Level: Why Greater Equality Makes Societies Stronger*. Harlow, England: Allen Lane/Penguin Books.

Wilson, Edward O. 1975. *Sociobiology: The New Synthesis.* Cambridge, MA: Harvard University Press.

Wilson, Edward O. 1998. *Consilience: The Unity of Knowledge.* New York: Alfred A. Knopf.

Wise, Justin. 2020. "Kudlow Says US Will Have to Make 'Difficult Tradeoffs' on Coronavirus: 'Cure Can't Be Worse than Disease.'" *The Hill,* March 23. https://thehill.com/homenews/administration /489064-kudlow-says-us-will-have-to-make-difficult-trade-offs-on-coronavirus.

Witters, Dan. 2019. "Hawaii Tops U.S. in Wellbeing for Record 7th Time." *Gallup,* February 27. https://news.gallup.com/poll/247034/ hawaii-tops-wellbeing-record-7th-time.aspx.

World Commission on Environment and Development. 1987. *Our Common Future.* Oxford, UK: Oxford University Press.

World Meteorological Organization. 2017. Greenhouse Gas Bulletin no. 13, WMO, October 30. https://ane4bf-datap1.s3-eu-west-1. amazonaws.com/wmocms/s3fs-public/ckedi- tor/files/GHG_Bulletin_13_EN_final_1_1. pdf?LGJNmHpwKkEG2Qw4mEQjdm6bWxgWAJHa.

Wright, Evelyn L., and Jon D. Erickson. 2003. "Climate Variability, Economic Adaptation, and Investment Timing." *International Journal of Global Environmental Issues* 3, no. 4: 357–68.

Yakusheva, Olga, Eline van den Broek-Altenburg, Gayle Brekke, and Adam Atherly. 2020. "The Cure Is Not Worse than the Disease: A Humanitarian Perspective." Social Science Research Network, July 1. https://ssrn.com/abstract=3638575.

Young, Iris Marion. 1990. *Justice and the Politics of Difference.* Princeton, NJ: Princeton University Press.

Zelizer, Julian C. 2001. "The Nation: Guns and Butter; Government Can Run More than a War." *The New York Times,* December 30. http://www.nytimes.com/2001/12/30/weekinreview/the-nation-guns-and-butter-government-can-run-more-than-a-war.html?mcubz=1.

Zencey, Eric. 2012. *The Other Road to Serfdom and the Path to Sustainable Democracy.* Lebanon, NH: University Press of New England.

Index

About the Author

Jon D. Erickson is the Blittersdorf Professor of Sustainability Science and Policy at the University of Vermont, faculty member of the Rubenstein School of Environment and Natural Resources, and Fellow of the Gund Institute for Environment. His previous co-authored and edited books include *Sustainable Wellbeing Futures*, *The Great Experiment in Conservation*, *Ecological Economics of Sustainable Watershed Management*, *Frontiers in Ecological Economic Theory and Application*, and *Ecological Economics: A Workbook for Problem-Based Learning*. He is also adjunct professor at the University of Iceland and has been a Fulbright Scholar in Tanzania, assistant professor of economics at Rensselaer Polytechnic Institute, and visiting professor in the Dominican Republic, Norway, Germany, and Slovakia. Outside the university, he is an Emmy-award-winning producer and director of documentary films, co-founder and board member of numerous nonprofit organizations, past-president of the U.S. Society for Ecological Economics, and advisor to state and national policymakers. Jon lives in Ferrisburgh, Vermont, with his wife, Pat, and a menagerie of dogs, cats, horses, chickens, and a donkey.